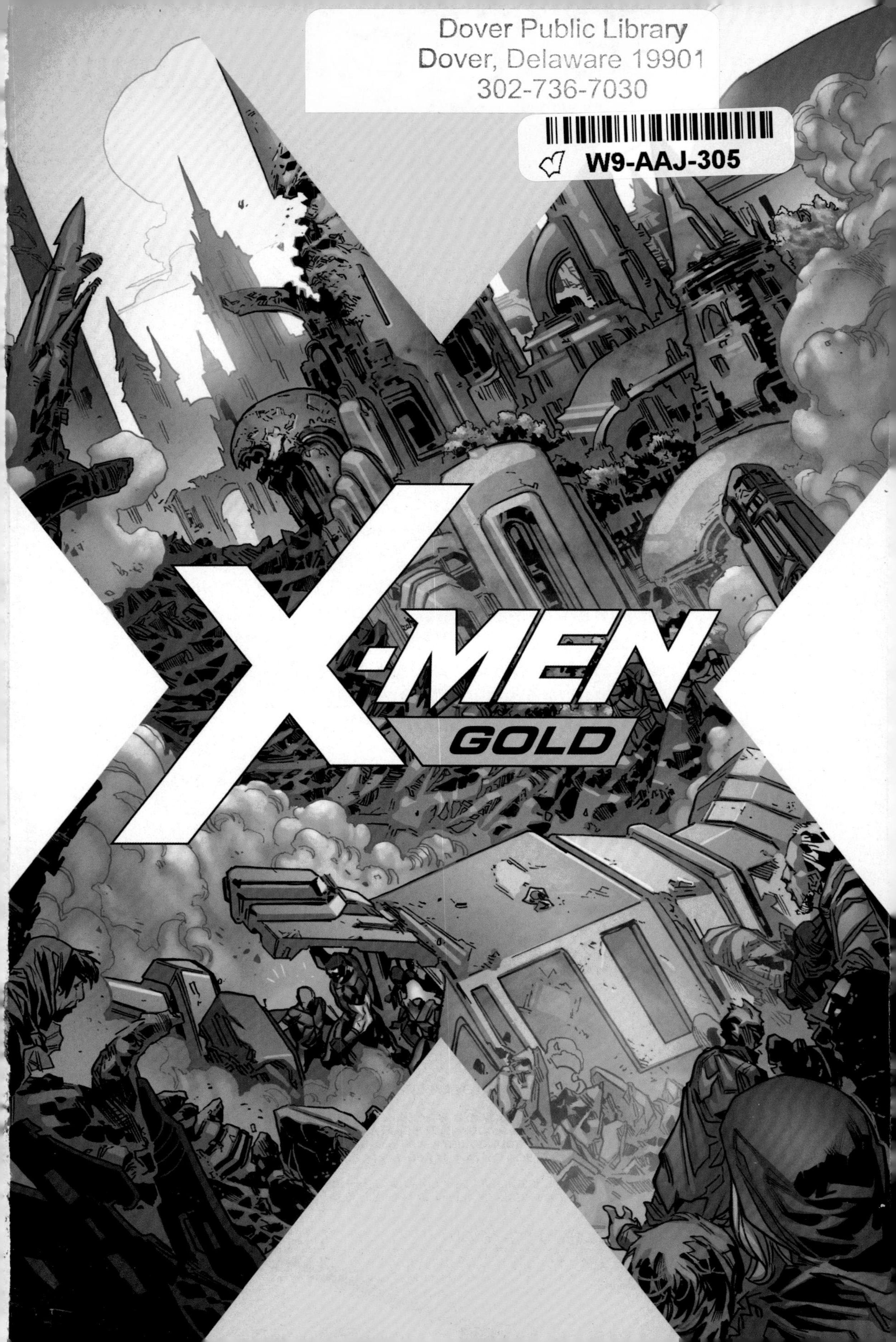
X-MEN
GOLD

RECENTLY, THE X-MEN QUASHED AN ATTACK ON THE
UNITED NATIONS BY A GROUP CLAIMING TO BE A NEWLY
REFORMED BROTHERHOOD OF EVIL MUTANTS — HOWEVER
IT WAS ULTIMATELY REVEALED TO BE MERELY A GROUP OF
UNWILLING MUTANTS UNDER THE TELEPATHIC THRALL OF
MESMERO, SAVE FOR ONE: AN EXTRATERRESTRIAL BEING
SPEAKING AN UNKNOWN LANGUAGE. IT WAS CAPTURED
AND HELD IN A SUBBASEMENT OF THE XAVIER INSTITUTE
FOR FURTHER ANALYSIS.

LATER, WHEN THE INSTITUTE WAS INFILTRATED BY A SERIAL
MUTANT-KILLER, THE MURDERER RELEASED THE ALIEN
FROM CAPTIVITY TO RETURN FROM WHENCE IT CAME...

X-MEN CREATED BY **STAN LEE** & **JACK KIRBY**

Collection Editor/**JENNIFER GRÜNWALD** · Assistant Editor/**CAITLIN O'CONNELL**
Associate Managing Editor/**KATERI WOODY** · Editor, Special Projects/**MARK D. BEAZLEY**
VP Production & Special Projects/**JEFF YOUNGQUIST** · SVP Print, Sales & Marketing/**DAVID GABRIEL**
Book Designer/**JAY BOWEN**

Editor in Chief/**C.B. CEBULSKI** · Chief Creative Officer/**JOE QUESADA**
President/**DAN BUCKLEY** · Executive Producer/**ALAN FINE**

X-MEN GOLD VOL. 4: THE NEGATIVE ZONE WAR. Contains material originally published in magazine form as X-MEN GOLD #12 and #16-20. First printing 2018. ISBN 978-1-302-90974-1. Published by MARVEL WORLDWIDE, INC.,
a subsidiary of MARVEL ENTERTAINMENT, LLC. OFFICE OF PUBLICATION: 135 West 50th Street, New York, NY 10020. Copyright © 2018 MARVEL No similarity between any of the names, characters, persons, and/or institutions in this
magazine with those of any living or dead person or institution is intended, and any such similarity which may exist is purely coincidental. **Printed in Canada.** DAN BUCKLEY, President, Marvel Entertainment; JOHN NEE, Publisher;
JOE QUESADA, Chief Creative Officer; TOM BREVOORT, SVP of Publishing; DAVID BOGART, SVP of Business Affairs & Operations, Publishing & Partnership; DAVID GABRIEL, SVP of Sales & Marketing, Publishing; JEFF YOUNGQUIST,
VP of Production & Special Projects; DAN CARR, Executive Director of Publishing Technology; ALEX MORALES, Director of Publishing Operations; SUSAN CRESPI, Production Manager; STAN LEE, Chairman Emeritus. For information
regarding advertising in Marvel Comics or on Marvel.com, please contact Vit DeBellis, Custom Solutions & Integrated Advertising Manager, at vdebellis@marvel.com. For Marvel subscription inquiries, please call 888-511-5480.
Manufactured between 2/2/2018 and 3/6/2018 by SOLISCO PRINTERS, SCOTT, QC, CANADA.
10 9 8 7 6 5 4 3 2 1

X-MEN GOLD

THE NEGATIVE ZONE WAR

Writer/**MARC GUGGENHEIM**

ISSUE #12

Artist/**LUKE ROSS**
Colorist/**FRANK MARTIN**
Cover Art/**KEN LASHLEY** & **NOLAN WOODARD**

ISSUE #16

Penciler/**LAN MEDINA**
Inkers/**JAY LEISTEN** & **CRAIG YEUNG**
Colorists/**FRANK MARTIN** & **ANDREW CROSSLEY**
Cover Art/**KEN LASHLEY** & **JUAN FERNANDEZ**

ISSUES #17-18

Artist/**KEN LASHLEY**
Colorists/**JUAN FERNANDEZ** (#17) & **ARIF PRIANTO** (#18)
Cover Art/**KEN LASHLEY** & **JUAN FERNANDEZ**

ISSUE #19

Penciler/**DIEGO BERNARD**
Inker/**JP MAYER**
Colorist/**CHRIS SOTOMAYOR**
Cover Art/**KEN LASHLEY** & **FEDERICO BLEE**

ISSUE #20

Penciler/**LAN MEDINA**
Inker/**CRAIG YEUNG**
Colorist/**FRANK MARTIN**
Cover Art/**KEN LASHLEY** & **FEDERICO BLEE**

Letterer/**VC's CORY PETIT**

Assistant Editors/**CHRIS ROBINSON**
& **CHRISTINA HARRINGTON**
Editor/**MARK PANICCIA**

X-MEN CREATED BY **STAN LEE** & **JACK KIRBY**

12

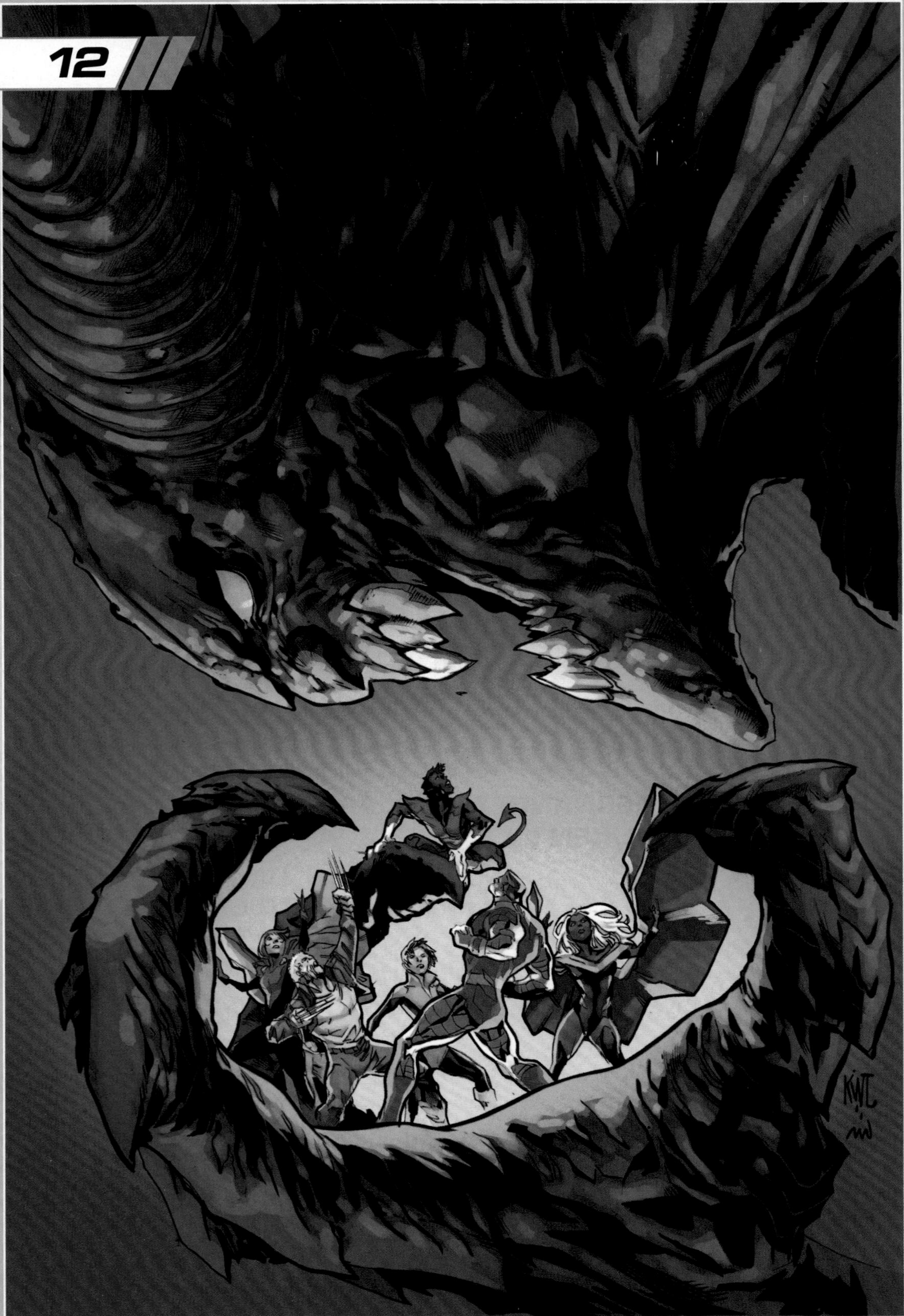

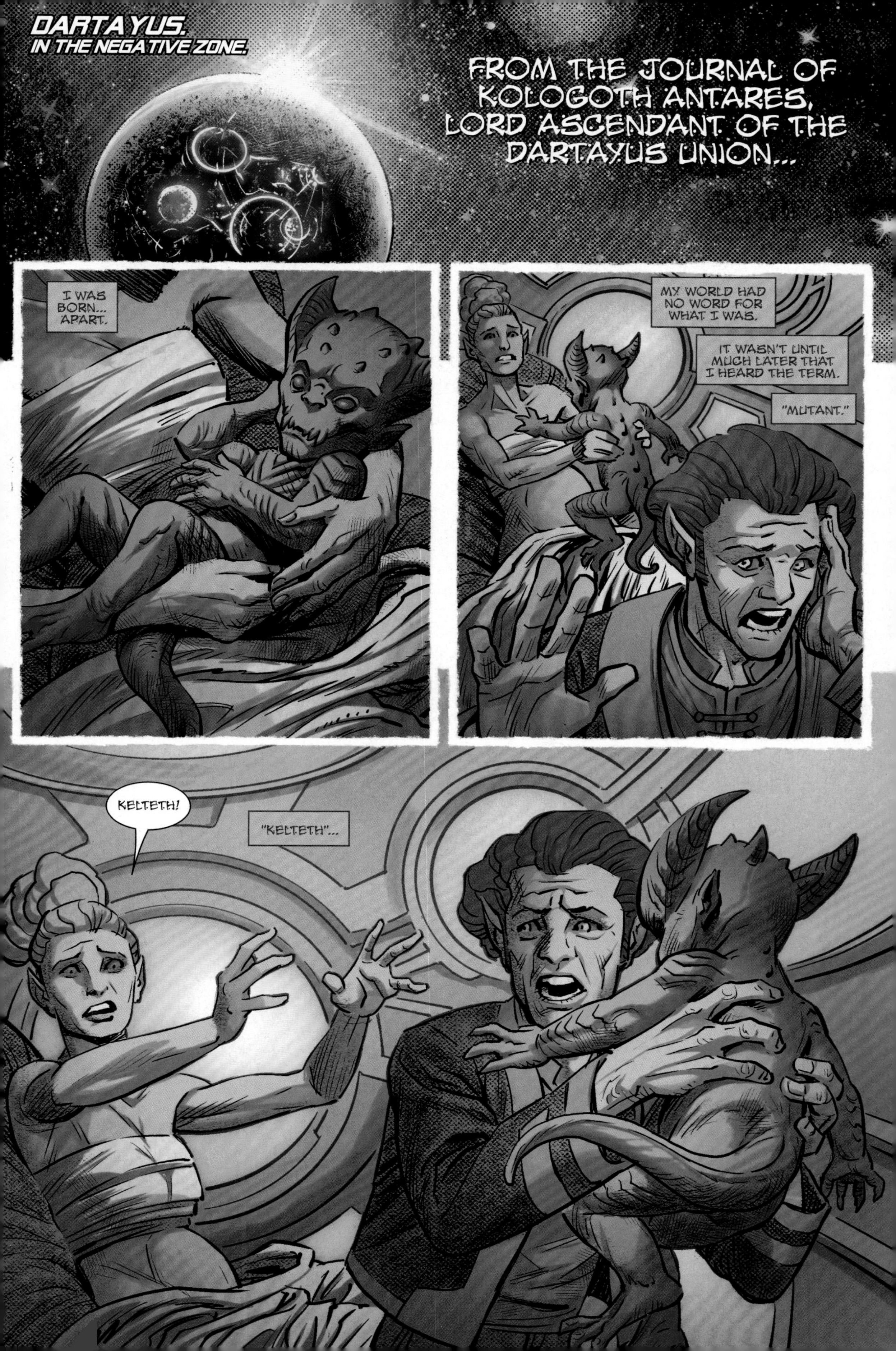

DARTAYUS.
IN THE NEGATIVE ZONE.
FROM THE JOURNAL OF KOLOGOTH ANTARES, LORD ASCENDANT OF THE DARTAYUS UNION...
I WAS BORN... APART.
MY WORLD HAD NO WORD FOR WHAT I WAS.
IT WASN'T UNTIL MUCH LATER THAT I HEARD THE TERM.
"MUTANT."
KELTETH!
"KELTETH"...

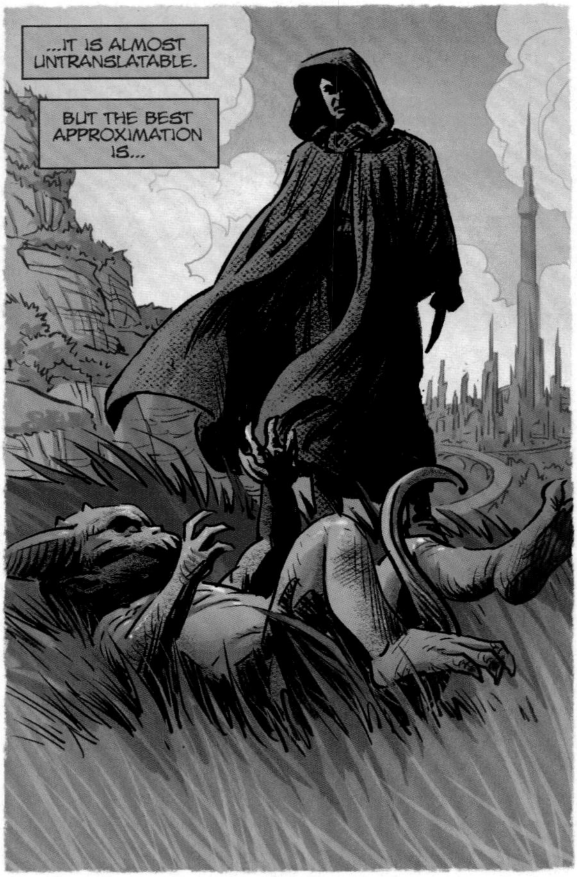
...IT IS ALMOST UNTRANSLATABLE.
BUT THE BEST APPROXIMATION IS...

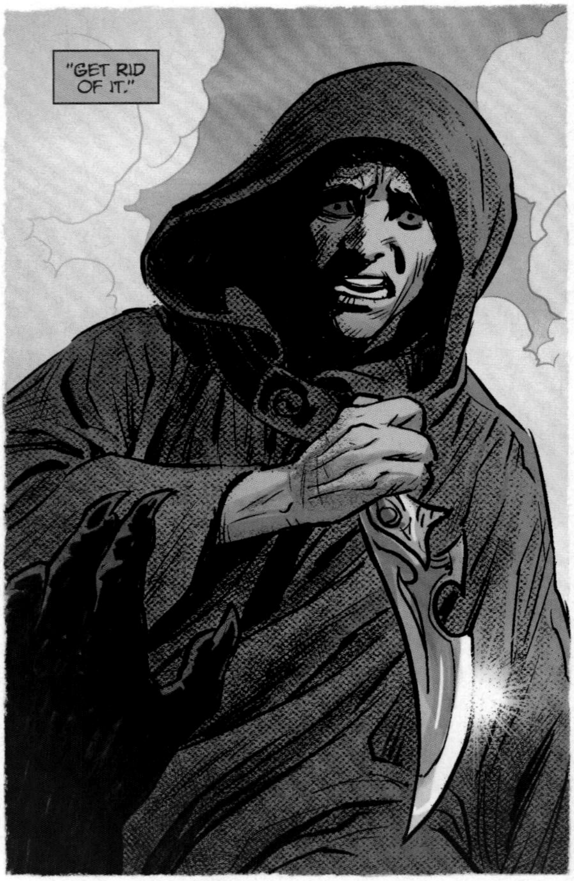
"GET RID OF IT."

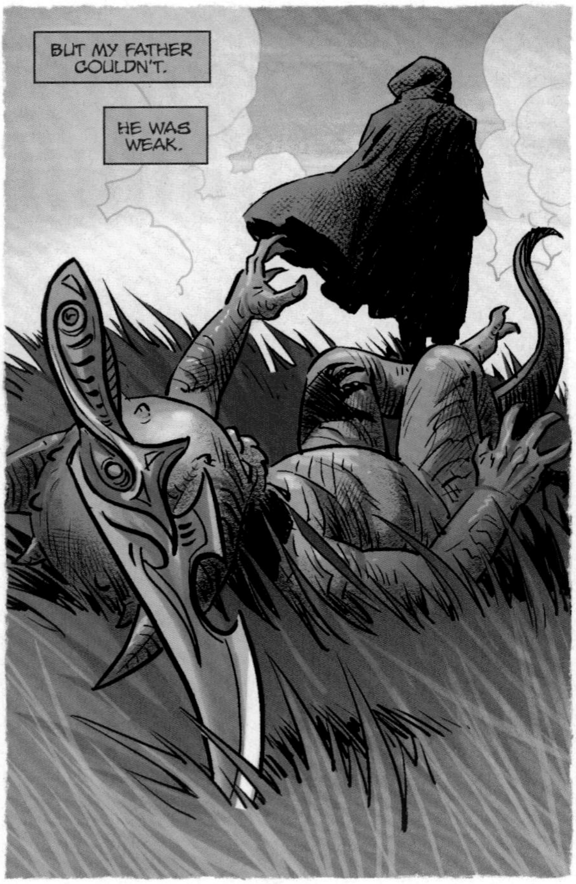
BUT MY FATHER COULDN'T.
HE WAS WEAK.

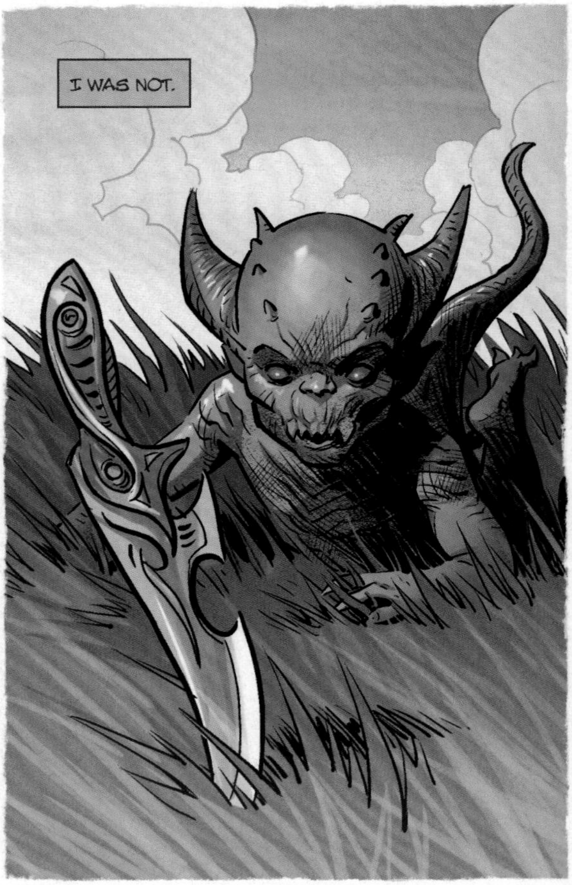
I WAS NOT.

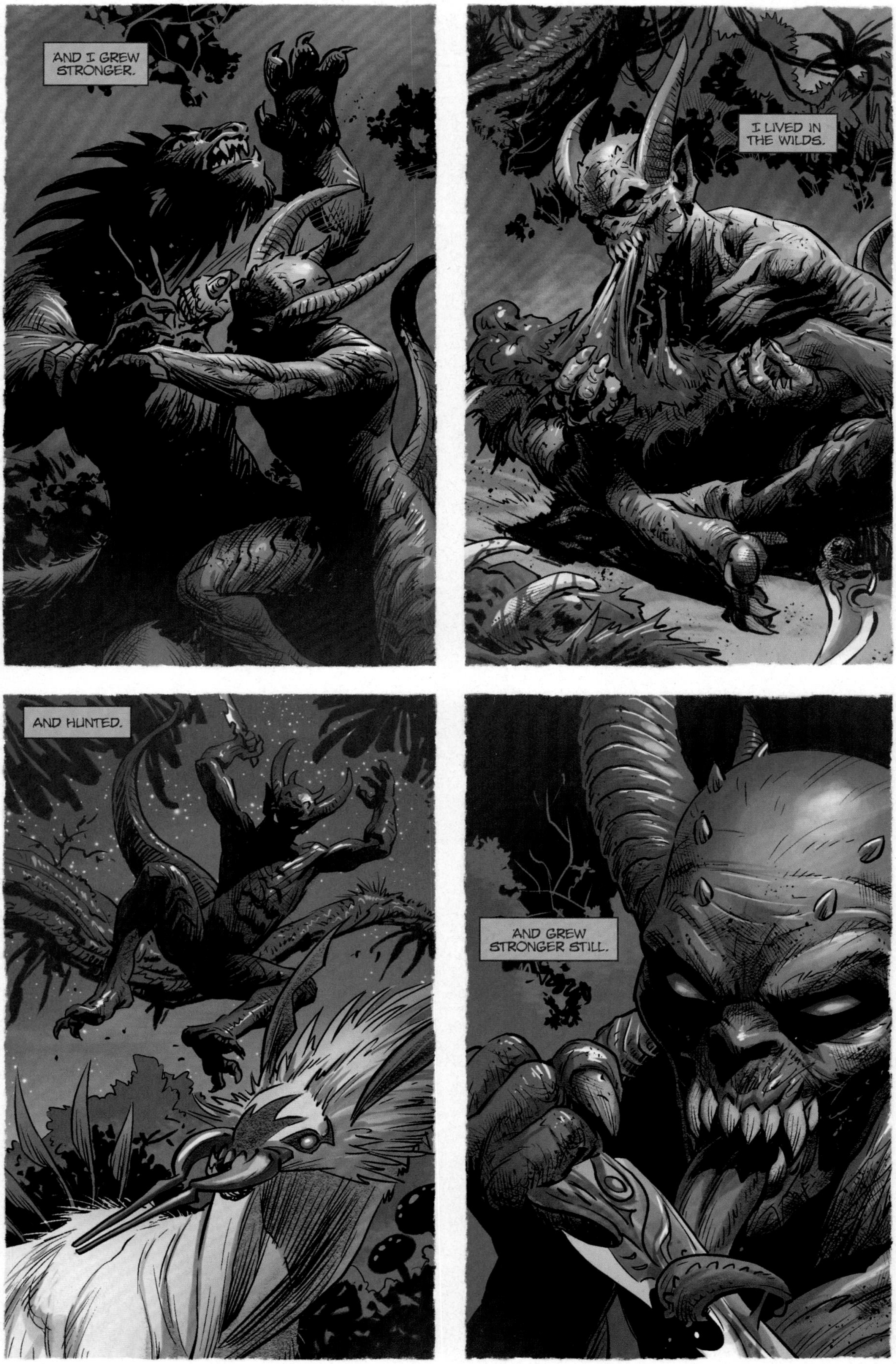
AND I GREW STRONGER.
I LIVED IN THE WILDS.
AND HUNTED.
AND GREW STRONGER STILL.

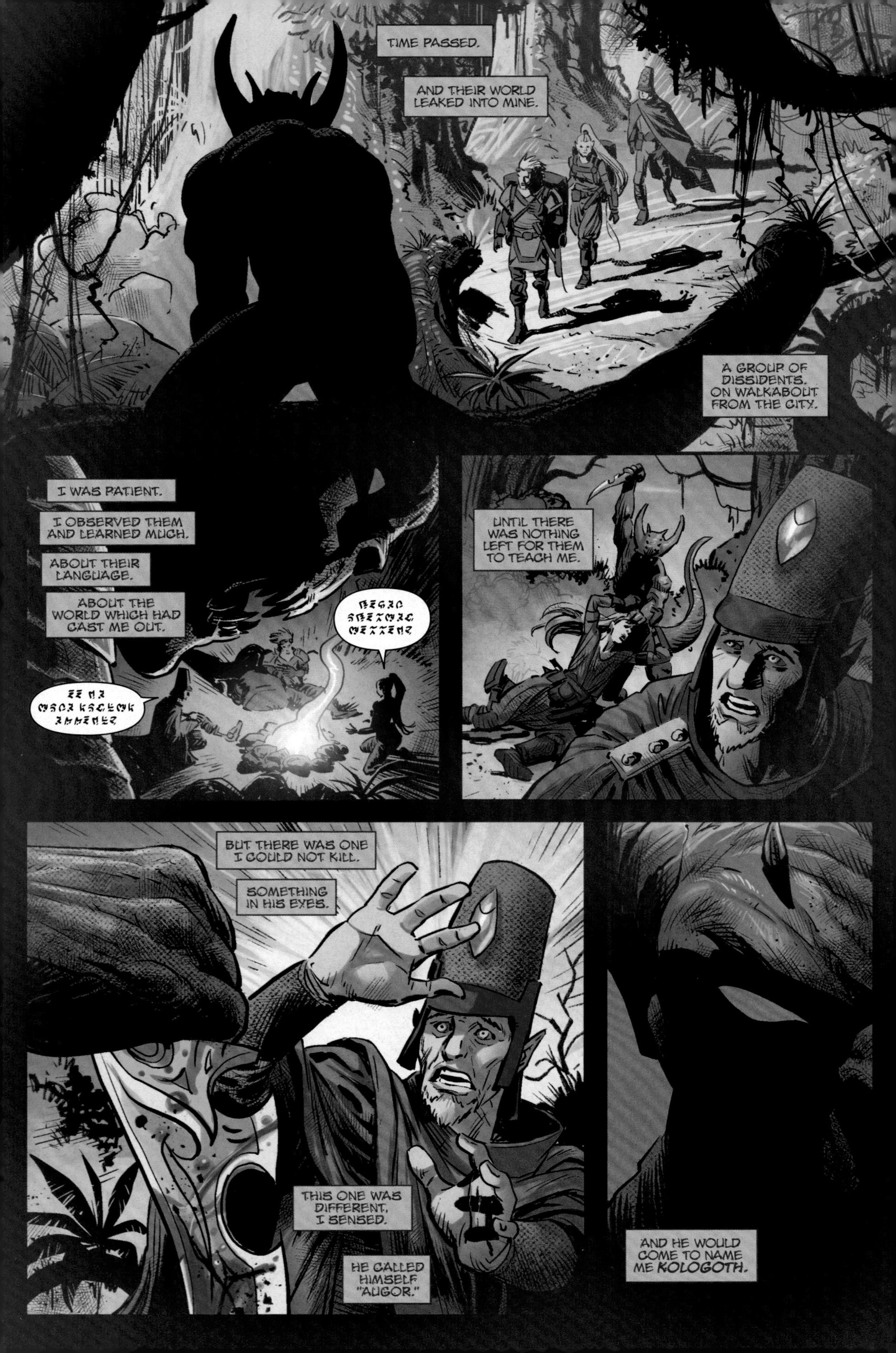
TIME PASSED.
AND THEIR WORLD LEAKED INTO MINE.
A GROUP OF DISSIDENTS, ON WALKABOUT FROM THE CITY.
I WAS PATIENT.
I OBSERVED THEM AND LEARNED MUCH.
ABOUT THEIR LANGUAGE.
ABOUT THE WORLD WHICH HAD CAST ME OUT.
UNTIL THERE WAS NOTHING LEFT FOR THEM TO TEACH ME.
BUT THERE WAS ONE I COULD NOT KILL.
SOMETHING IN HIS EYES.
THIS ONE WAS DIFFERENT, I SENSED.
HE CALLED HIMSELF "AUGOR."
AND HE WOULD COME TO NAME ME KOLOGOTH.

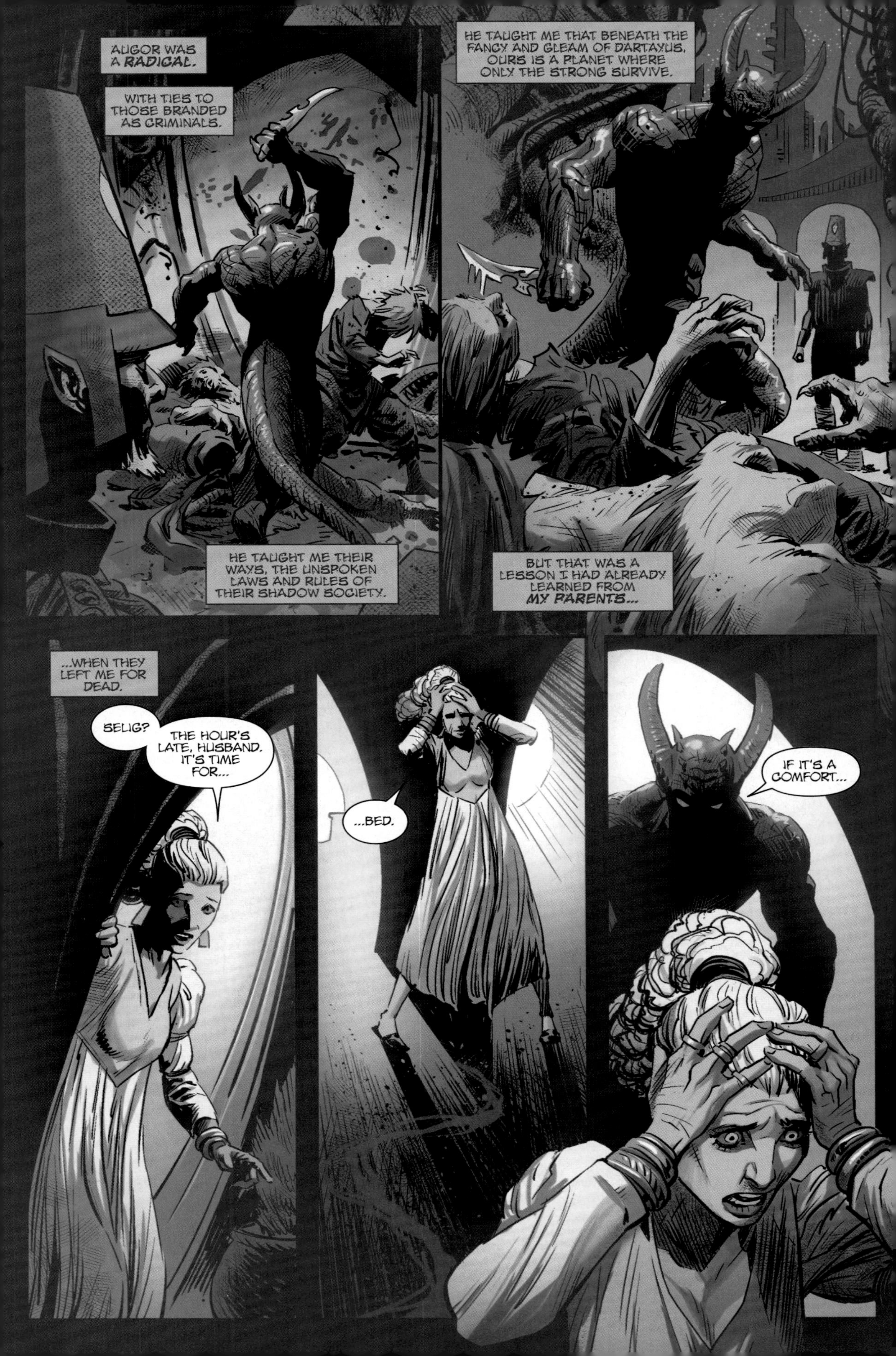
AUGOR WAS A RADICAL.
WITH TIES TO THOSE BRANDED AS CRIMINALS.
HE TAUGHT ME THEIR WAYS, THE UNSPOKEN LAWS AND RULES OF THEIR SHADOW SOCIETY.
HE TAUGHT ME THAT BENEATH THE FANCY AND GLEAM OF DARTAYUS, OURS IS A PLANET WHERE ONLY THE STRONG SURVIVE.
BUT THAT WAS A LESSON I HAD ALREADY LEARNED FROM MY PARENTS...
...WHEN THEY LEFT ME FOR DEAD.
SELIG?
THE HOUR'S LATE, HUSBAND. IT'S TIME FOR...
...BED.
IF IT'S A COMFORT...

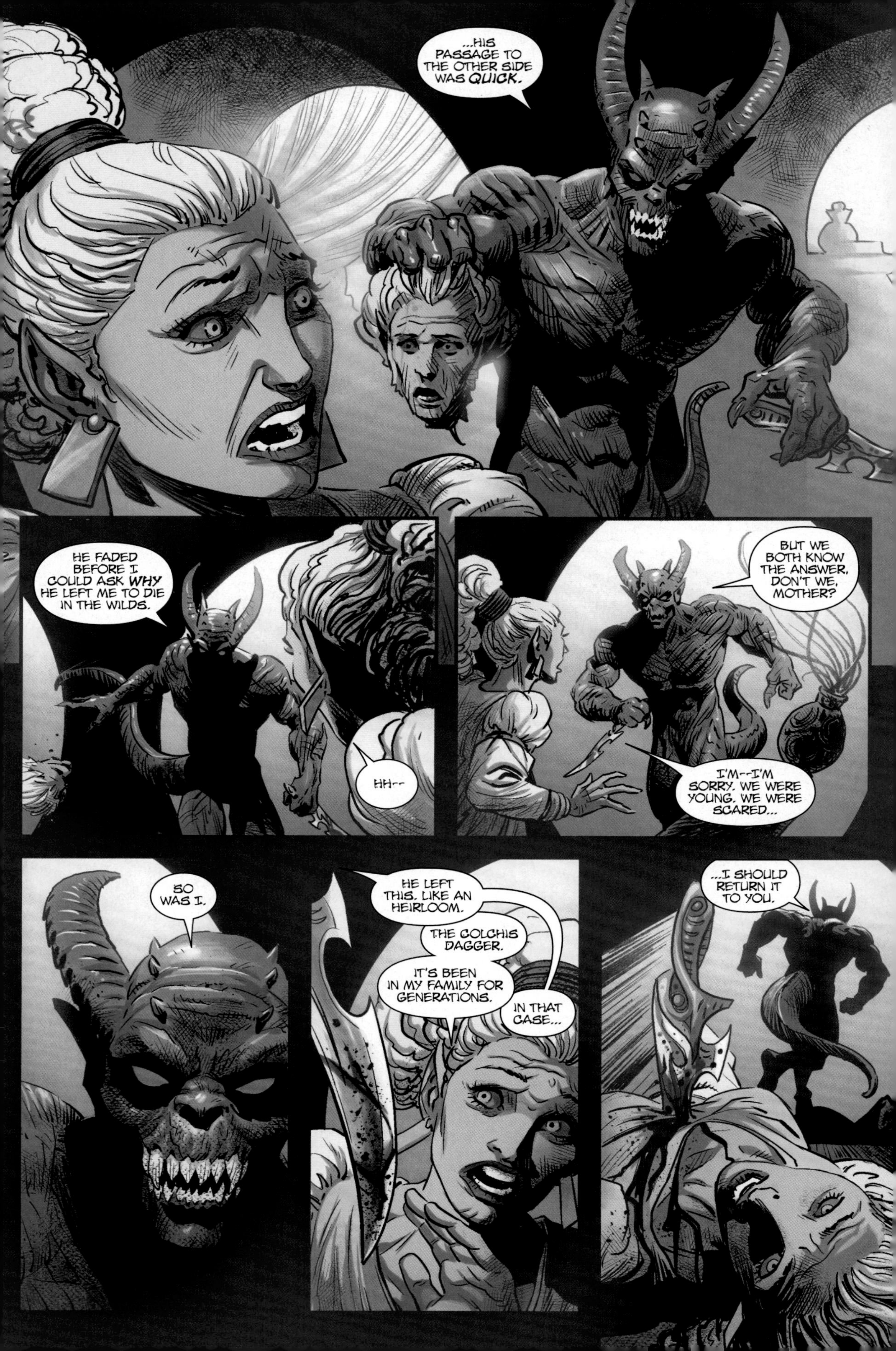
...HIS PASSAGE TO THE OTHER SIDE WAS QUICK.
HE FADED BEFORE I COULD ASK WHY HE LEFT ME TO DIE IN THE WILDS.
HH--
BUT WE BOTH KNOW THE ANSWER, DON'T WE, MOTHER?
I'M--I'M SORRY. WE WERE YOUNG. WE WERE SCARED...
SO WAS I.
HE LEFT THIS. LIKE AN HEIRLOOM.
THE COLCHIS DAGGER.
IT'S BEEN IN MY FAMILY FOR GENERATIONS.
IN THAT CASE...
...I SHOULD RETURN IT TO YOU.

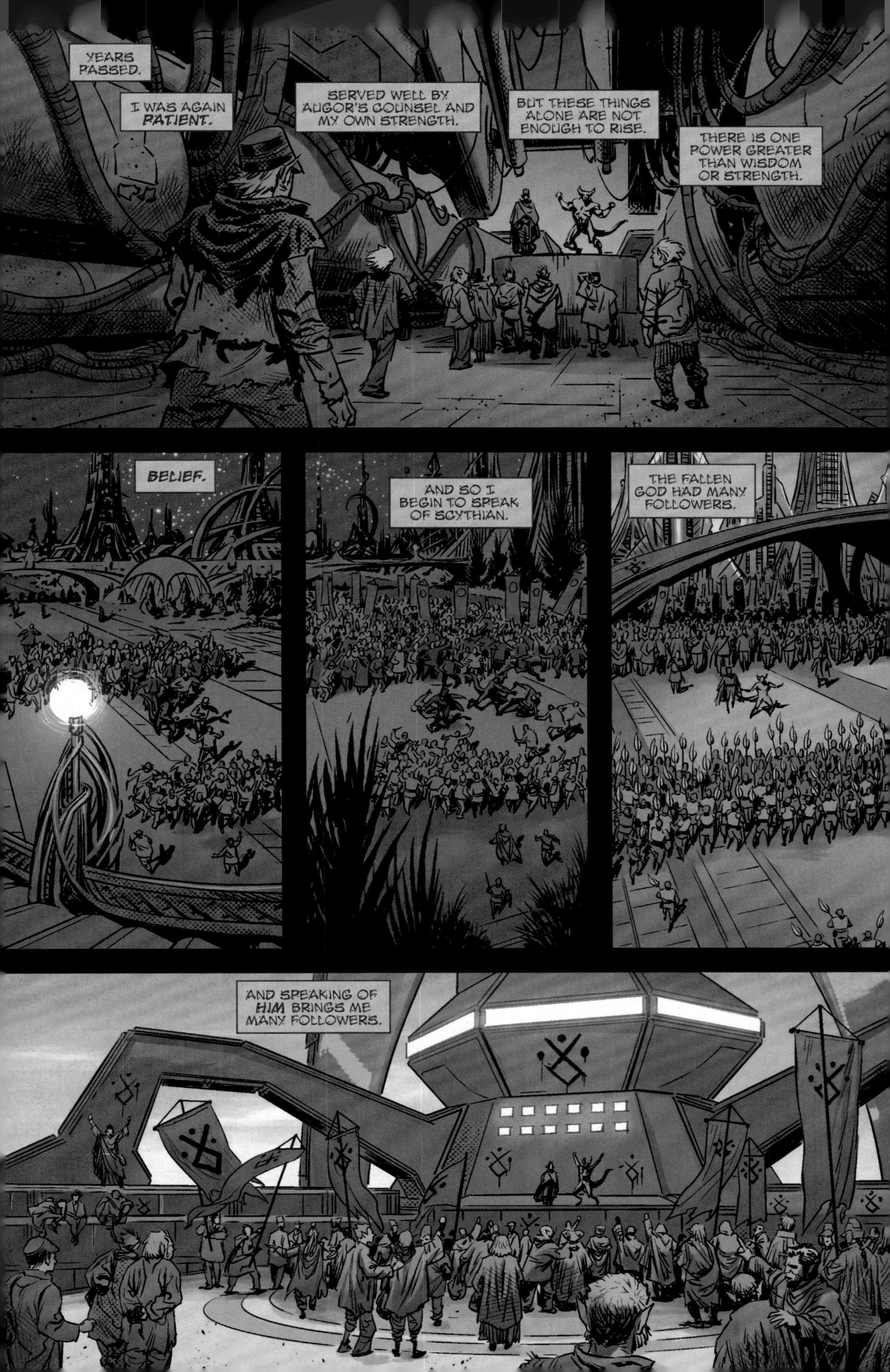
YEARS PASSED.
I WAS AGAIN PATIENT.
SERVED WELL BY AUGOR'S COUNSEL AND MY OWN STRENGTH.
BUT THESE THINGS ALONE ARE NOT ENOUGH TO RISE.
THERE IS ONE POWER GREATER THAN WISDOM OR STRENGTH.
BELIEF.
AND SO I BEGIN TO SPEAK OF SCYTHIAN.
THE FALLEN GOD HAD MANY FOLLOWERS.
AND SPEAKING OF HIM BRINGS ME MANY FOLLOWERS.

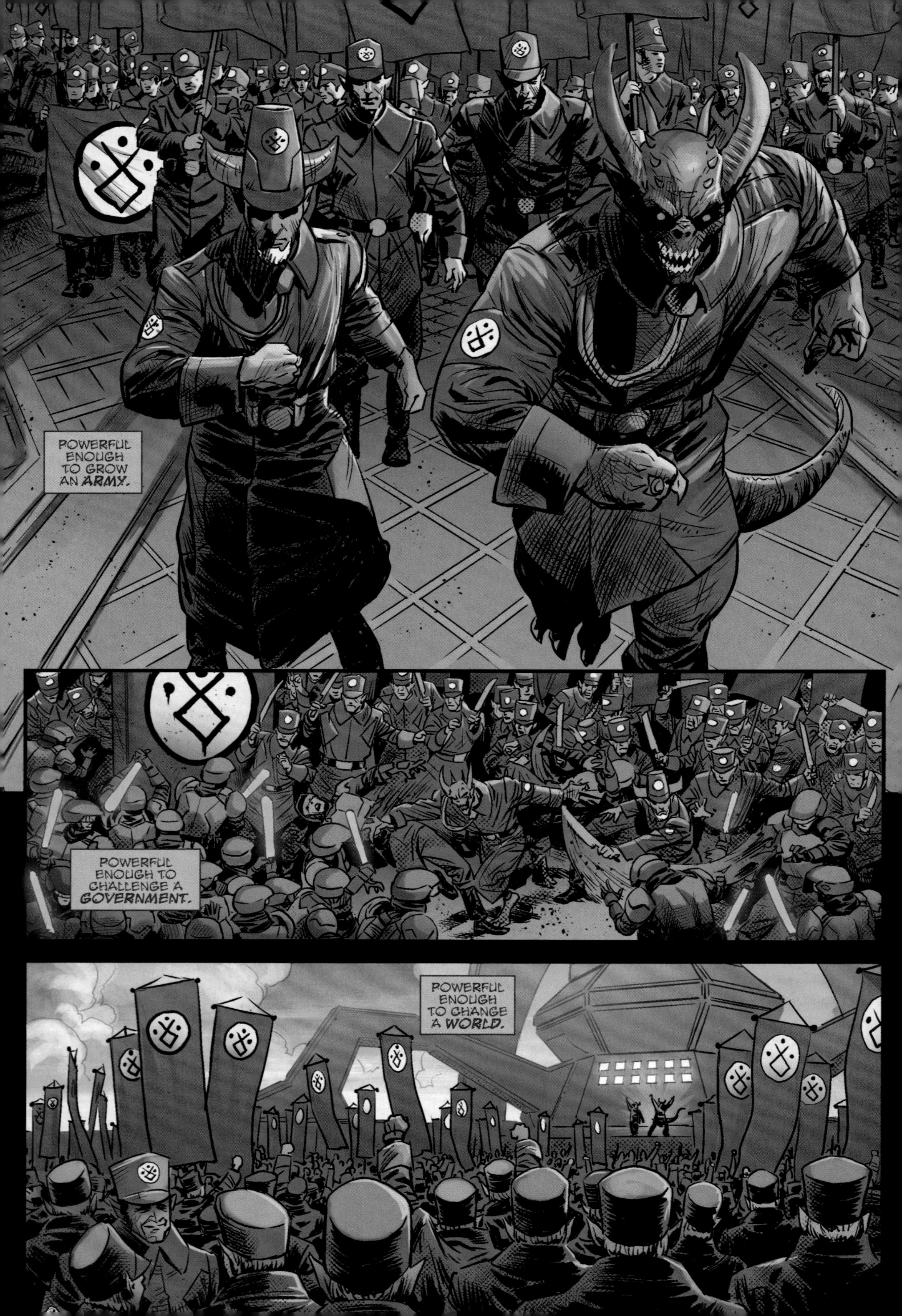
POWERFUL ENOUGH TO GROW AN ARMY.
POWERFUL ENOUGH TO CHALLENGE A GOVERNMENT.
POWERFUL ENOUGH TO CHANGE A WORLD.

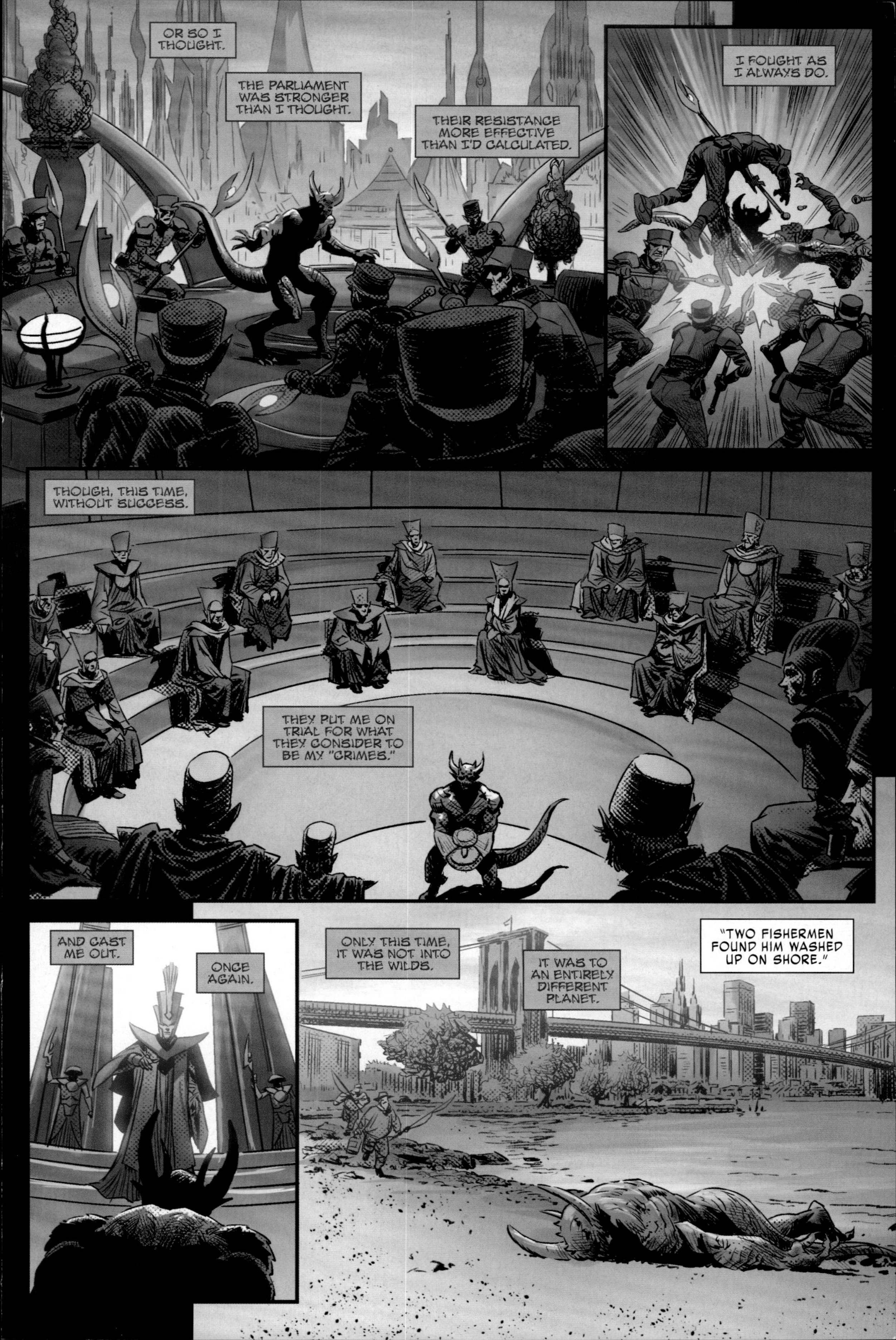

OR SO I THOUGHT.
THE PARLIAMENT WAS STRONGER THAN I THOUGHT.
THEIR RESISTANCE MORE EFFECTIVE THAN I'D CALCULATED.
I FOUGHT AS I ALWAYS DO.
THOUGH, THIS TIME, WITHOUT SUCCESS.
THEY PUT ME ON TRIAL FOR WHAT THEY CONSIDER TO BE MY "CRIMES."
AND CAST ME OUT.
ONCE AGAIN.
ONLY THIS TIME, IT WAS NOT INTO THE WILDS.
IT WAS TO AN ENTIRELY DIFFERENT PLANET.
"TWO FISHERMEN FOUND HIM WASHED UP ON SHORE."

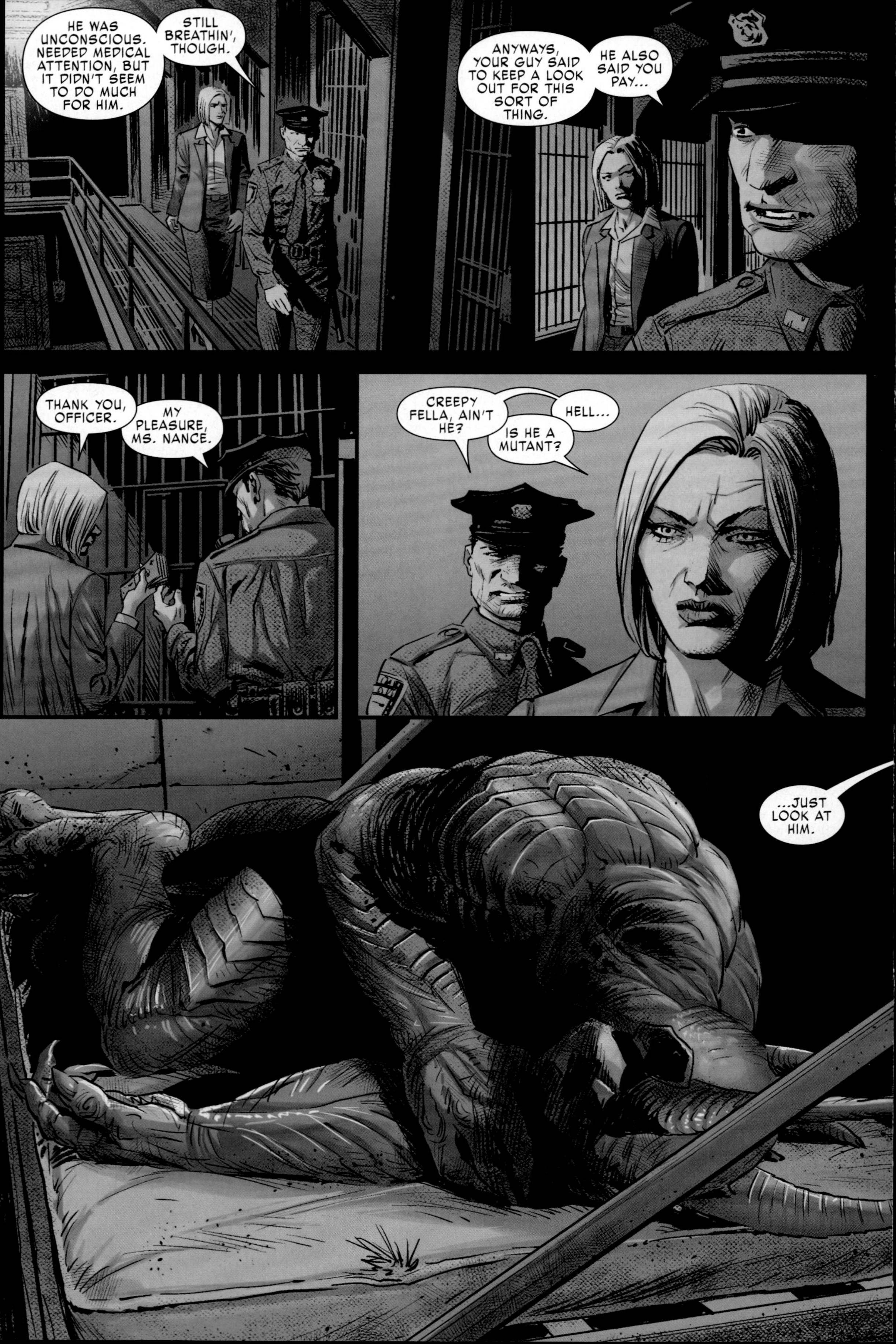

HE WAS UNCONSCIOUS. NEEDED MEDICAL ATTENTION, BUT IT DIDN'T SEEM TO DO MUCH FOR HIM.
STILL BREATHIN', THOUGH.
ANYWAYS, YOUR GUY SAID TO KEEP A LOOK OUT FOR THIS SORT OF THING.
HE ALSO SAID YOU PAY...
THANK YOU, OFFICER.
MY PLEASURE, MS. NANCE.
CREEPY FELLA, AIN'T HE?
HELL...
IS HE A MUTANT?
...JUST LOOK AT HIM.

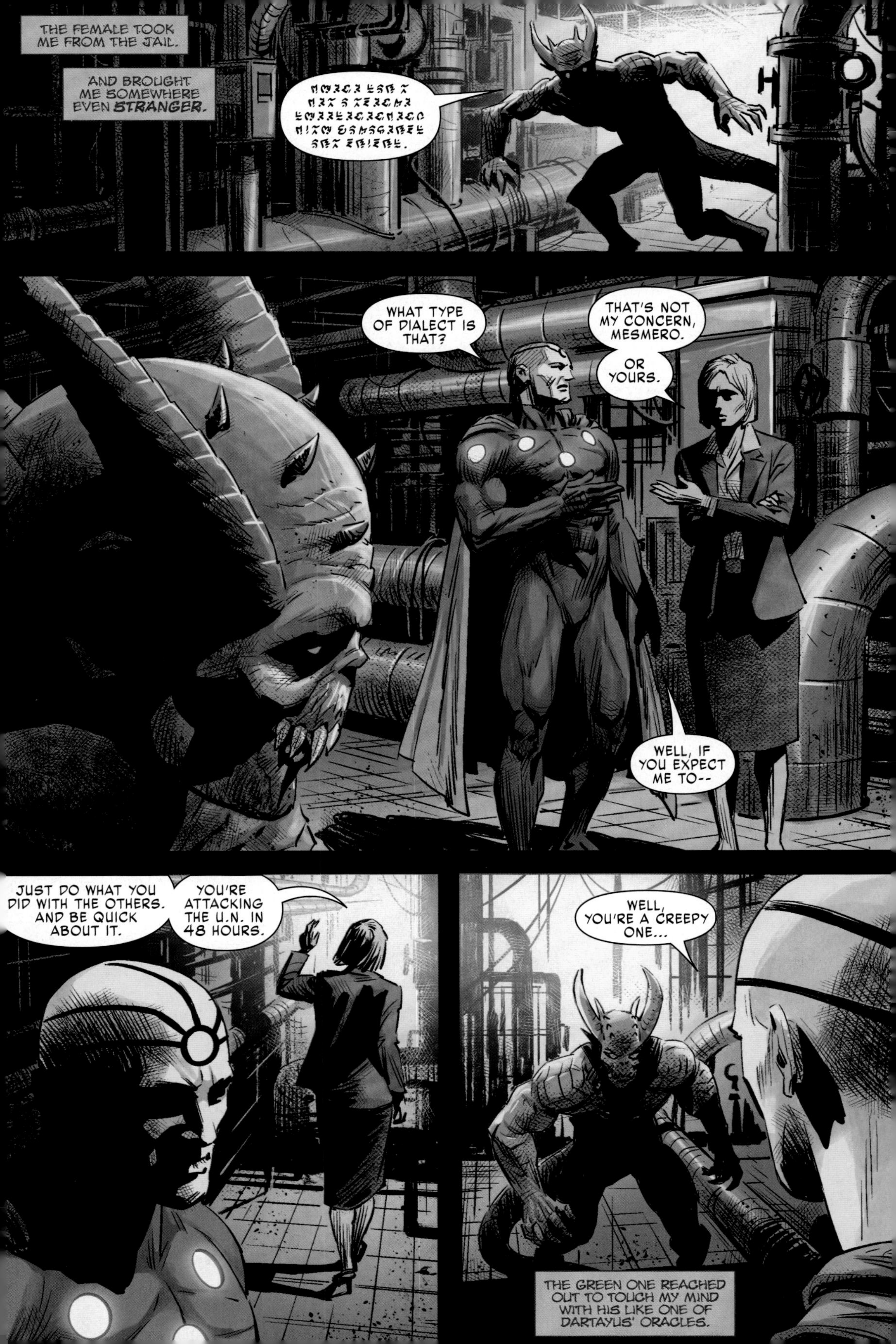
THE FEMALE TOOK ME FROM THE JAIL.
AND BROUGHT ME SOMEWHERE EVEN STRANGER.
WHAT TYPE OF DIALECT IS THAT?
THAT'S NOT MY CONCERN, MESMERO.
OR YOURS.
WELL, IF YOU EXPECT ME TO--
JUST DO WHAT YOU DID WITH THE OTHERS. AND BE QUICK ABOUT IT.
YOU'RE ATTACKING THE U.N. IN 48 HOURS.
WELL, YOU'RE A CREEPY ONE...
THE GREEN ONE REACHED OUT TO TOUCH MY MIND WITH HIS LIKE ONE OF DARTAYUS' ORACLES.

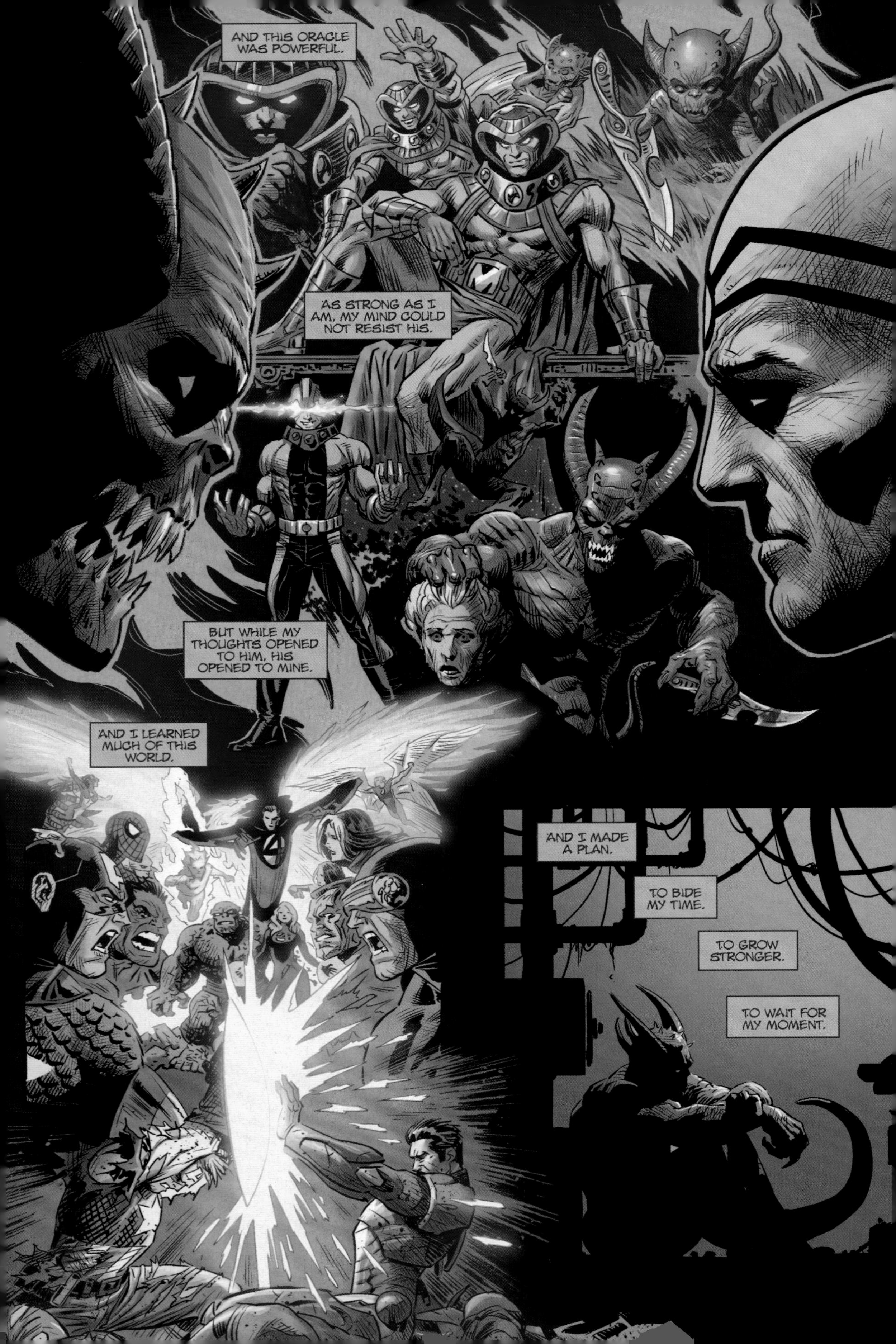
AND THIS ORACLE WAS POWERFUL.
AS STRONG AS I AM, MY MIND COULD NOT RESIST HIS.
BUT WHILE MY THOUGHTS OPENED TO HIM, HIS OPENED TO MINE.
AND I LEARNED MUCH OF THIS WORLD.
AND I MADE A PLAN.
TO BIDE MY TIME.
TO GROW STRONGER.
TO WAIT FOR MY MOMENT.

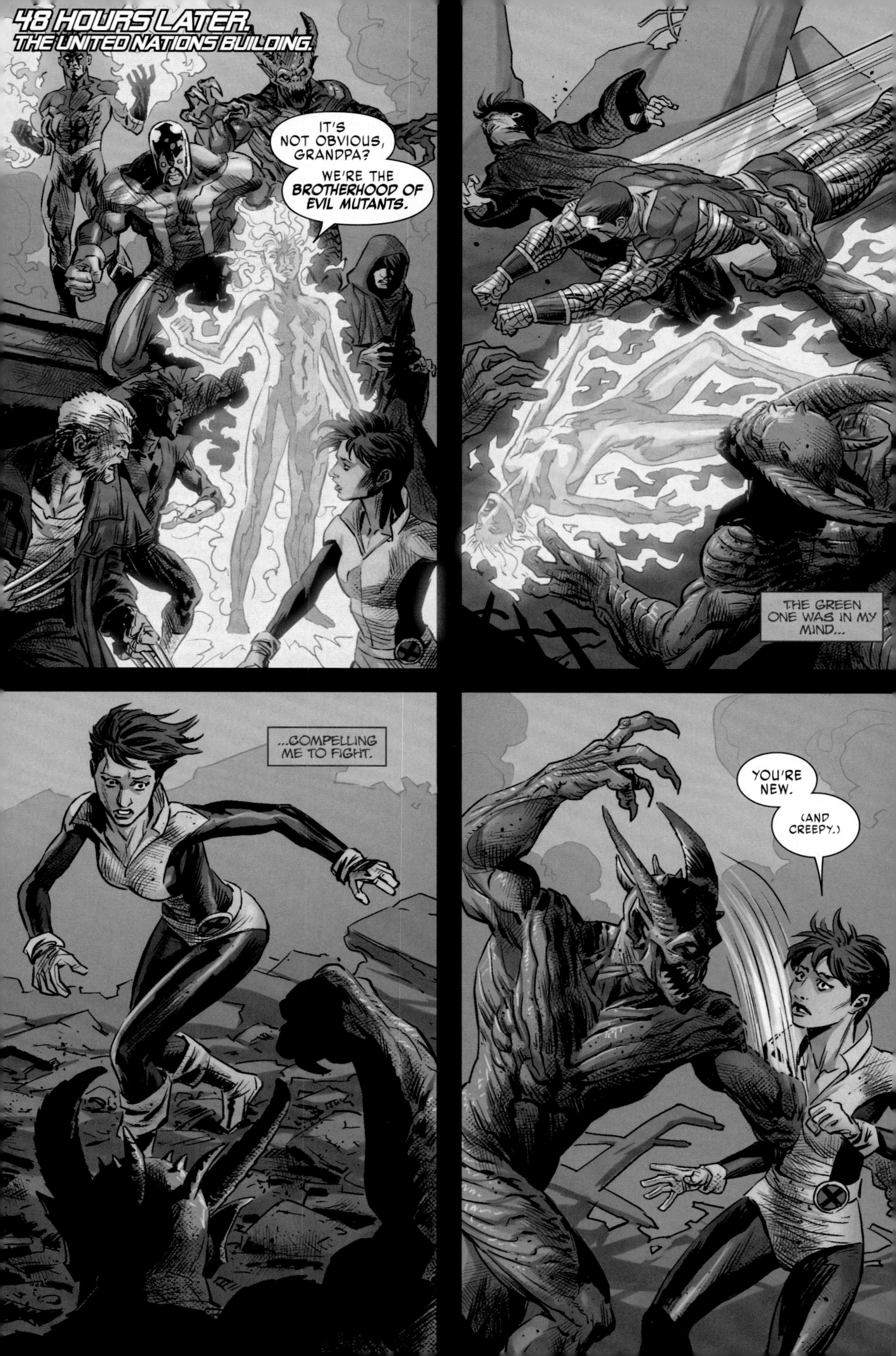
48 HOURS LATER.
THE UNITED NATIONS BUILDING.
IT'S NOT OBVIOUS, GRANDPA?
WE'RE THE BROTHERHOOD OF EVIL MUTANTS.
THE GREEN ONE WAS IN MY MIND...
...COMPELLING ME TO FIGHT.
YOU'RE NEW.
(AND CREEPY.)

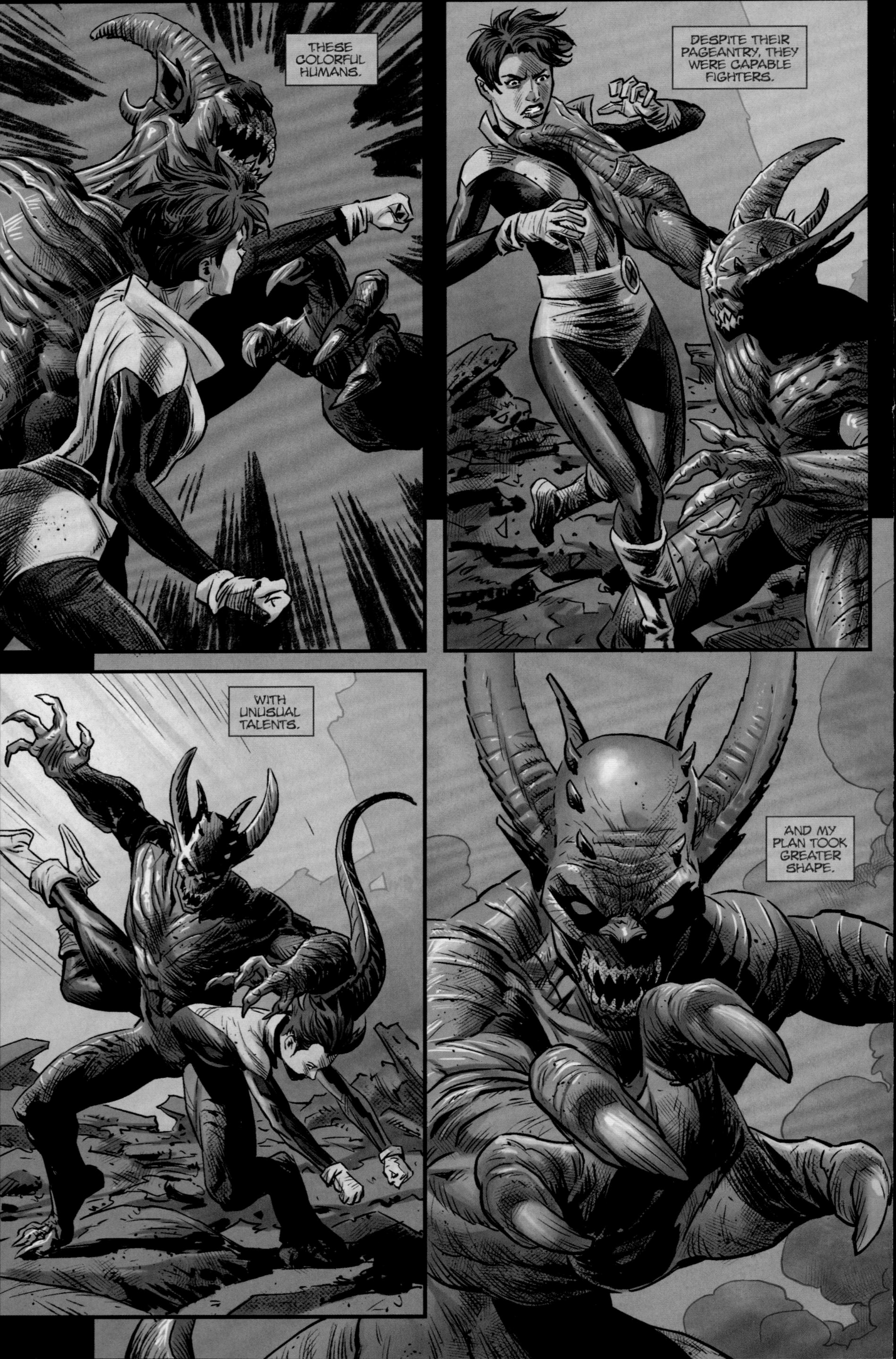
THESE COLORFUL HUMANS.
DESPITE THEIR PAGEANTRY, THEY WERE CAPABLE FIGHTERS.
WITH UNUSUAL TALENTS.
AND MY PLAN TOOK GREATER SHAPE.

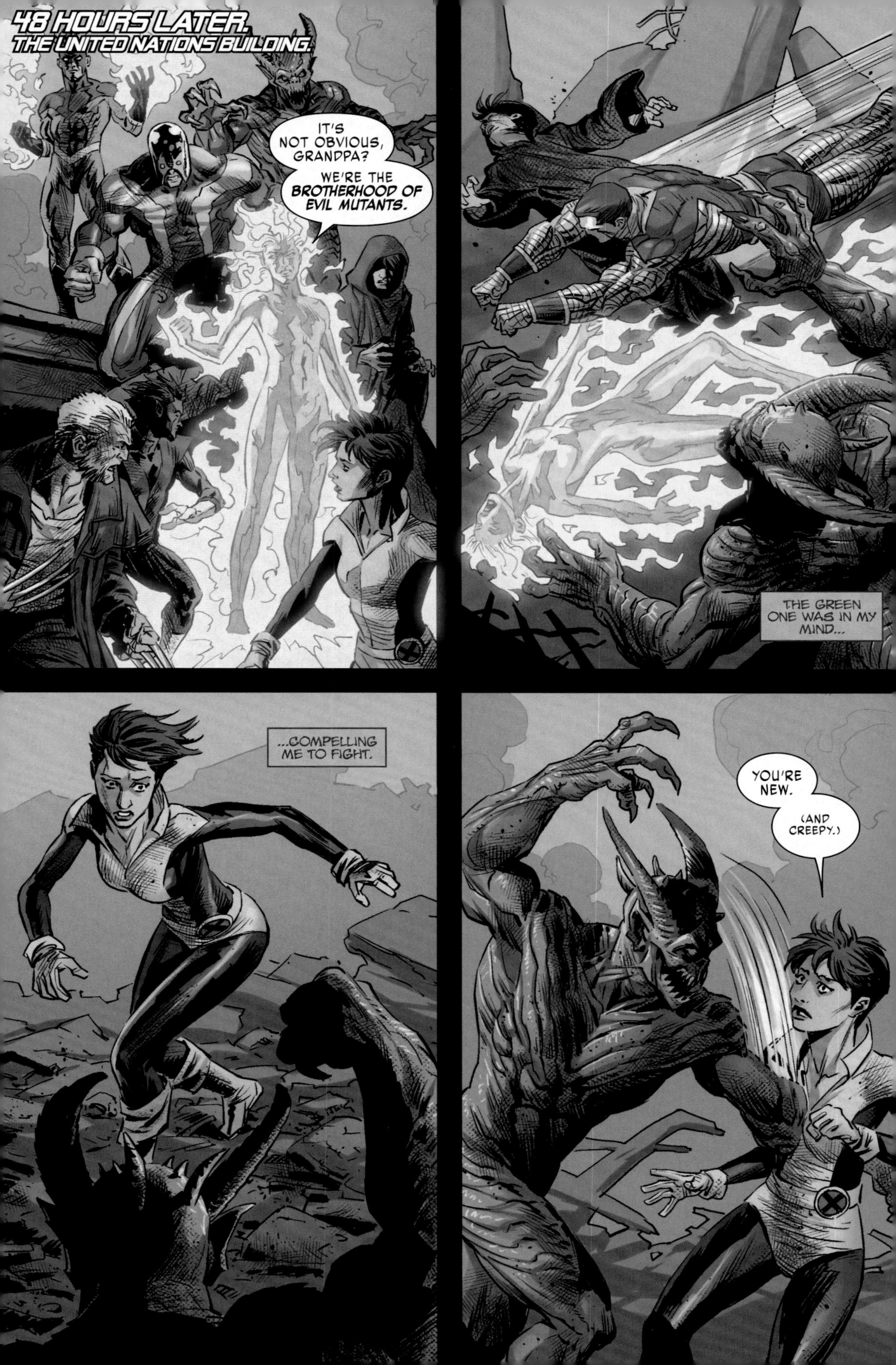
48 HOURS LATER.
THE UNITED NATIONS BUILDING.
IT'S NOT OBVIOUS, GRANDPA?
WE'RE THE BROTHERHOOD OF EVIL MUTANTS.
THE GREEN ONE WAS IN MY MIND...
...COMPELLING ME TO FIGHT.
YOU'RE NEW.
(AND CREEPY.)

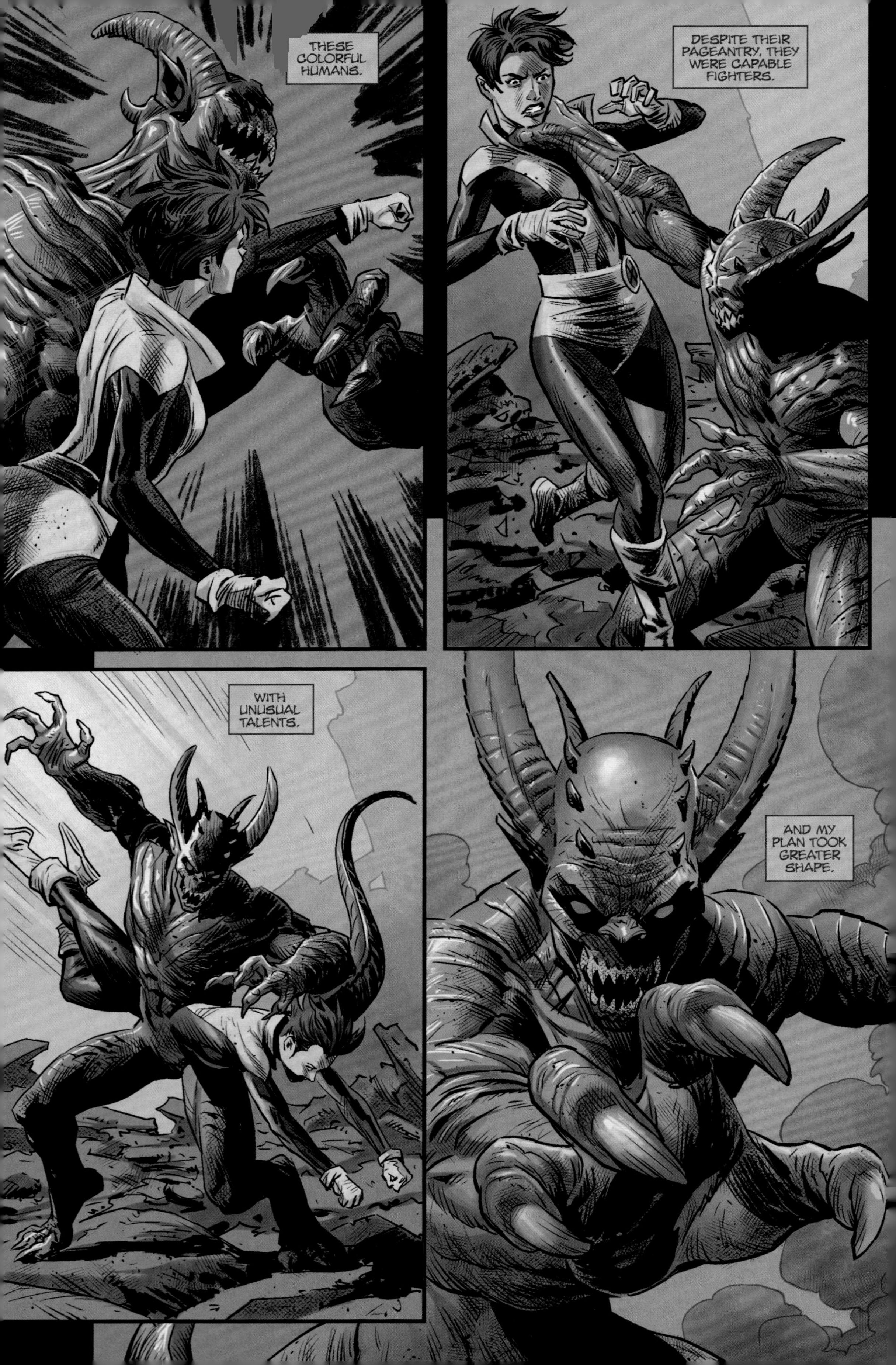
THESE COLORFUL HUMANS.
DESPITE THEIR PAGEANTRY, THEY WERE CAPABLE FIGHTERS.
WITH UNUSUAL TALENTS.
AND MY PLAN TOOK GREATER SHAPE.

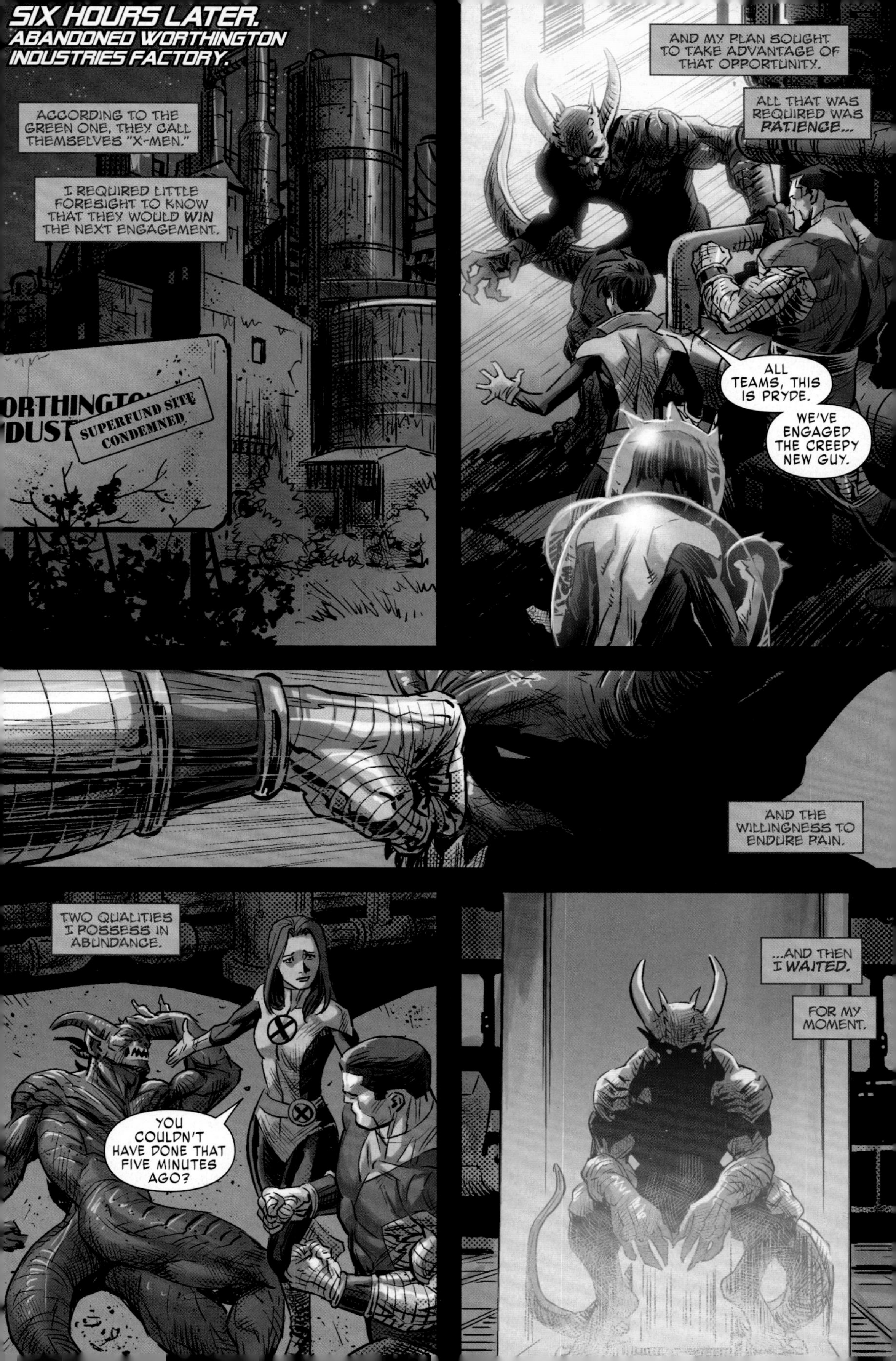
SIX HOURS LATER.
ABANDONED WORTHINGTON INDUSTRIES FACTORY.
ACCORDING TO THE GREEN ONE, THEY CALL THEMSELVES "X-MEN."
I REQUIRED LITTLE FORESIGHT TO KNOW THAT THEY WOULD WIN THE NEXT ENGAGEMENT.
ORTHINGTO
DUST
SUPERFUND SITE CONDEMNED
AND MY PLAN SOUGHT TO TAKE ADVANTAGE OF THAT OPPORTUNITY.
ALL THAT WAS REQUIRED WAS PATIENCE...
ALL TEAMS, THIS IS PRYDE.
WE'VE ENGAGED THE CREEPY NEW GUY.
AND THE WILLINGNESS TO ENDURE PAIN.
TWO QUALITIES I POSSESS IN ABUNDANCE.
YOU COULDN'T HAVE DONE THAT FIVE MINUTES AGO?
...AND THEN I WAITED.
FOR MY MOMENT.

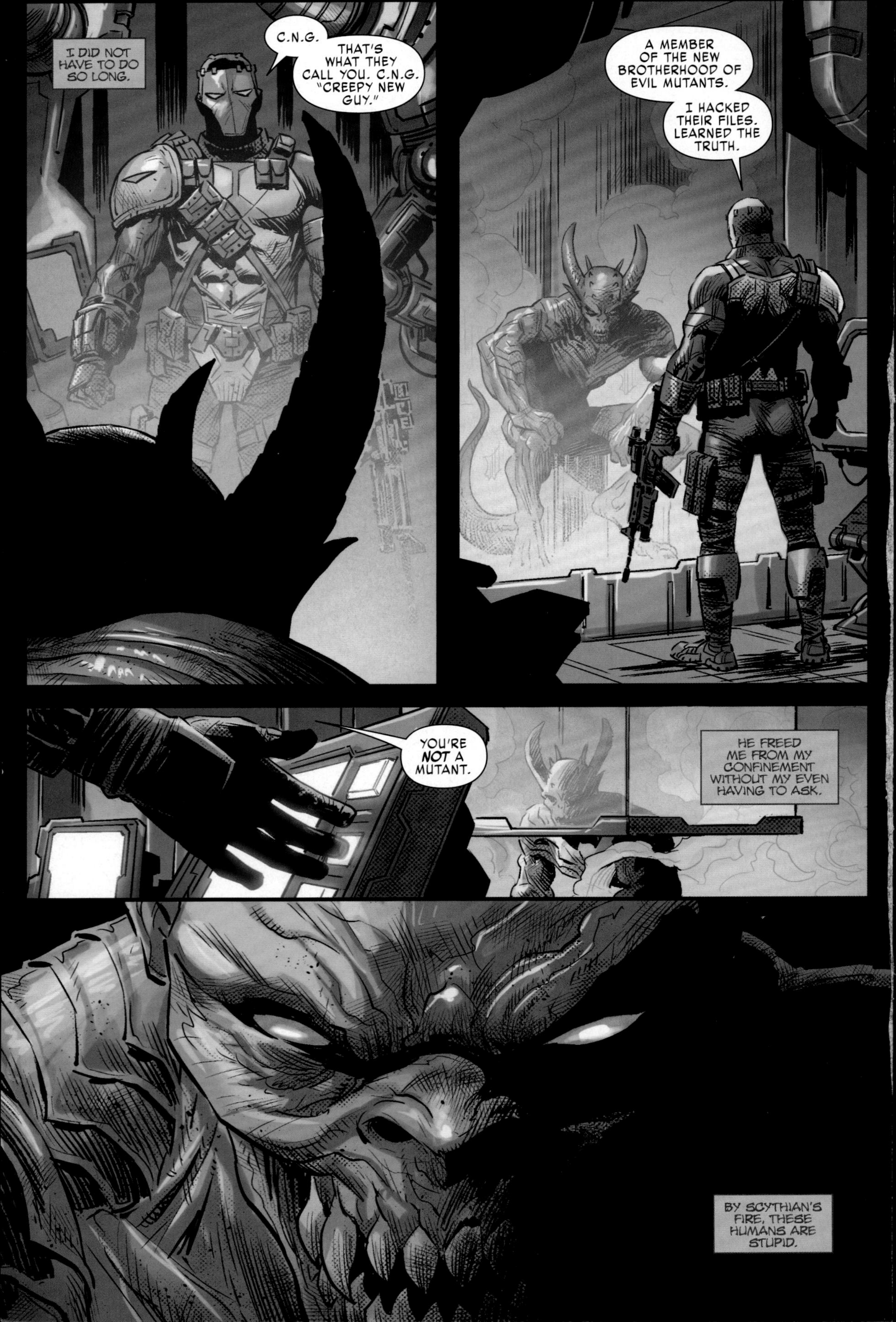
I DID NOT HAVE TO DO SO LONG.
C.N.G.
THAT'S WHAT THEY CALL YOU. C.N.G. "CREEPY NEW GUY."
A MEMBER OF THE NEW BROTHERHOOD OF EVIL MUTANTS.
I HACKED THEIR FILES. LEARNED THE TRUTH.
YOU'RE NOT A MUTANT.
HE FREED ME FROM MY CONFINEMENT WITHOUT MY EVEN HAVING TO ASK.
BY SCYTHIAN'S FIRE, THESE HUMANS ARE STUPID.

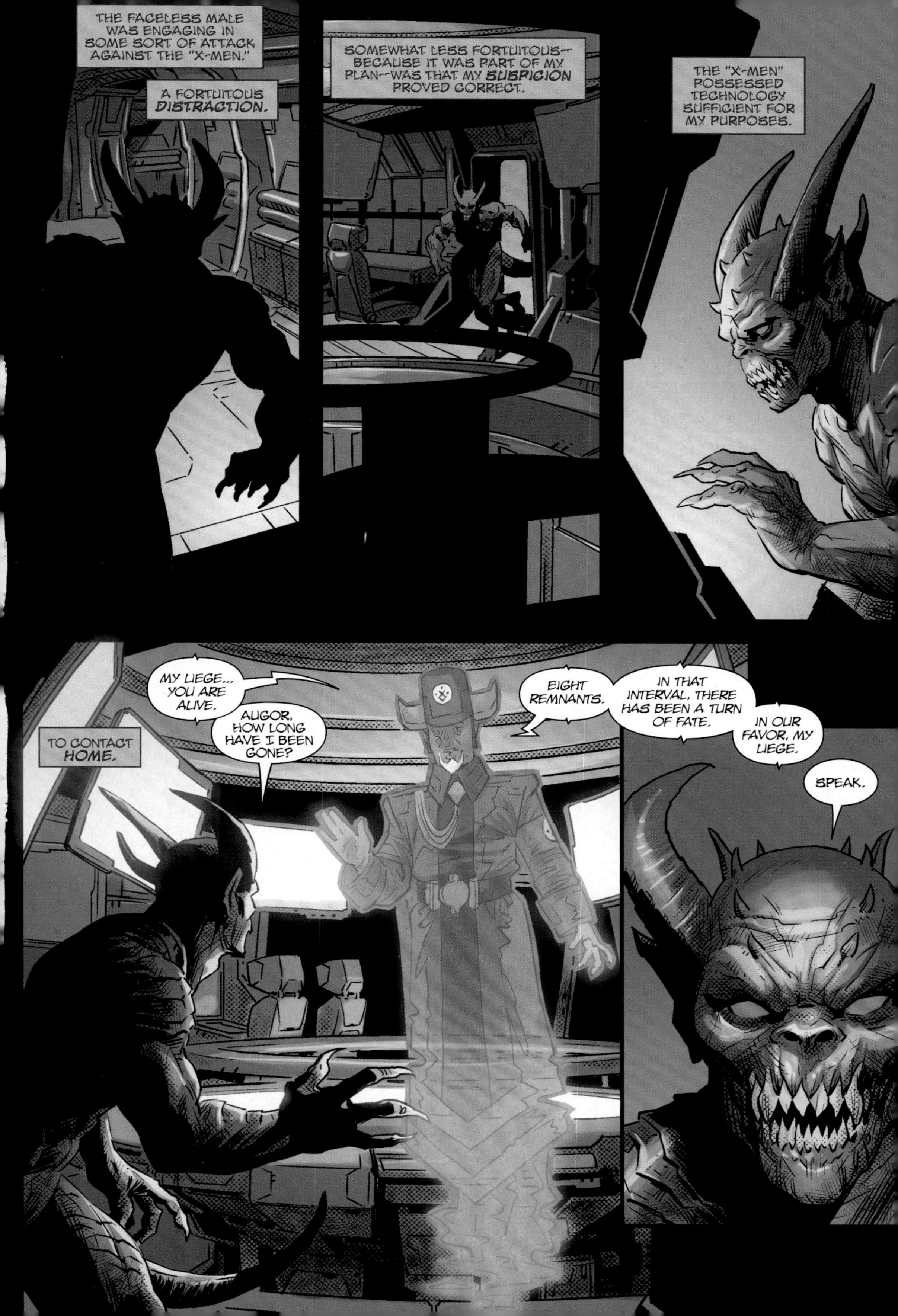
THE FACELESS MALE WAS ENGAGING IN SOME SORT OF ATTACK AGAINST THE "X-MEN."
A FORTUITOUS DISTRACTION.
SOMEWHAT LESS FORTUITOUS--BECAUSE IT WAS PART OF MY PLAN--WAS THAT MY SUSPICION PROVED CORRECT.
THE "X-MEN" POSSESSED TECHNOLOGY SUFFICIENT FOR MY PURPOSES.
TO CONTACT HOME.
MY LIEGE... YOU ARE ALIVE.
AUGOR, HOW LONG HAVE I BEEN GONE?
EIGHT REMNANTS.
IN THAT INTERVAL, THERE HAS BEEN A TURN OF FATE.
IN OUR FAVOR, MY LIEGE.
SPEAK.

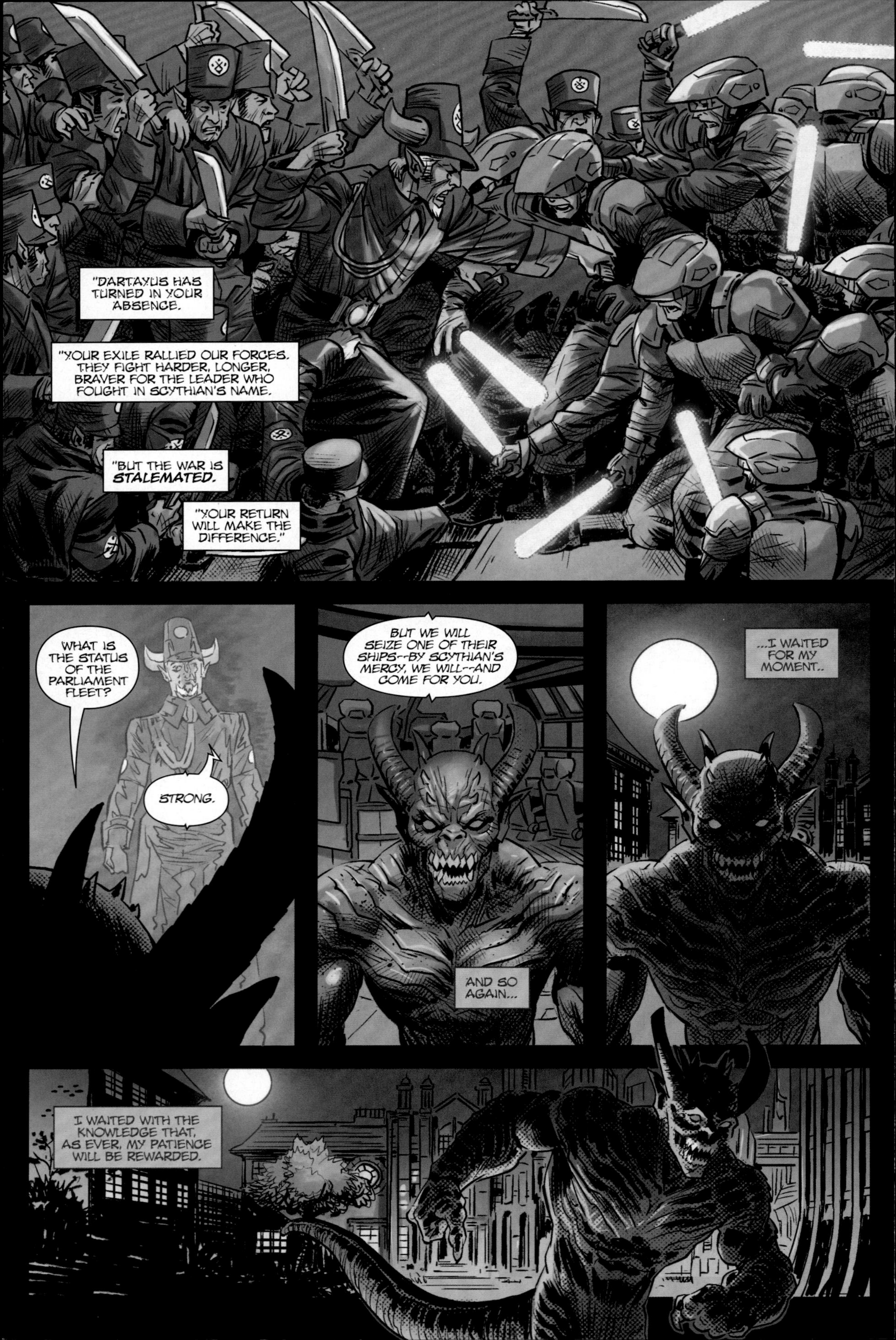
"DARTAYUS HAS TURNED IN YOUR ABSENCE.
"YOUR EXILE RALLIED OUR FORCES. THEY FIGHT HARDER, LONGER, BRAVER FOR THE LEADER WHO FOUGHT IN SCYTHIAN'S NAME.
"BUT THE WAR IS STALEMATED.
"YOUR RETURN WILL MAKE THE DIFFERENCE."
WHAT IS THE STATUS OF THE PARLIAMENT FLEET?
STRONG.
BUT WE WILL SEIZE ONE OF THEIR SHIPS--BY SCYTHIAN'S MERCY, WE WILL--AND COME FOR YOU.
AND SO AGAIN...
...I WAITED FOR MY MOMENT..
I WAITED WITH THE KNOWLEDGE THAT, AS EVER, MY PATIENCE WILL BE REWARDED.

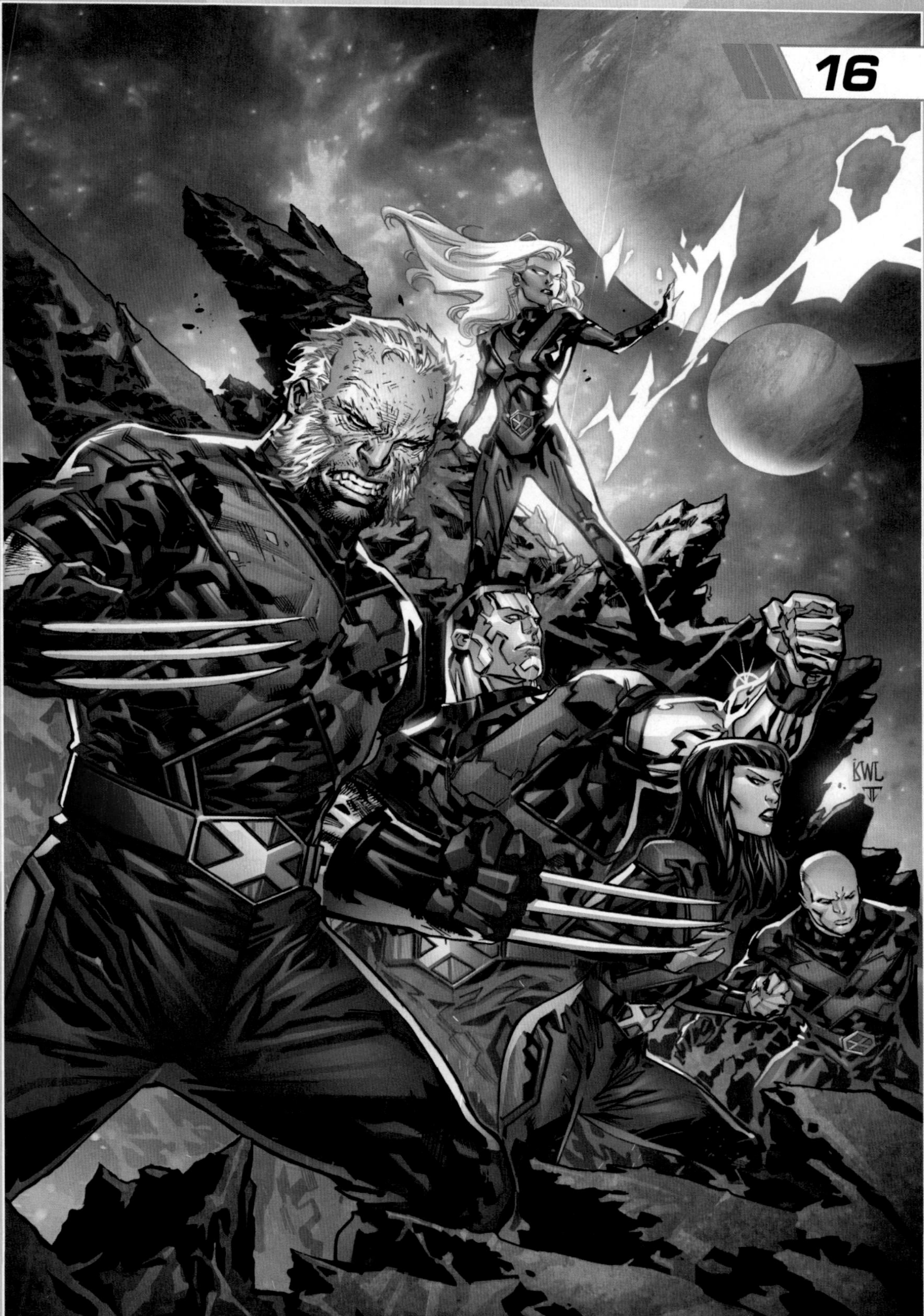
16

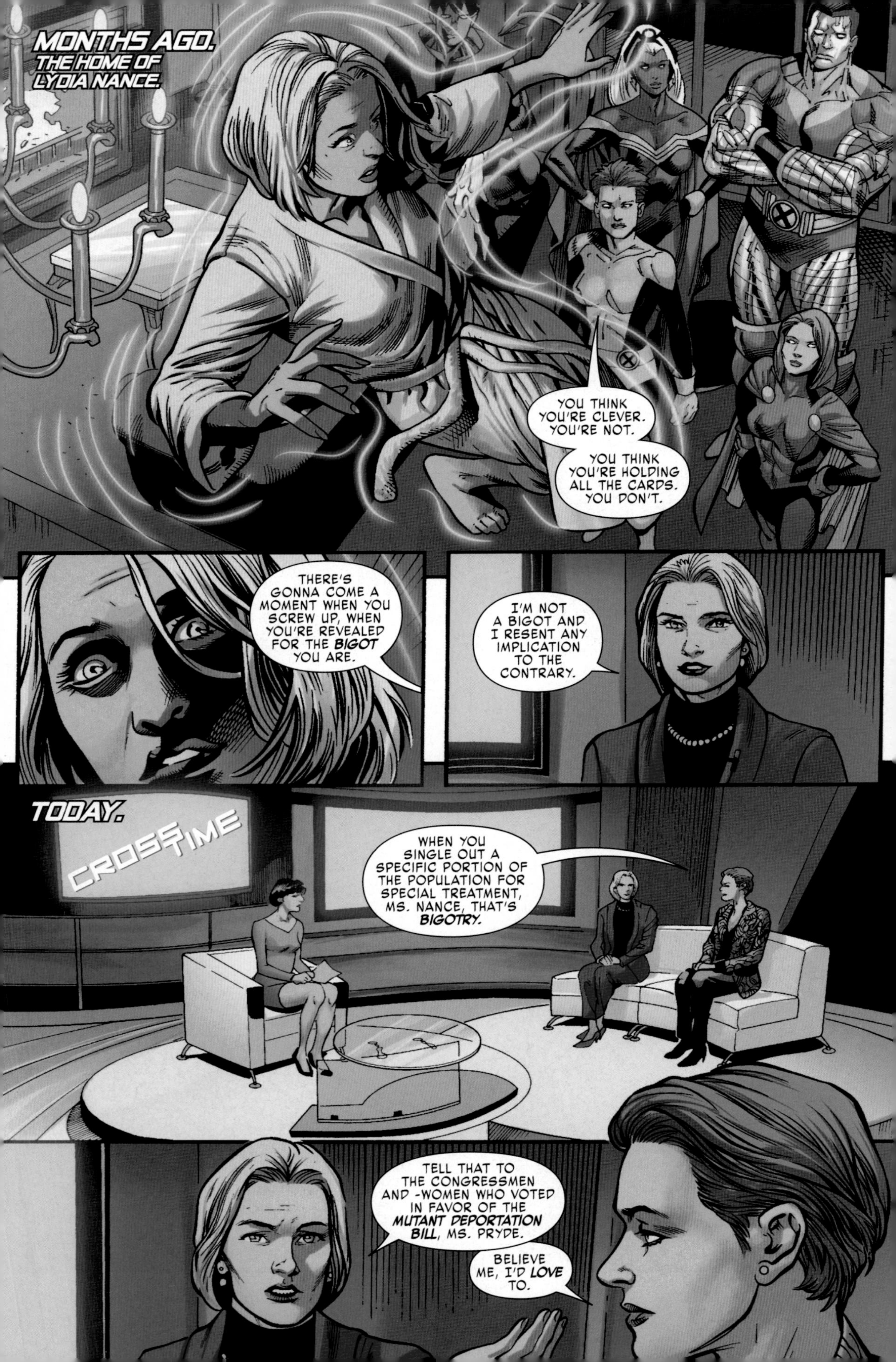
MONTHS AGO. THE HOME OF LYDIA NANCE.
YOU THINK YOU'RE CLEVER. YOU'RE NOT.
YOU THINK YOU'RE HOLDING ALL THE CARDS. YOU DON'T.
THERE'S GONNA COME A MOMENT WHEN YOU SCREW UP, WHEN YOU'RE REVEALED FOR THE BIGOT YOU ARE.
I'M NOT A BIGOT AND I RESENT ANY IMPLICATION TO THE CONTRARY.
TODAY.
CROSS TIME
WHEN YOU SINGLE OUT A SPECIFIC PORTION OF THE POPULATION FOR SPECIAL TREATMENT, MS. NANCE, THAT'S BIGOTRY.
TELL THAT TO THE CONGRESSMEN AND -WOMEN WHO VOTED IN FAVOR OF THE MUTANT DEPORTATION BILL, MS. PRYDE.
BELIEVE ME, I'D LOVE TO.

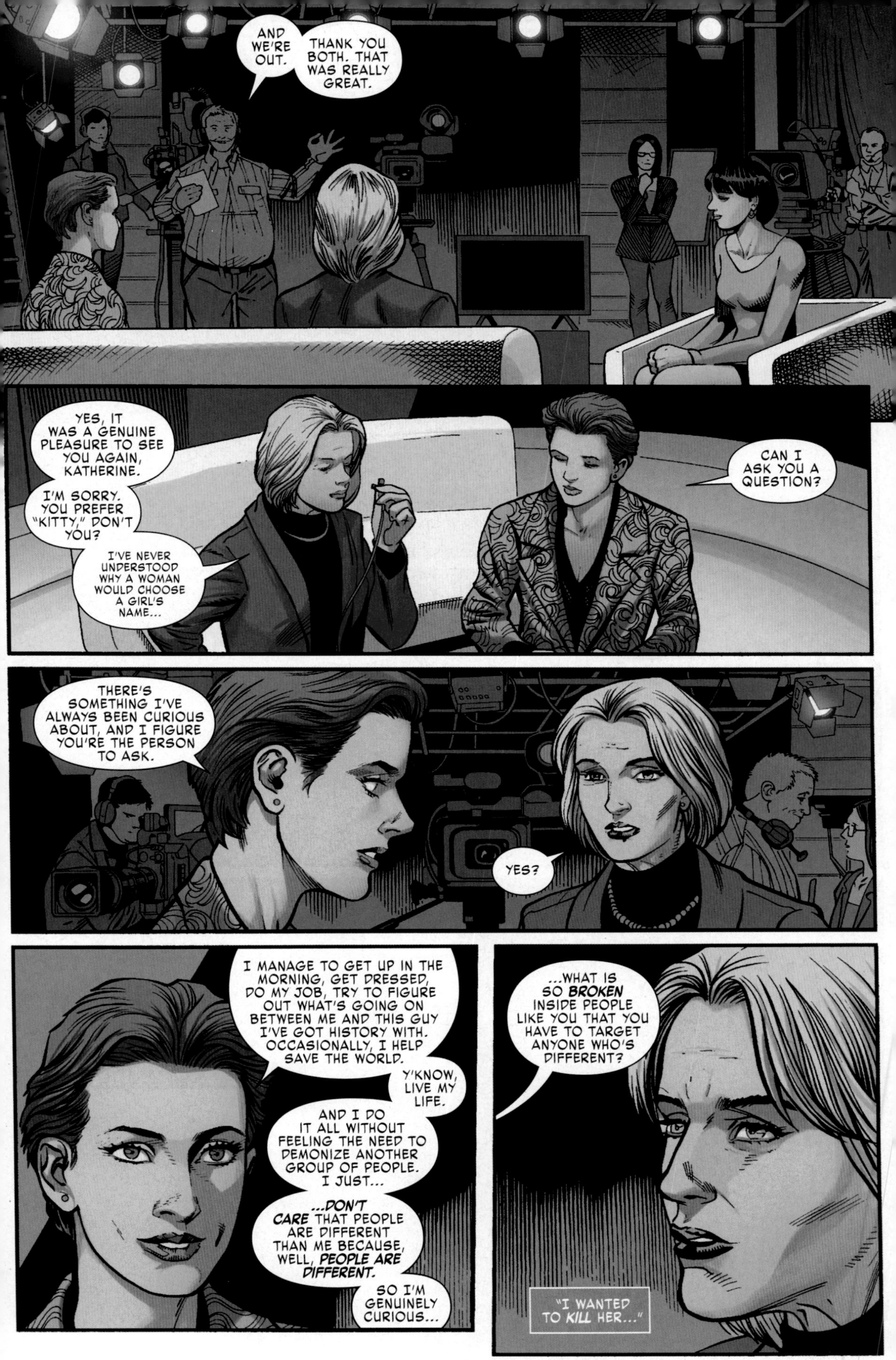
AND WE'RE OUT.
THANK YOU BOTH. THAT WAS REALLY GREAT.
YES, IT WAS A GENUINE PLEASURE TO SEE YOU AGAIN, KATHERINE.
I'M SORRY. YOU PREFER "KITTY," DON'T YOU?
I'VE NEVER UNDERSTOOD WHY A WOMAN WOULD CHOOSE A GIRL'S NAME...
CAN I ASK YOU A QUESTION?
THERE'S SOMETHING I'VE ALWAYS BEEN CURIOUS ABOUT, AND I FIGURE YOU'RE THE PERSON TO ASK.
YES?
I MANAGE TO GET UP IN THE MORNING, GET DRESSED, DO MY JOB, TRY TO FIGURE OUT WHAT'S GOING ON BETWEEN ME AND THIS GUY I'VE GOT HISTORY WITH. OCCASIONALLY, I HELP SAVE THE WORLD.
Y'KNOW, LIVE MY LIFE.
AND I DO IT ALL WITHOUT FEELING THE NEED TO DEMONIZE ANOTHER GROUP OF PEOPLE. I JUST...
...DON'T CARE THAT PEOPLE ARE DIFFERENT THAN ME BECAUSE, WELL, PEOPLE ARE DIFFERENT.
SO I'M GENUINELY CURIOUS...
...WHAT IS SO BROKEN INSIDE PEOPLE LIKE YOU THAT YOU HAVE TO TARGET ANYONE WHO'S DIFFERENT?
"I WANTED TO KILL HER..."

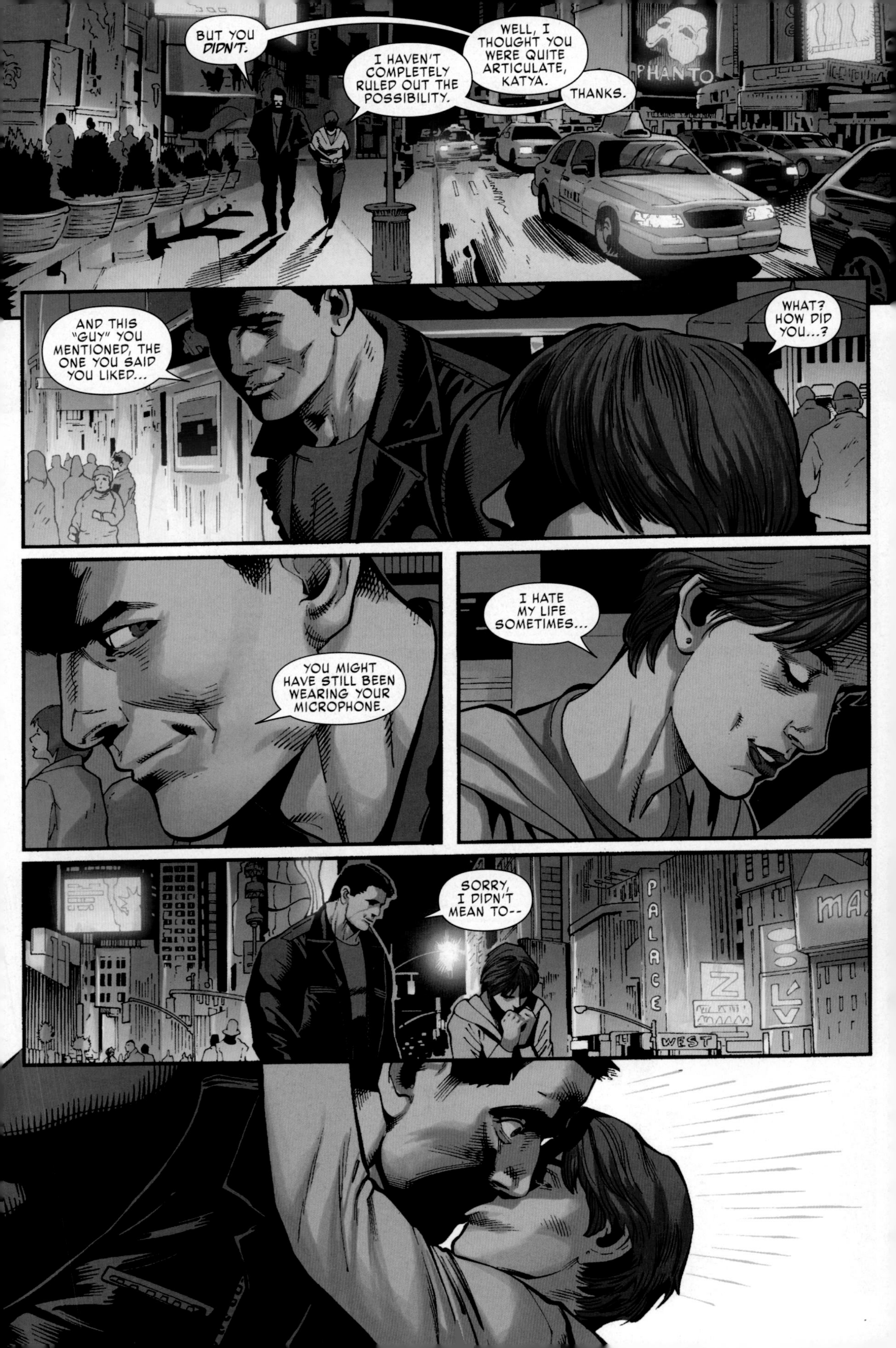

BUT YOU *DIDN'T*.
I HAVEN'T COMPLETELY RULED OUT THE POSSIBILITY.
WELL, I THOUGHT YOU WERE QUITE ARTICULATE, KATYA.
THANKS.
PHANTO
AND THIS "GUY" YOU MENTIONED, THE ONE YOU SAID YOU LIKED...
WHAT? HOW DID YOU...?
YOU MIGHT HAVE STILL BEEN WEARING YOUR MICROPHONE.
I HATE MY LIFE SOMETIMES...
SORRY, I DIDN'T MEAN TO--
PALACE
WEST

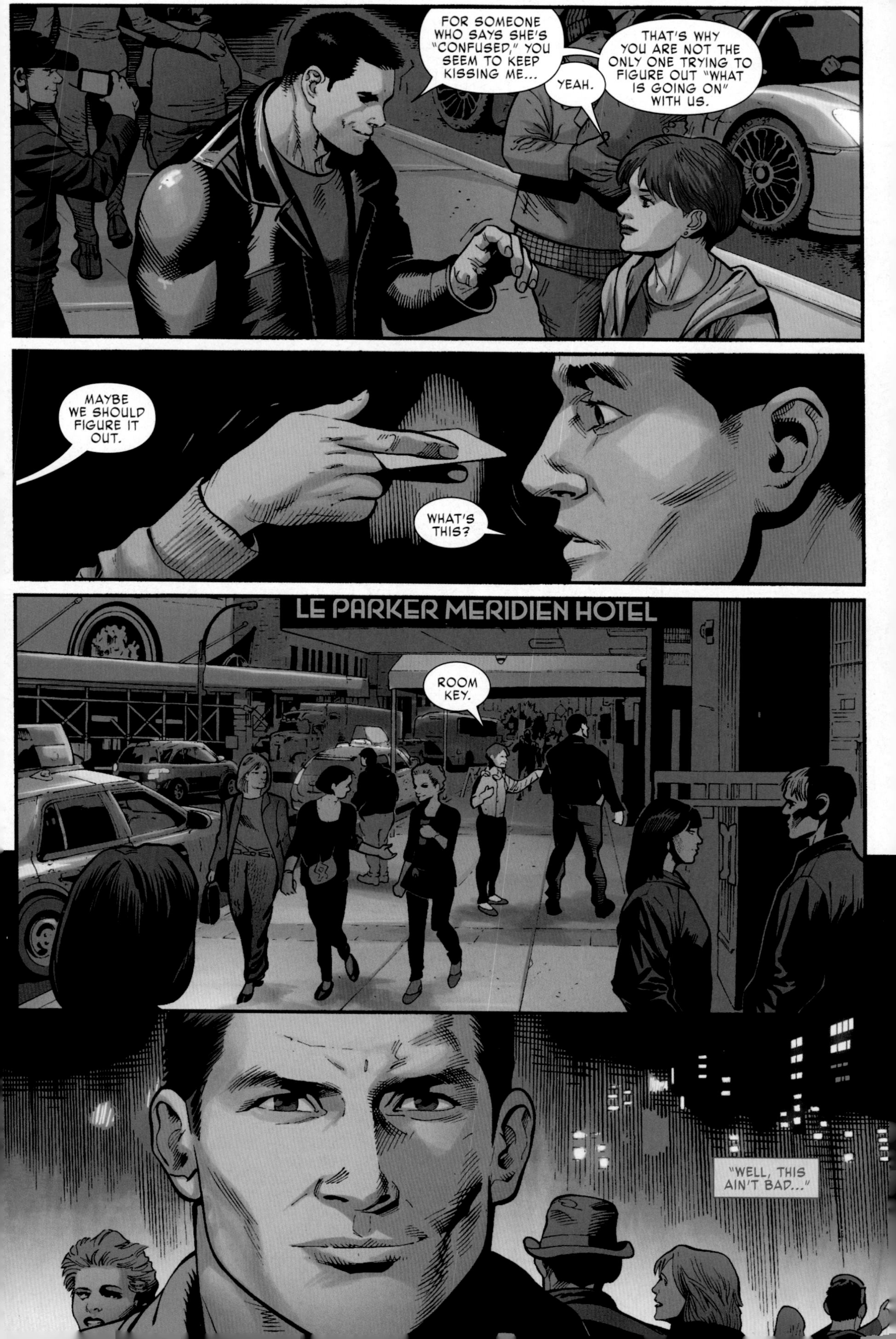
FOR SOMEONE WHO SAYS SHE'S "CONFUSED," YOU SEEM TO KEEP KISSING ME...
YEAH.
THAT'S WHY YOU ARE NOT THE ONLY ONE TRYING TO FIGURE OUT "WHAT IS GOING ON" WITH US.
MAYBE WE SHOULD FIGURE IT OUT.
WHAT'S THIS?
LE PARKER MERIDIEN HOTEL
ROOM KEY.
"WELL, THIS AIN'T BAD..."

NO, I GOTTA SAY...

...THIS AIN'T BAD AT ALL.

MUTANTS = AMERICANS

FIRST THEY CAME FOR THE MUTANTS

NO MUTANT DEPORTATION

X-MEN ARE HUMAN

EQUALITY FOR ALL

WE'RE ALL MUTANTS

RESIST

UNITY

CENTRAL PARK. MANHATTAN.

THINK SOMEBODY OUGHTA GO OUT THERE, SAY A FEW WORDS?

YOU KNOW ME BETTER'N THAT, 'RO.

ARE YOU VOLUNTEERING, LOGAN?

FIRST THEY CAME FOR THE MUTANTS

WHERE'S KÄTZCHEN? SHE REALLY SHOULD SEE THIS...

I HOPE EVERYTHING'S ALL RIGHT...

SHE DID THE CROSSTIME SHOW LAST NIGHT. I'M NOT SURE IF SHE MADE IT BACK TO THE MANSION...

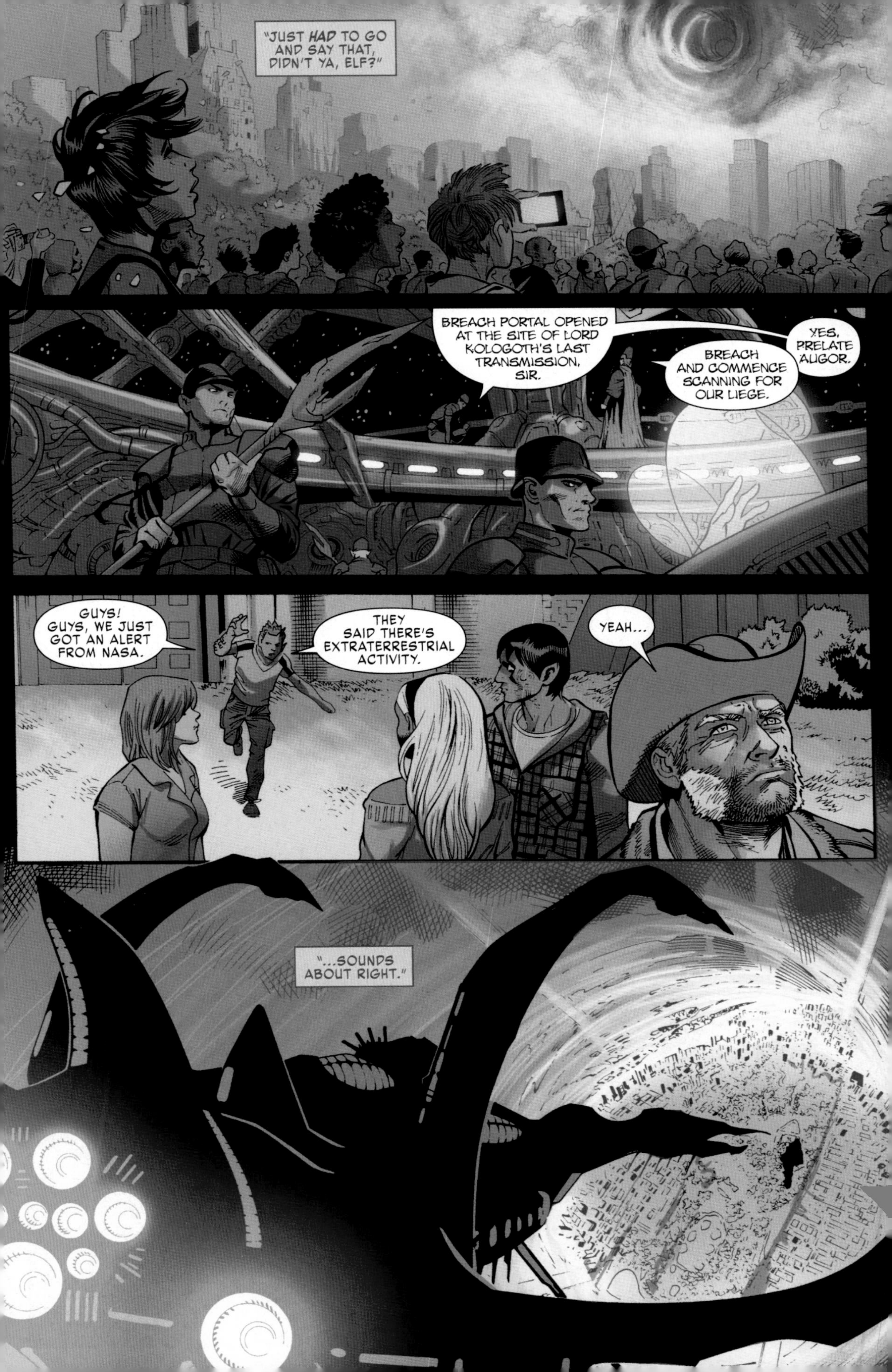
"JUST HAD TO GO AND SAY THAT, DIDN'T YA, ELF?"
BREACH PORTAL OPENED AT THE SITE OF LORD KOLOGOTH'S LAST TRANSMISSION, SIR.
BREACH AND COMMENCE SCANNING FOR OUR LIEGE.
YES, PRELATE AUGOR.
GUYS! GUYS, WE JUST GOT AN ALERT FROM NASA.
THEY SAID THERE'S EXTRATERRESTRIAL ACTIVITY.
YEAH...
"...SOUNDS ABOUT RIGHT."

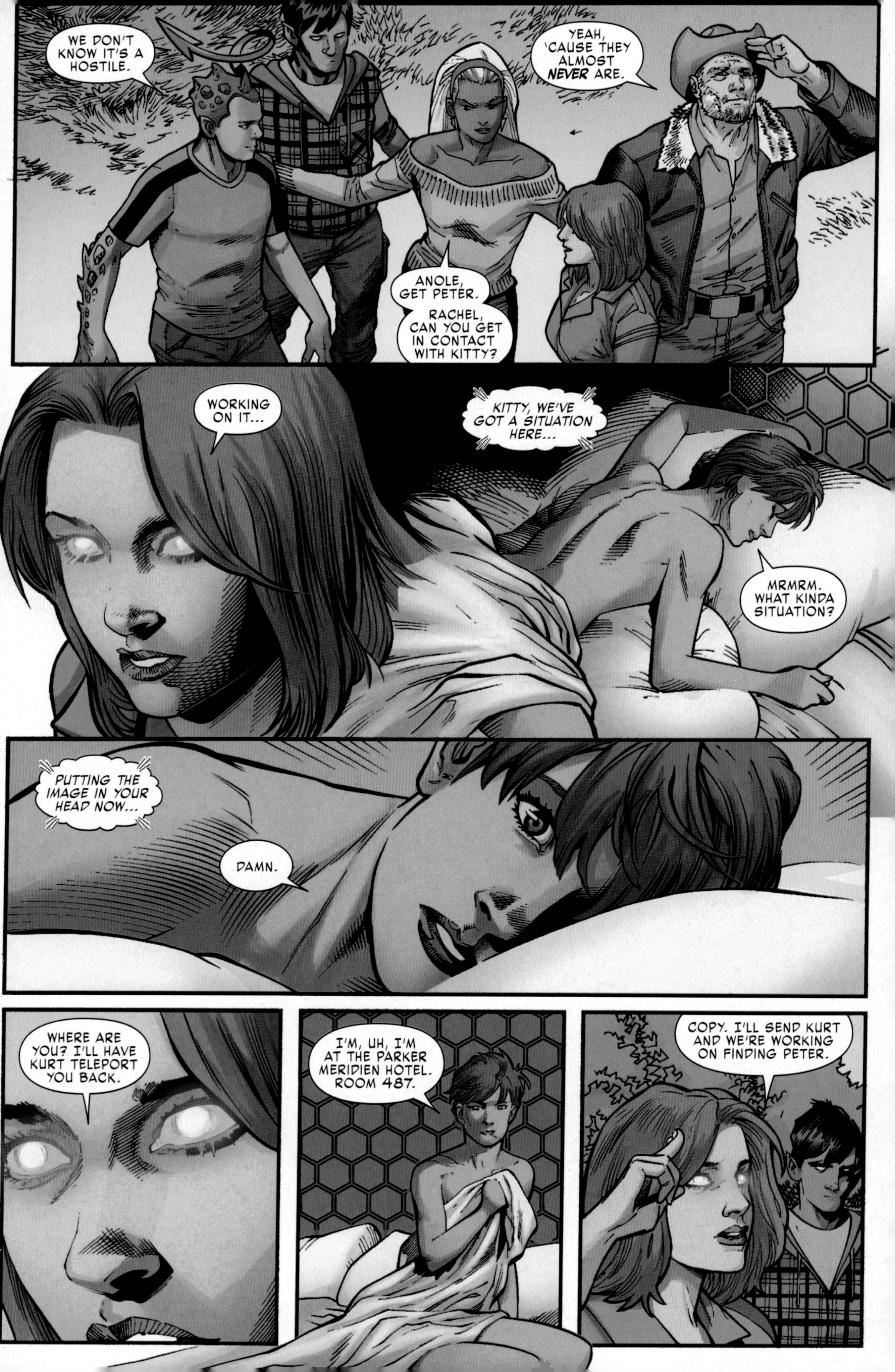
WE DON'T KNOW IT'S A HOSTILE.
YEAH, 'CAUSE THEY ALMOST *NEVER* ARE.
ANOLE, GET PETER.
RACHEL, CAN YOU GET IN CONTACT WITH KITTY?
WORKING ON IT...
KITTY, WE'VE GOT A SITUATION HERE...
MRMRM. WHAT KINDA SITUATION?
PUTTING THE IMAGE IN YOUR HEAD NOW...
DAMN.
WHERE ARE YOU? I'LL HAVE KURT TELEPORT YOU BACK.
I'M, UH, I'M AT THE PARKER MERIDIEN HOTEL. ROOM 487.
COPY. I'LL SEND KURT AND WE'RE WORKING ON FINDING PETER.

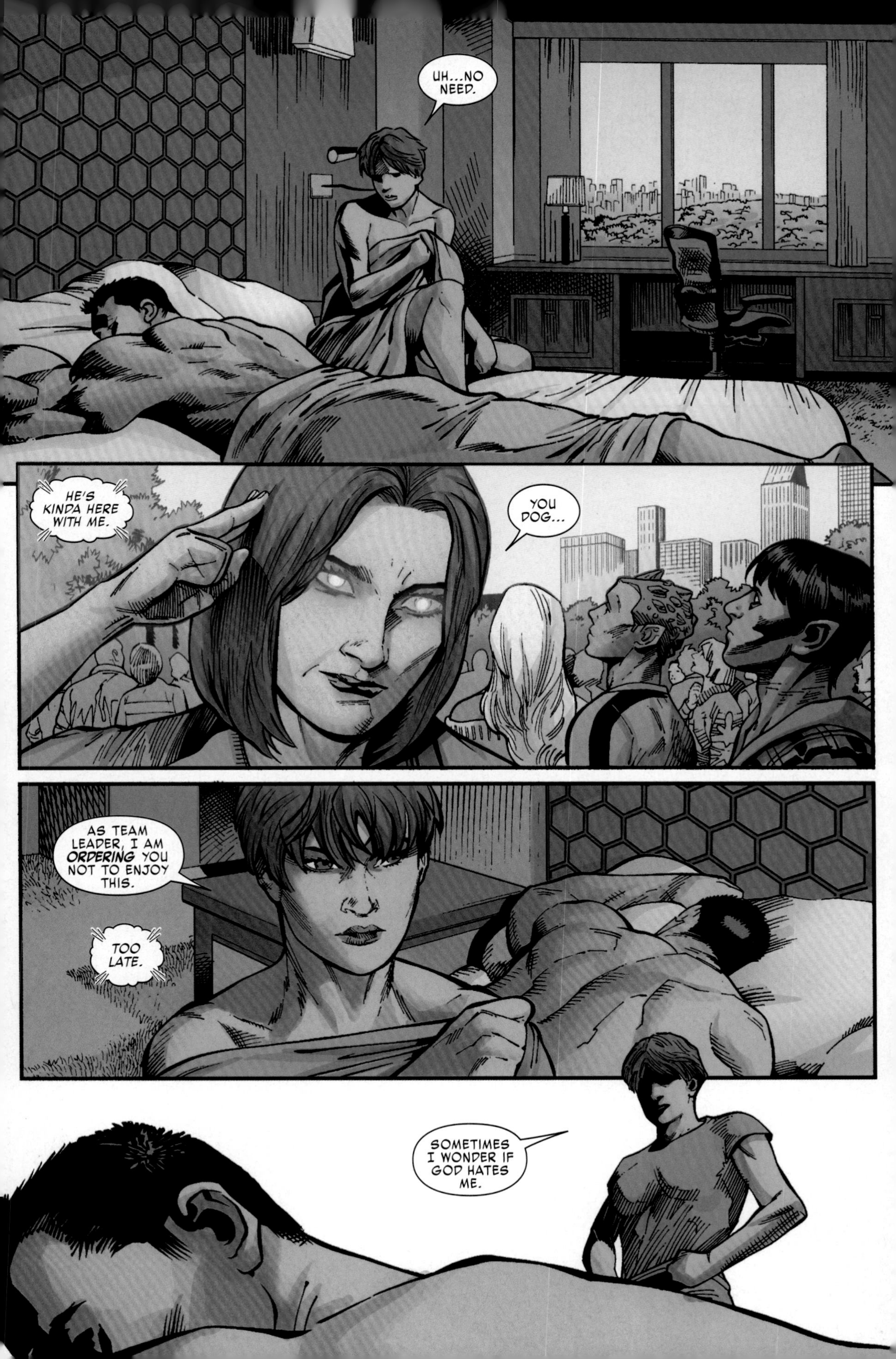
UH...NO NEED.
HE'S KINDA HERE WITH ME.
YOU DOG...
AS TEAM LEADER, I AM ORDERING YOU NOT TO ENJOY THIS.
TOO LATE.
SOMETIMES I WONDER IF GOD HATES ME.

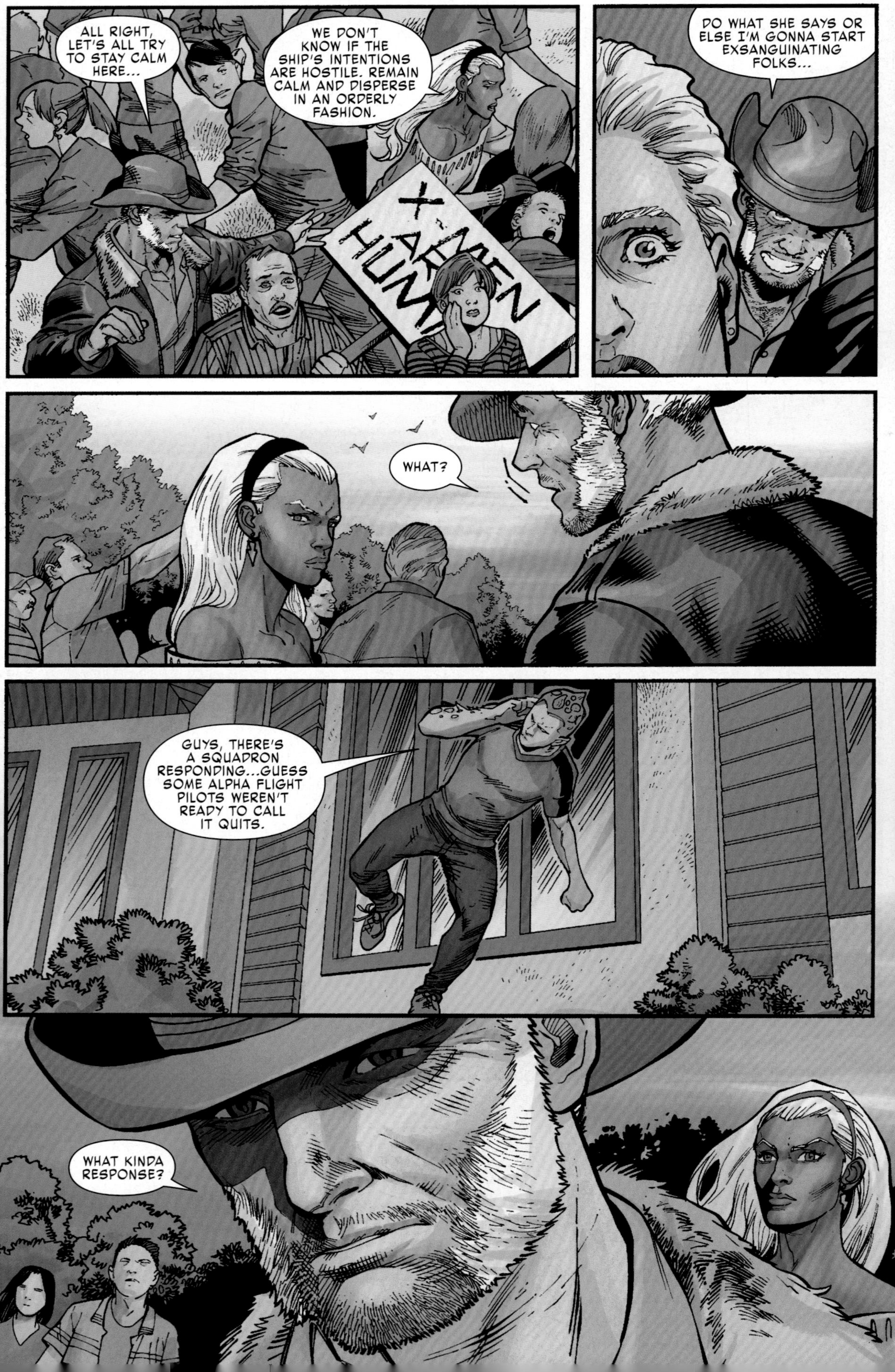
ALL RIGHT, LET'S ALL TRY TO STAY CALM HERE...
WE DON'T KNOW IF THE SHIP'S INTENTIONS ARE HOSTILE. REMAIN CALM AND DISPERSE IN AN ORDERLY FASHION.
DO WHAT SHE SAYS OR ELSE I'M GONNA START EXSANGUINATING FOLKS...
WHAT?
GUYS, THERE'S A SQUADRON RESPONDING...GUESS SOME ALPHA FLIGHT PILOTS WEREN'T READY TO CALL IT QUITS.
WHAT KINDA RESPONSE?

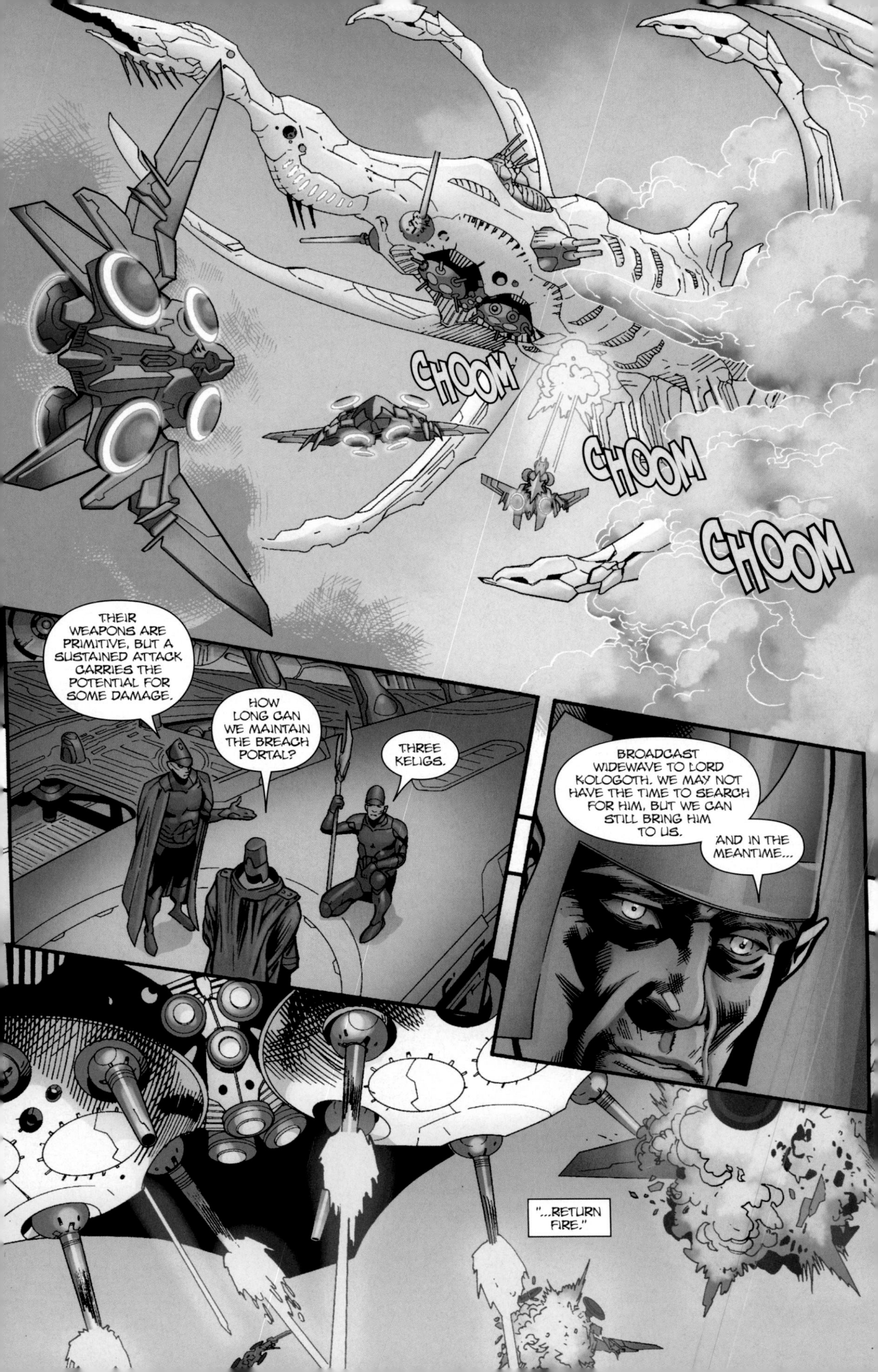
CHOOM
CHOOM
CHOOM
THEIR WEAPONS ARE PRIMITIVE, BUT A SUSTAINED ATTACK CARRIES THE POTENTIAL FOR SOME DAMAGE.
HOW LONG CAN WE MAINTAIN THE BREACH PORTAL?
THREE KELIGS.
BROADCAST WIDEWAVE TO LORD KOLOGOTH. WE MAY NOT HAVE THE TIME TO SEARCH FOR HIM, BUT WE CAN STILL BRING HIM TO US.
AND IN THE MEANTIME...
"...RETURN FIRE."

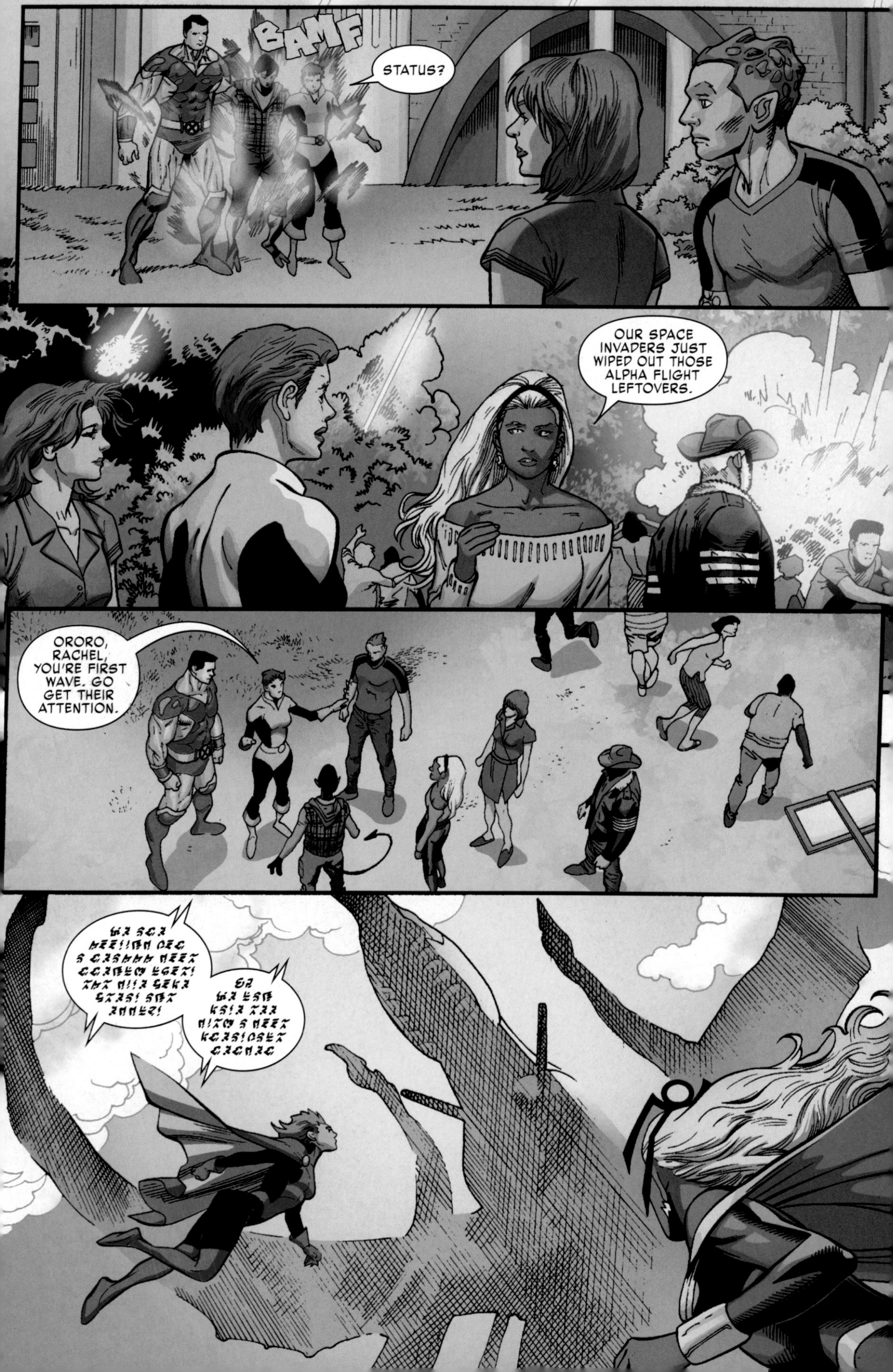
BAMF
STATUS?
OUR SPACE INVADERS JUST WIPED OUT THOSE ALPHA FLIGHT LEFTOVERS.
ORORO, RACHEL, YOU'RE FIRST WAVE. GO GET THEIR ATTENTION.

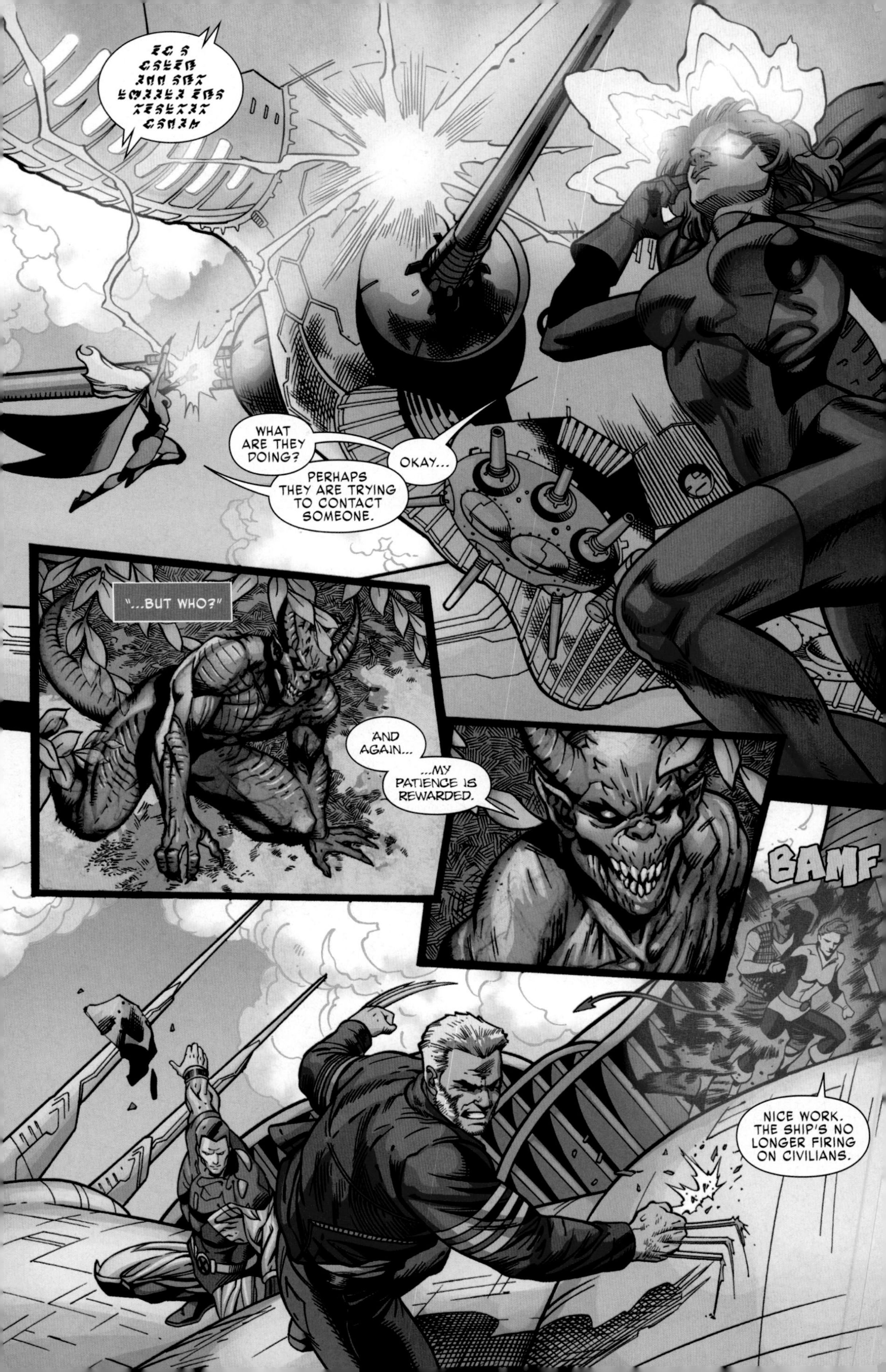
WHAT ARE THEY DOING?
OKAY...
PERHAPS THEY ARE TRYING TO CONTACT SOMEONE.
"...BUT WHO?"
AND AGAIN...
...MY PATIENCE IS REWARDED.
BAMF
NICE WORK. THE SHIP'S NO LONGER FIRING ON CIVILIANS.

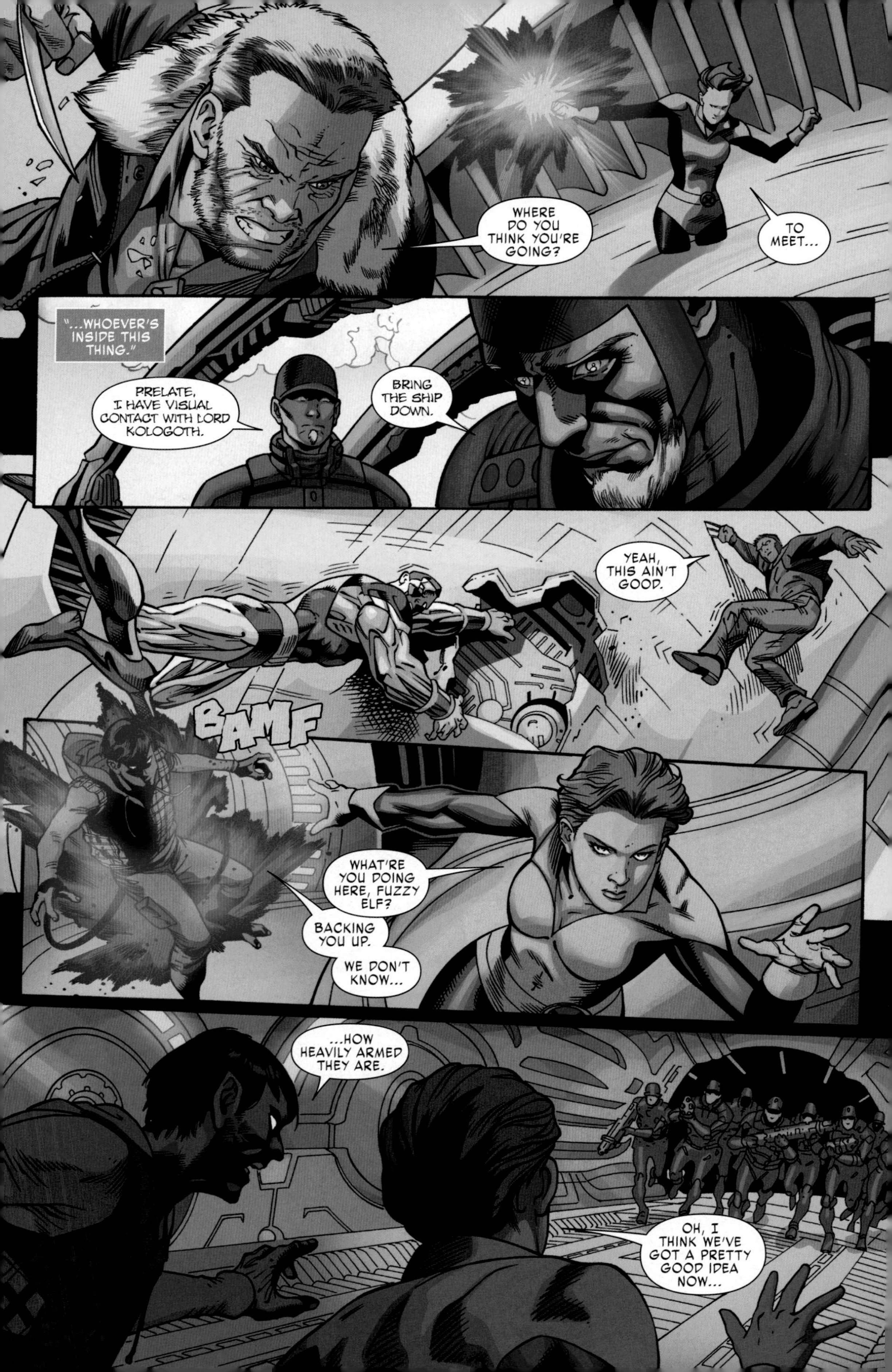
WHERE DO YOU THINK YOU'RE GOING?
TO MEET...
"...WHOEVER'S INSIDE THIS THING."
PRELATE, I HAVE VISUAL CONTACT WITH LORD KOLOGOTH.
BRING THE SHIP DOWN.
YEAH, THIS AIN'T GOOD.
BAMF
WHAT'RE YOU DOING HERE, FUZZY ELF?
BACKING YOU UP.
WE DON'T KNOW...
...HOW HEAVILY ARMED THEY ARE.
OH, I THINK WE'VE GOT A PRETTY GOOD IDEA NOW...

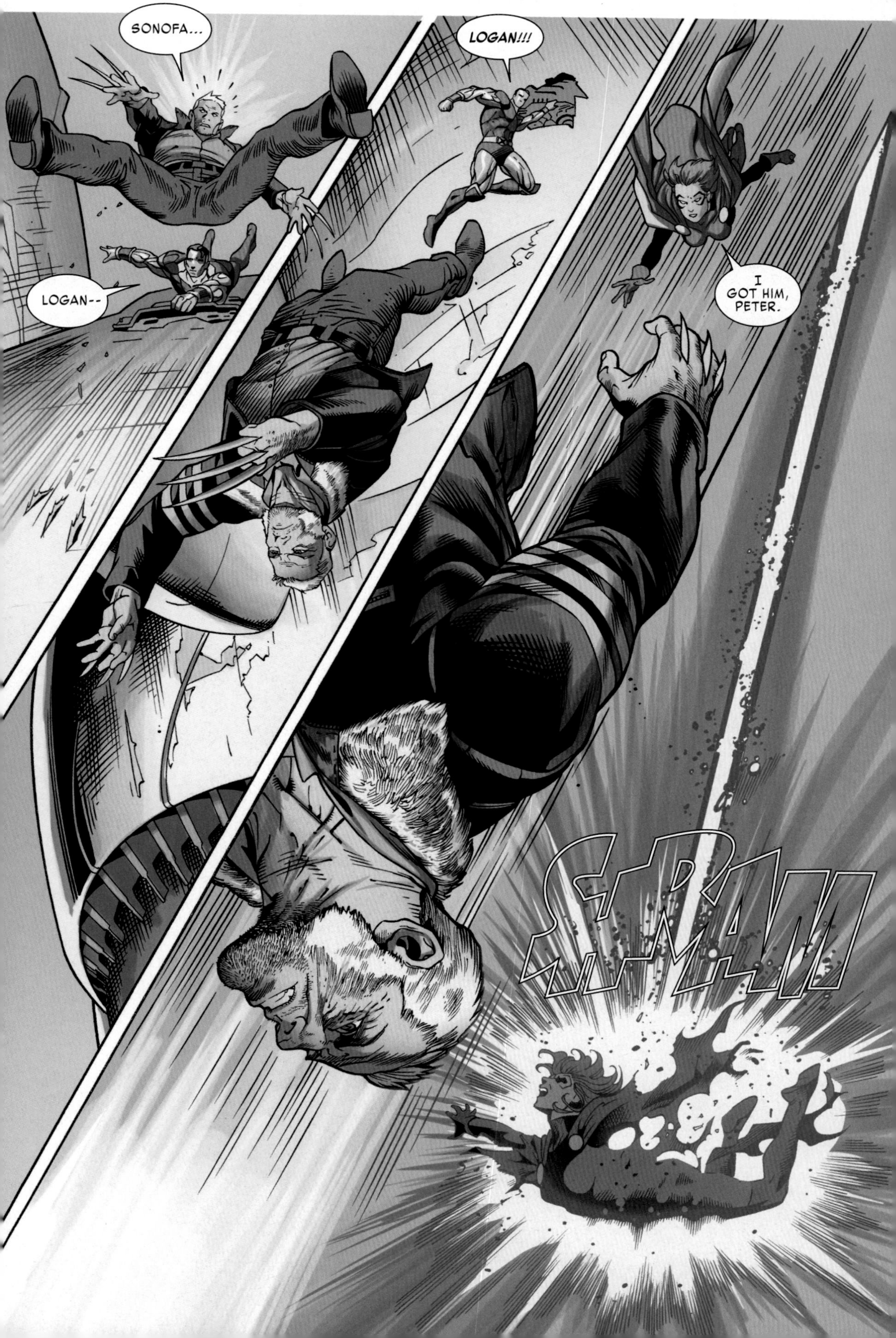
SONOFA...
LOGAN--
LOGAN!!!
I GOT HIM, PETER.
SPAM

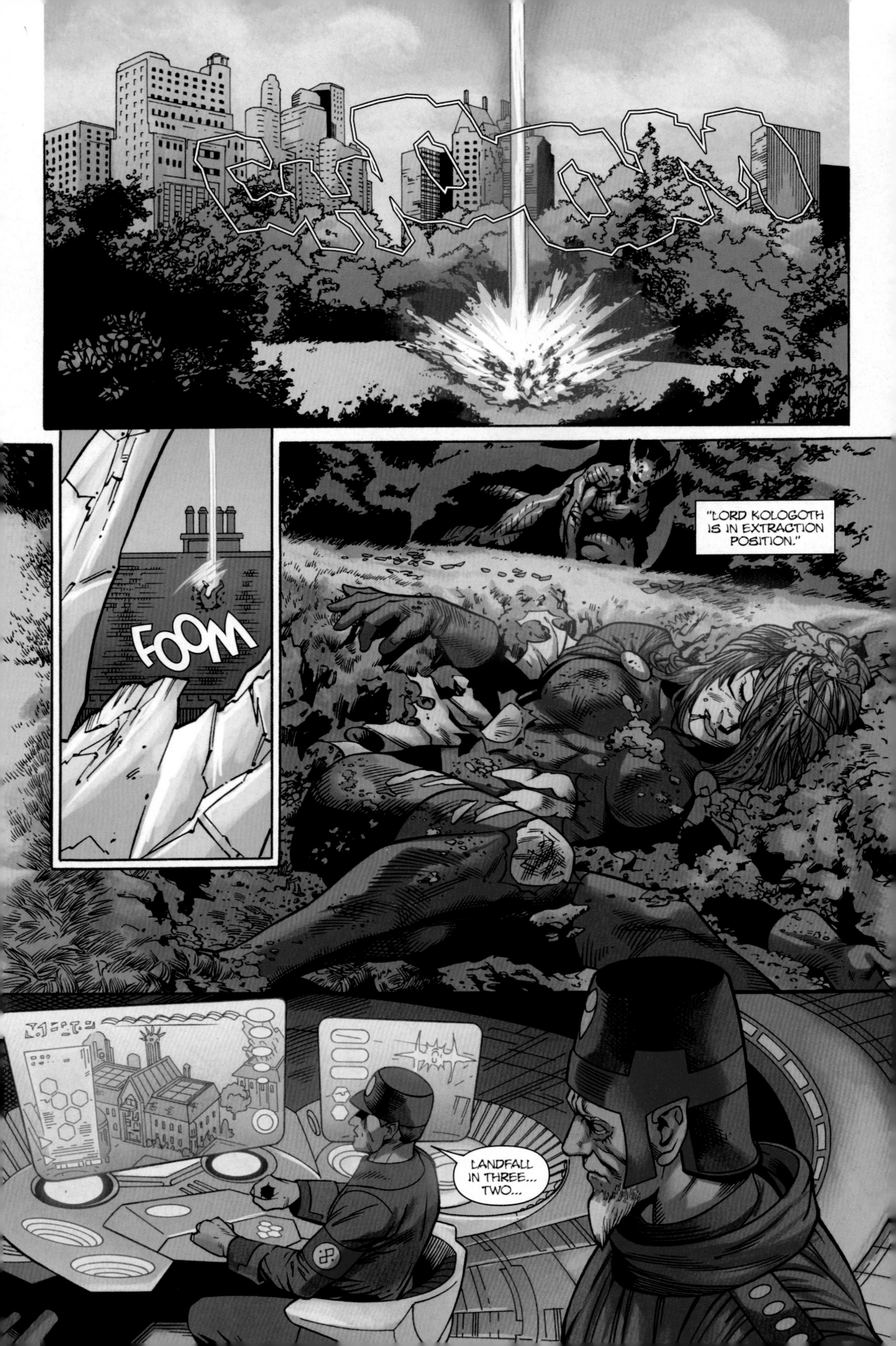
FOOM
"LORD KOLOGOTH IS IN EXTRACTION POSITION."
LANDFALL IN THREE... TWO...

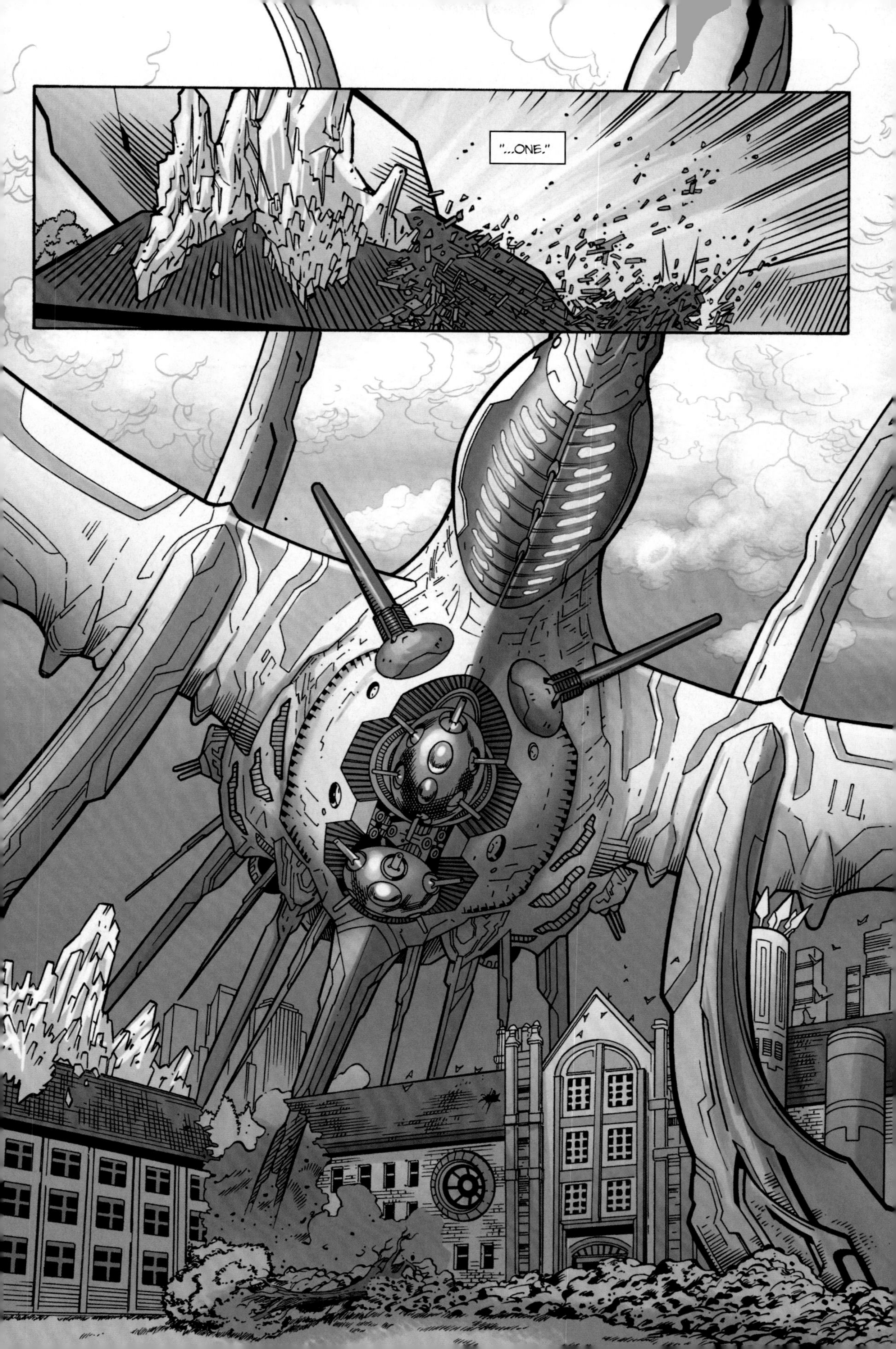
"...ONE."

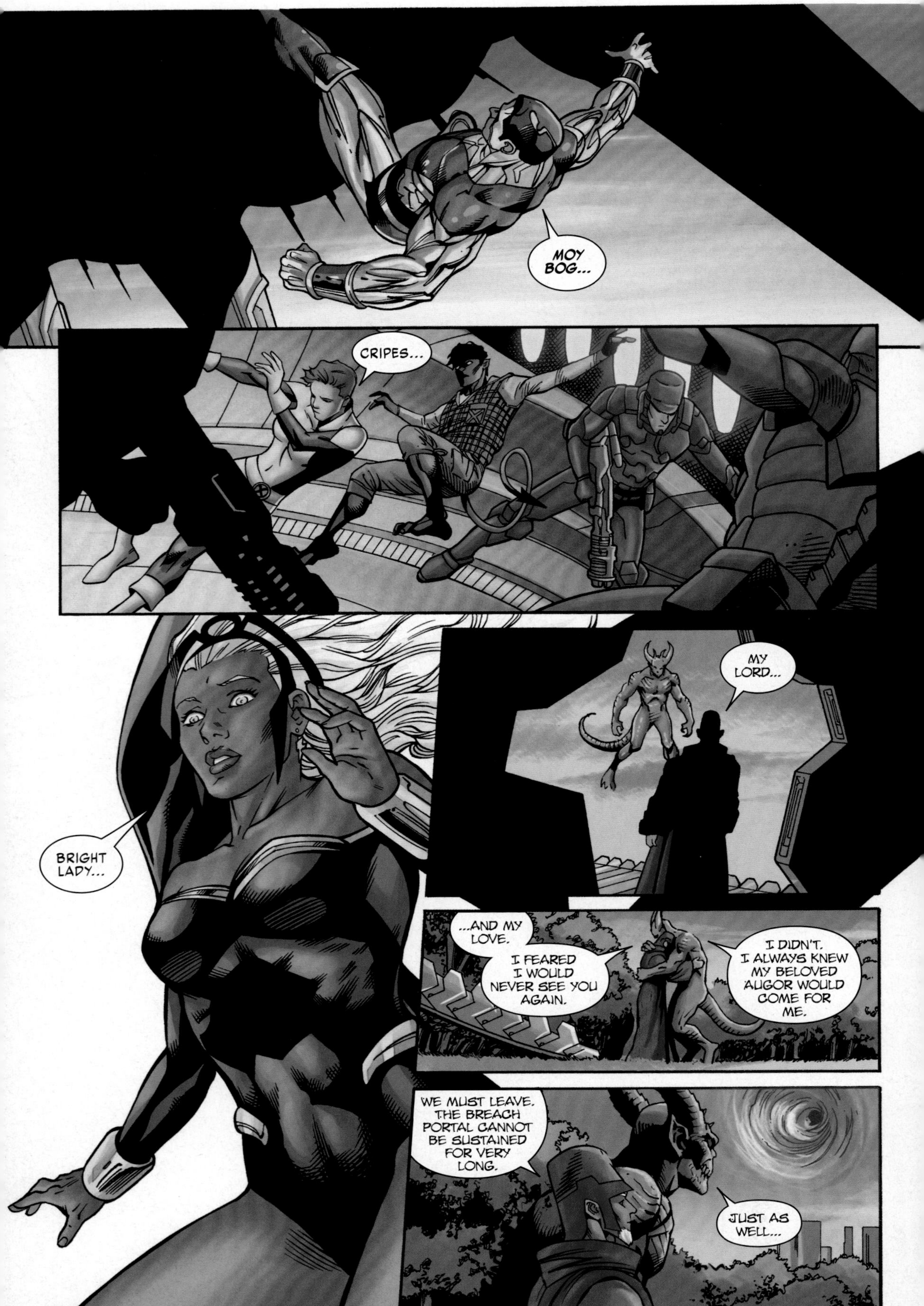
MOY BOG...
CRIPES...
BRIGHT LADY...
MY LORD...
...AND MY LOVE.
I FEARED I WOULD NEVER SEE YOU AGAIN.
I DIDN'T. I ALWAYS KNEW MY BELOVED AUGOR WOULD COME FOR ME.
WE MUST LEAVE. THE BREACH PORTAL CANNOT BE SUSTAINED FOR VERY LONG.
JUST AS WELL...

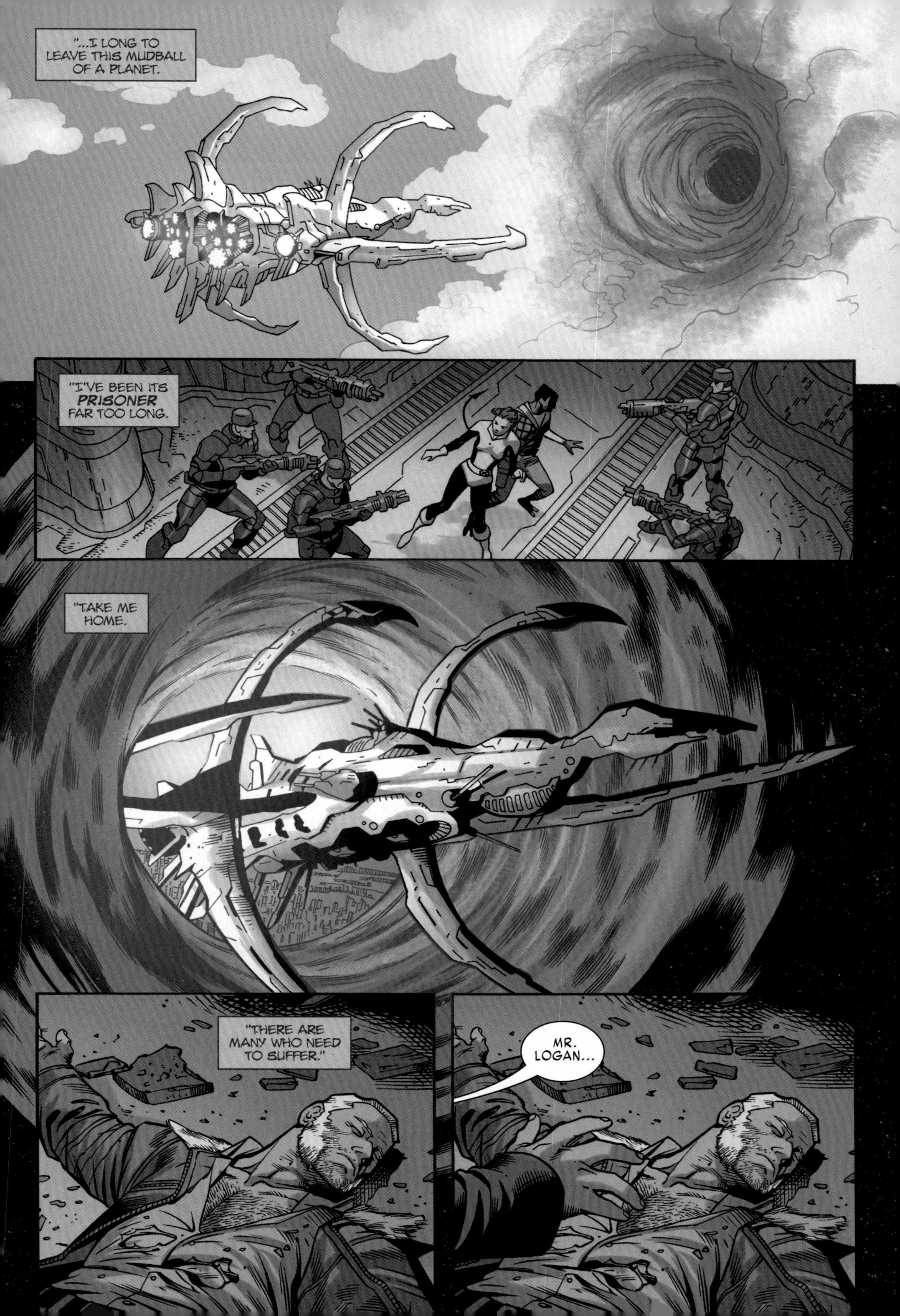
"...I LONG TO LEAVE THIS MUDBALL OF A PLANET.
"I'VE BEEN ITS PRISONER FAR TOO LONG.
"TAKE ME HOME.
"THERE ARE MANY WHO NEED TO SUFFER."
MR. LOGAN...

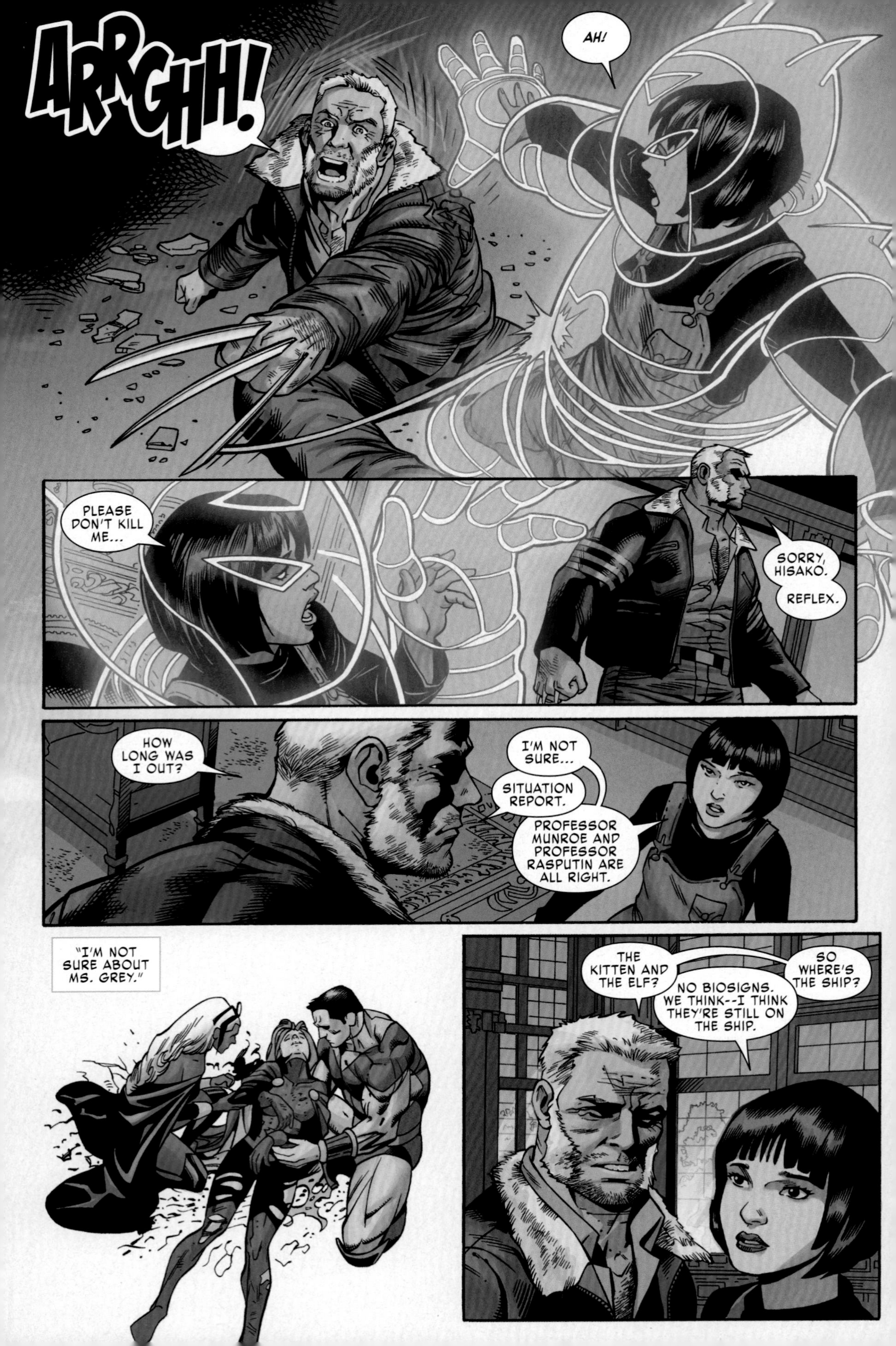
ARRGHH!
AH!
PLEASE DON'T KILL ME...
SORRY, HISAKO.
REFLEX.
HOW LONG WAS I OUT?
I'M NOT SURE...
SITUATION REPORT.
PROFESSOR MUNROE AND PROFESSOR RASPUTIN ARE ALL RIGHT.
"I'M NOT SURE ABOUT MS. GREY."
THE KITTEN AND THE ELF?
NO BIOSIGNS. WE THINK--I THINK THEY'RE STILL ON THE SHIP.
SO WHERE'S THE SHIP?

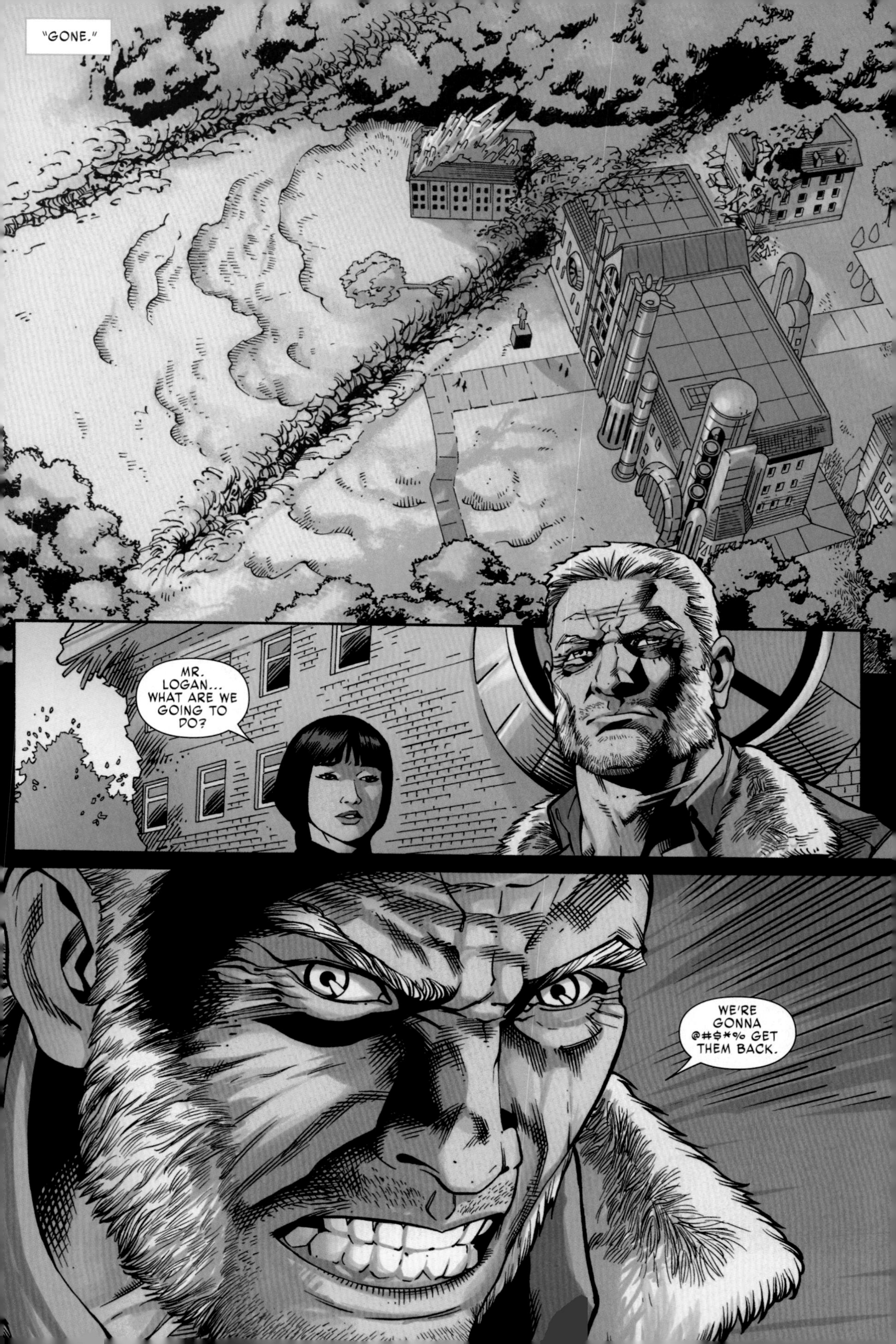
"GONE."
MR. LOGAN... WHAT ARE WE GOING TO DO?
WE'RE GONNA @#$*% GET THEM BACK.

17

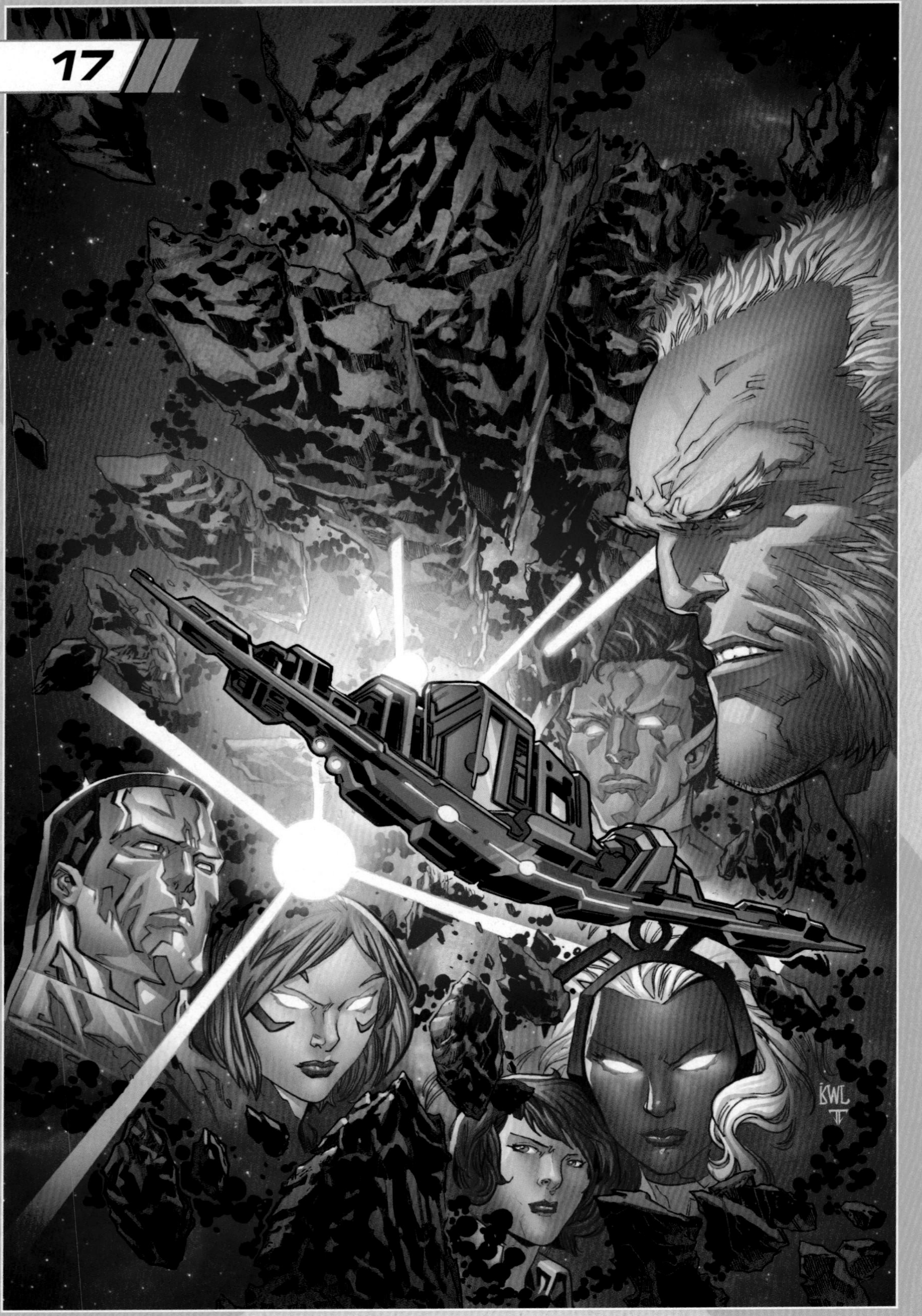

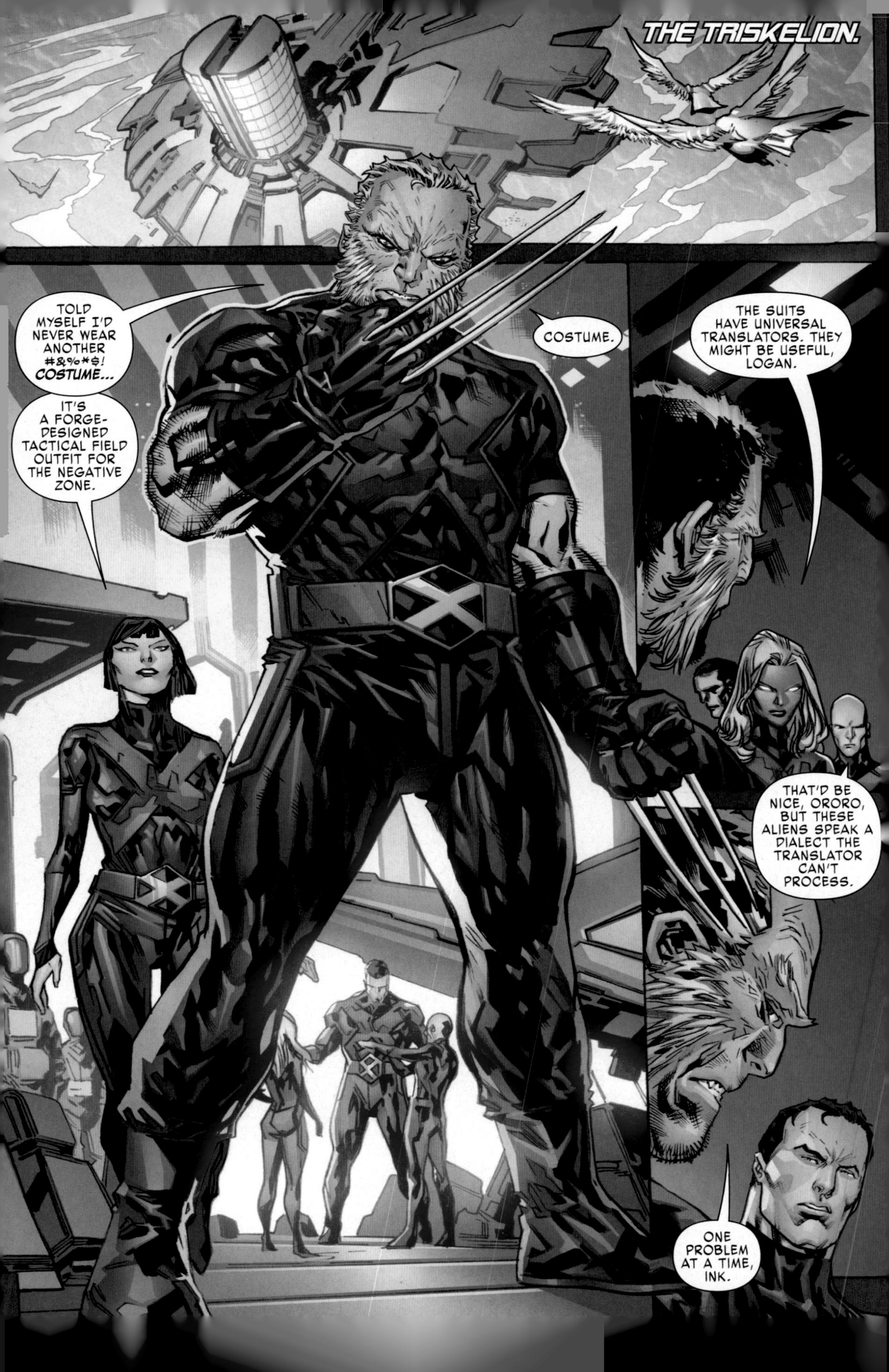
THE TRISKELION.
TOLD MYSELF I'D NEVER WEAR ANOTHER #&%*$! COSTUME...
IT'S A FORGE-DESIGNED TACTICAL FIELD OUTFIT FOR THE NEGATIVE ZONE.
COSTUME.
THE SUITS HAVE UNIVERSAL TRANSLATORS. THEY MIGHT BE USEFUL, LOGAN.
THAT'D BE NICE, ORORO, BUT THESE ALIENS SPEAK A DIALECT THE TRANSLATOR CAN'T PROCESS.
ONE PROBLEM AT A TIME, INK.

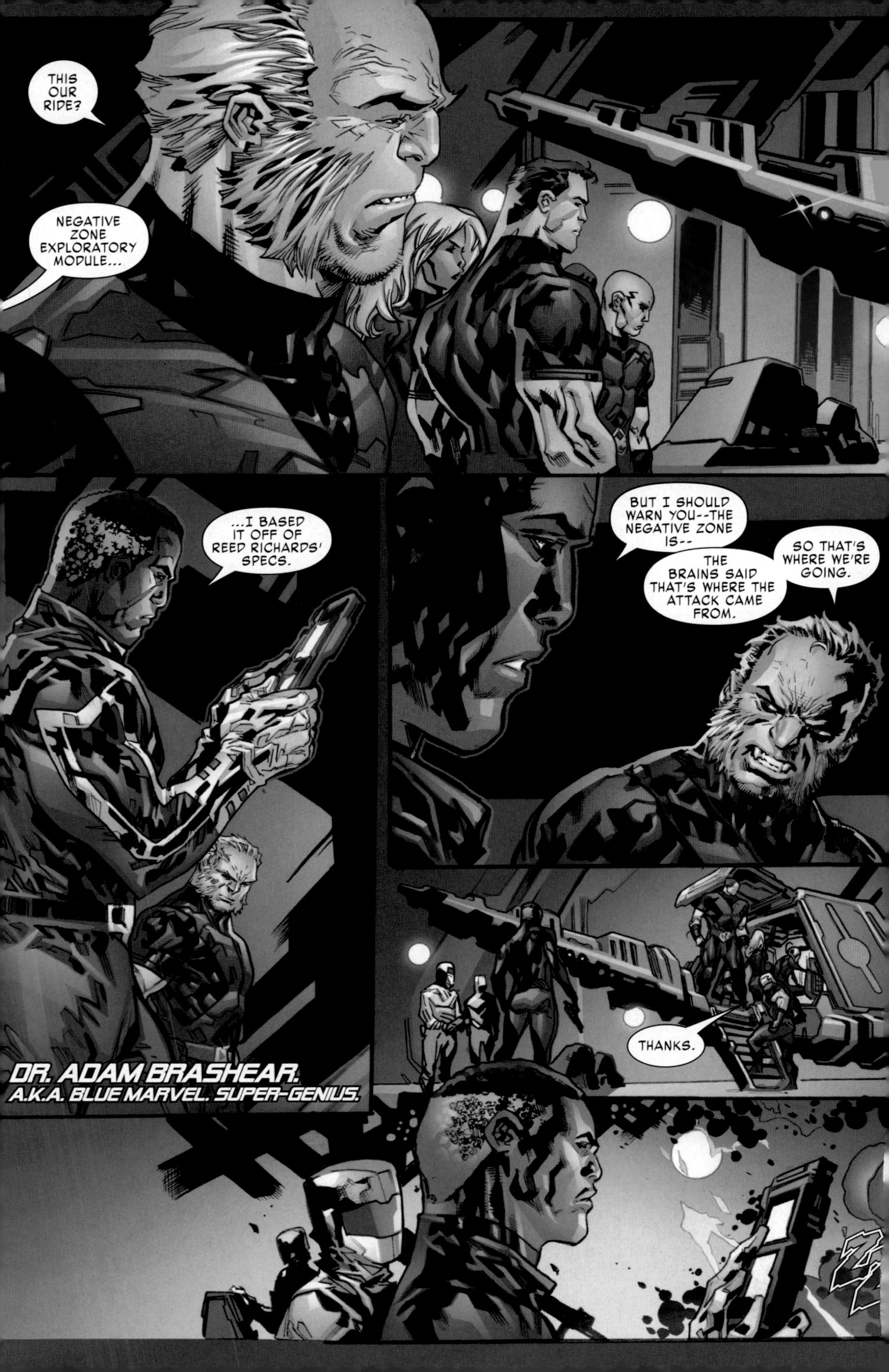
THIS OUR RIDE?
NEGATIVE ZONE EXPLORATORY MODULE...
...I BASED IT OFF OF REED RICHARDS' SPECS.
DR. ADAM BRASHEAR. A.K.A. BLUE MARVEL. SUPER-GENIUS.
BUT I SHOULD WARN YOU--THE NEGATIVE ZONE IS--
THE BRAINS SAID THAT'S WHERE THE ATTACK CAME FROM.
SO THAT'S WHERE WE'RE GOING.
THANKS.

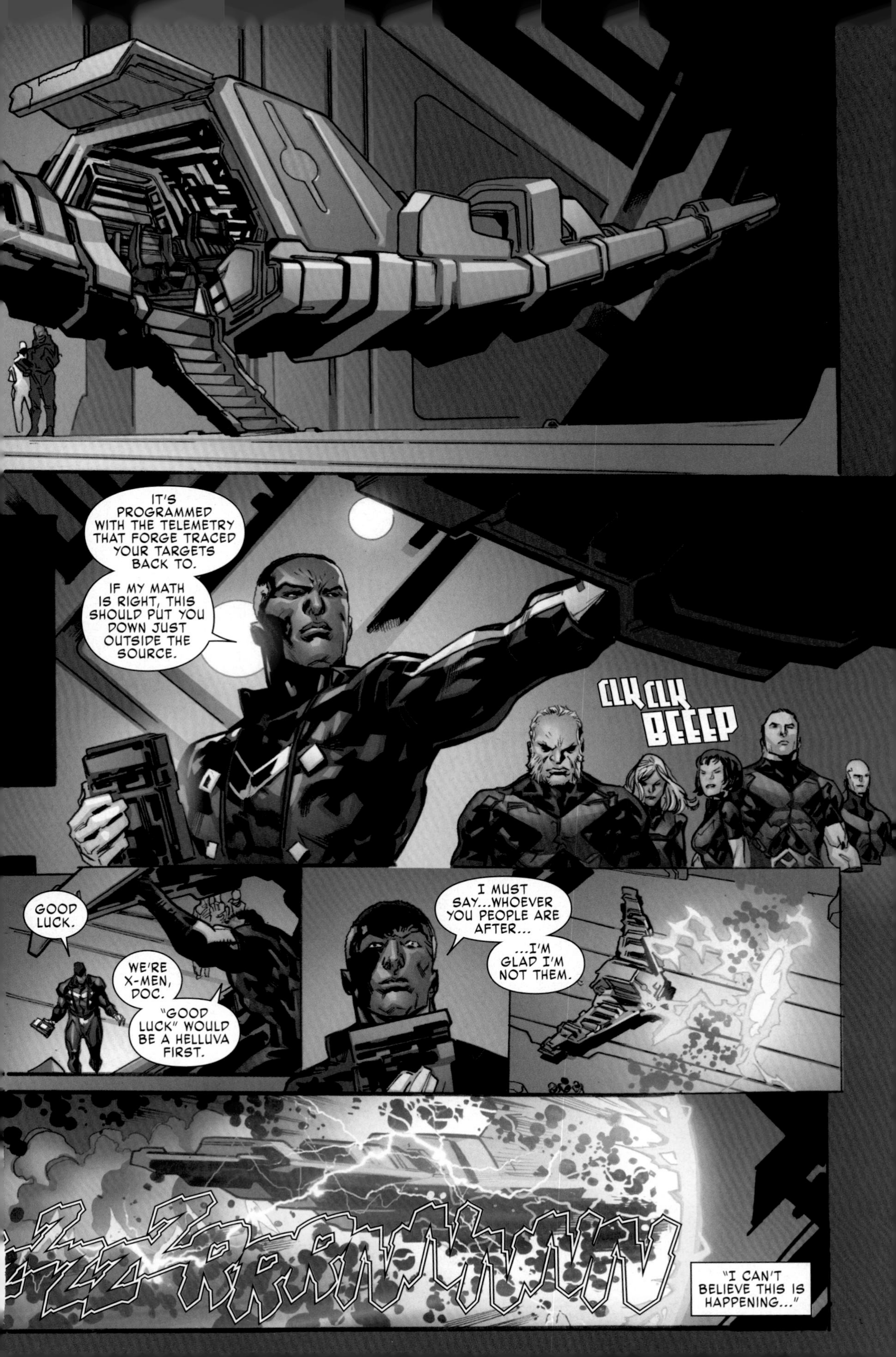
IT'S PROGRAMMED WITH THE TELEMETRY THAT FORGE TRACED YOUR TARGETS BACK TO.
IF MY MATH IS RIGHT, THIS SHOULD PUT YOU DOWN JUST OUTSIDE THE SOURCE.
CLK CLK BEEEP
GOOD LUCK.
WE'RE X-MEN, DOC.
"GOOD LUCK" WOULD BE A HELLUVA FIRST.
I MUST SAY...WHOEVER YOU PEOPLE ARE AFTER...
...I'M GLAD I'M NOT THEM.
"I CAN'T BELIEVE THIS IS HAPPENING..."

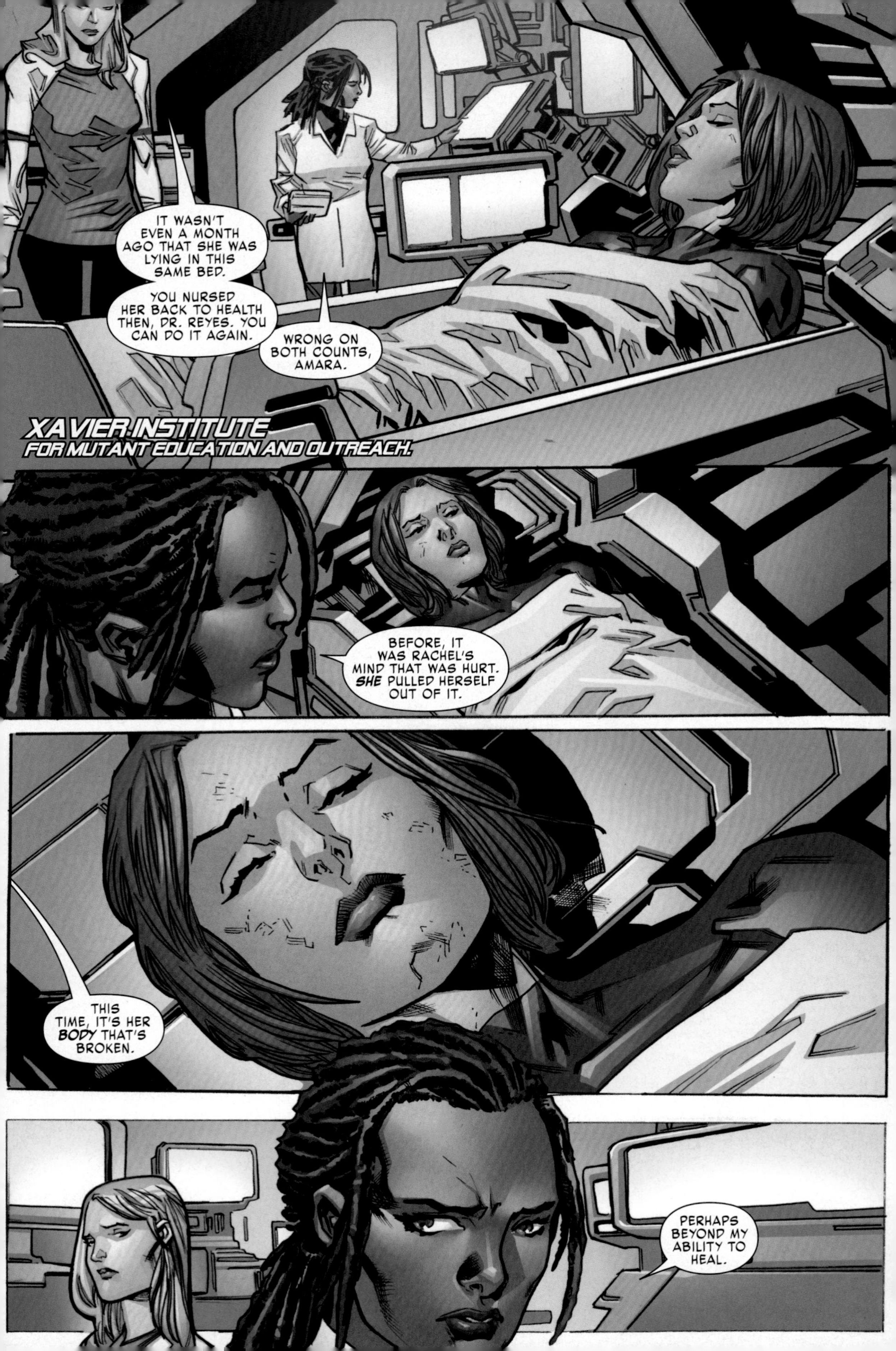
IT WASN'T EVEN A MONTH AGO THAT SHE WAS LYING IN THIS SAME BED.
YOU NURSED HER BACK TO HEALTH THEN, DR. REYES. YOU CAN DO IT AGAIN.
WRONG ON BOTH COUNTS, AMARA.
XAVIER INSTITUTE FOR MUTANT EDUCATION AND OUTREACH.
BEFORE, IT WAS RACHEL'S MIND THAT WAS HURT. SHE PULLED HERSELF OUT OF IT.
THIS TIME, IT'S HER BODY THAT'S BROKEN.
PERHAPS BEYOND MY ABILITY TO HEAL.

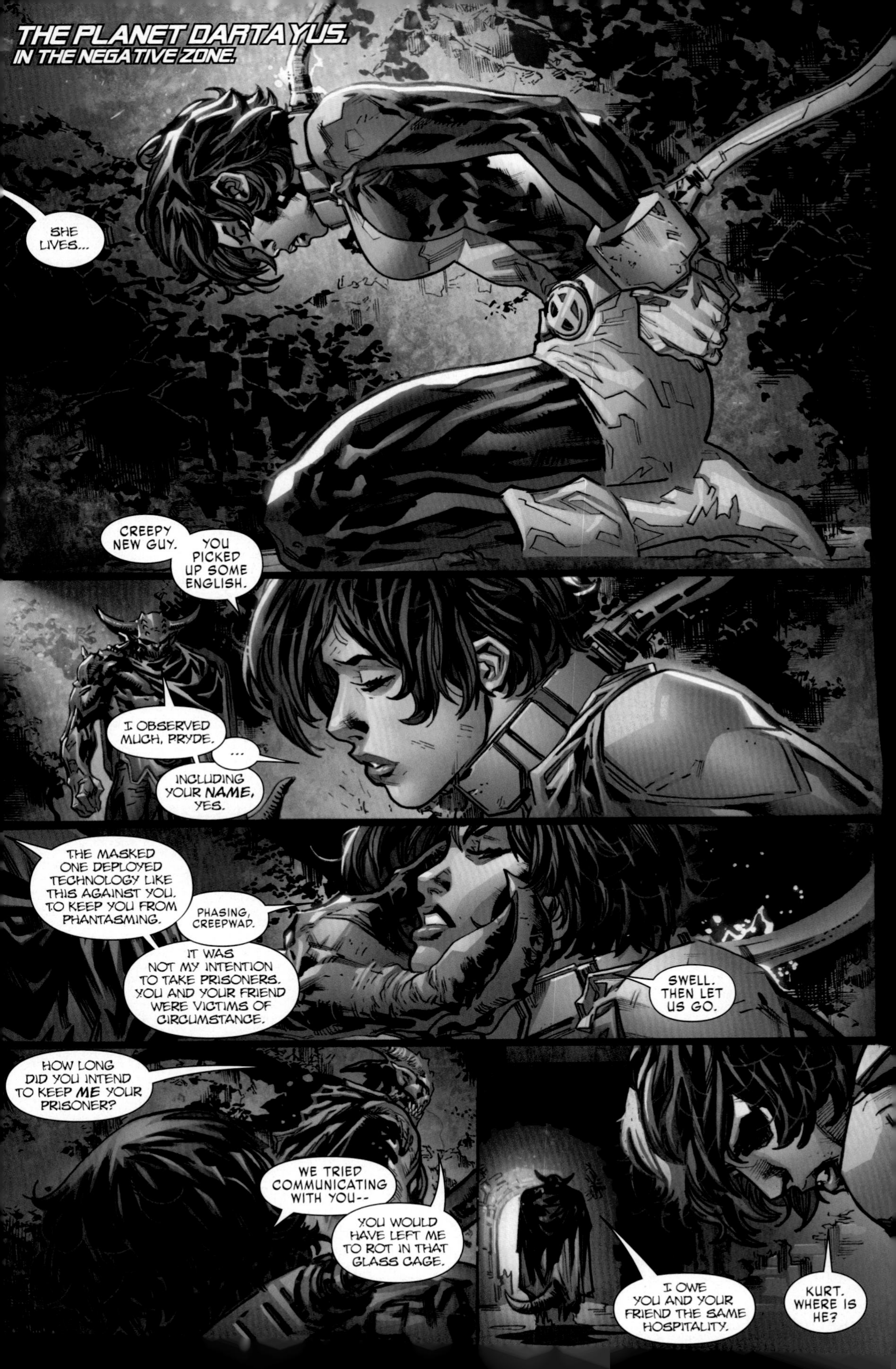
THE PLANET DARTAYUS. IN THE NEGATIVE ZONE.
SHE LIVES...
CREEPY NEW GUY.
YOU PICKED UP SOME ENGLISH.
I OBSERVED MUCH, PRYDE.
...
INCLUDING YOUR NAME, YES.
THE MASKED ONE DEPLOYED TECHNOLOGY LIKE THIS AGAINST YOU, TO KEEP YOU FROM PHANTASMING.
PHASING, CREEPWAD.
IT WAS NOT MY INTENTION TO TAKE PRISONERS. YOU AND YOUR FRIEND WERE VICTIMS OF CIRCUMSTANCE.
SWELL. THEN LET US GO.
HOW LONG DID YOU INTEND TO KEEP ME YOUR PRISONER?
WE TRIED COMMUNICATING WITH YOU--
YOU WOULD HAVE LEFT ME TO ROT IN THAT GLASS CAGE.
I OWE YOU AND YOUR FRIEND THE SAME HOSPITALITY.
KURT. WHERE IS HE?

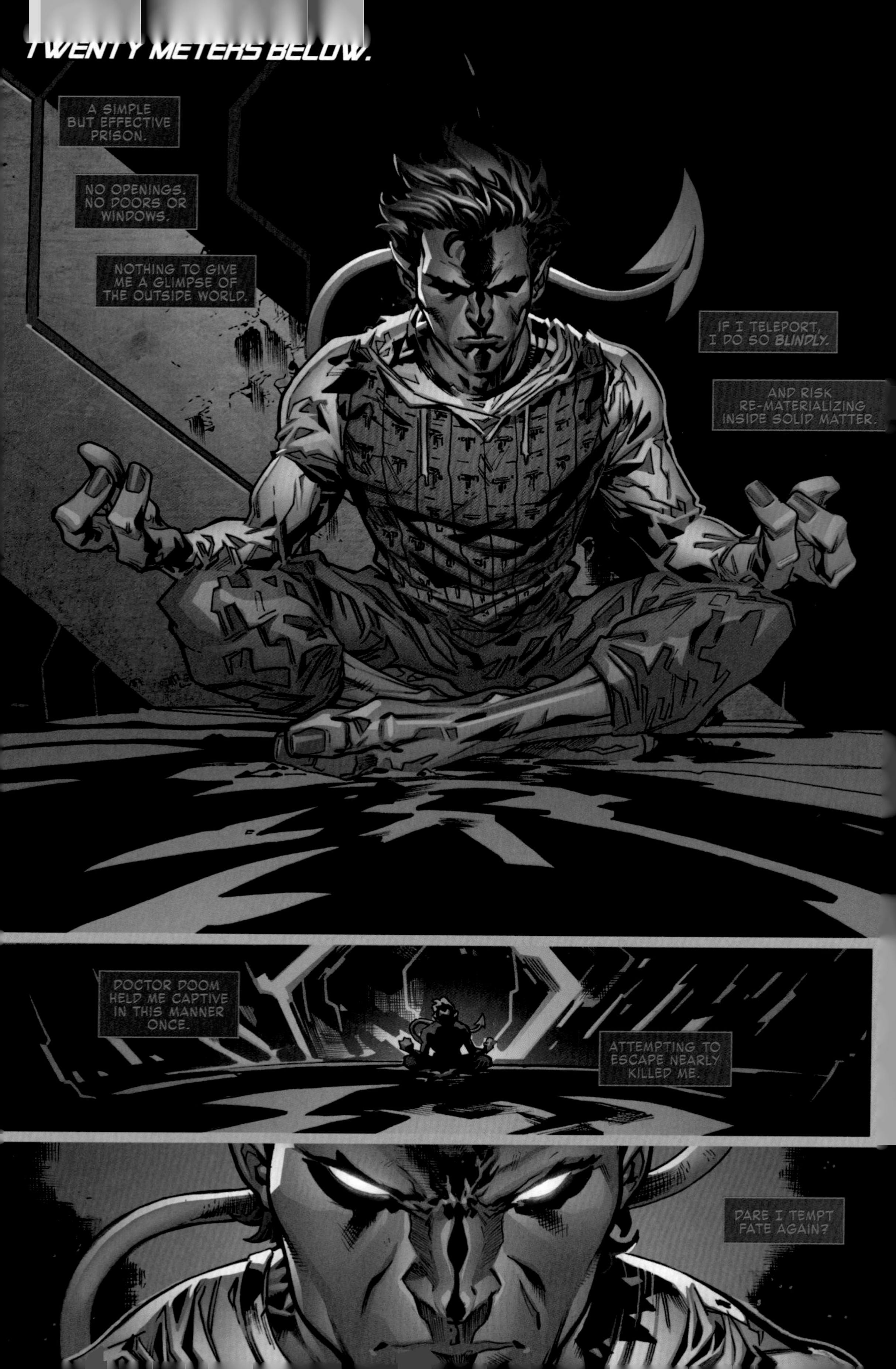
TWENTY METERS BELOW.
A SIMPLE BUT EFFECTIVE PRISON.
NO OPENINGS. NO DOORS OR WINDOWS.
NOTHING TO GIVE ME A GLIMPSE OF THE OUTSIDE WORLD.
IF I TELEPORT, I DO SO BLINDLY.
AND RISK RE-MATERIALIZING INSIDE SOLID MATTER.
DOCTOR DOOM HELD ME CAPTIVE IN THIS MANNER ONCE.
ATTEMPTING TO ESCAPE NEARLY KILLED ME.
DARE I TEMPT FATE AGAIN?

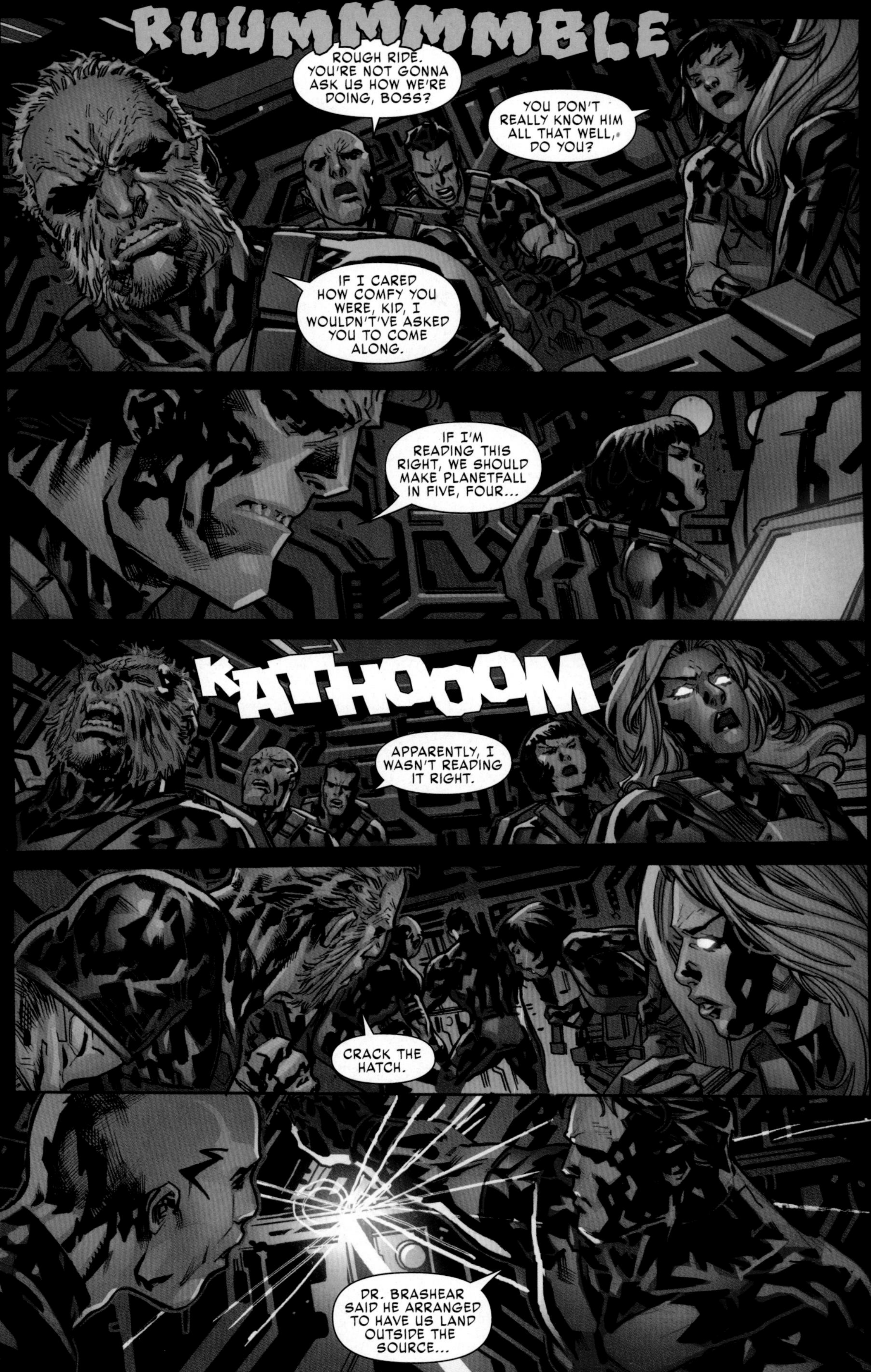
RUUMMMMBLE
ROUGH RIDE. YOU'RE NOT GONNA ASK US HOW WE'RE DOING, BOSS?
YOU DON'T REALLY KNOW HIM ALL THAT WELL, DO YOU?
IF I CARED HOW COMFY YOU WERE, KID, I WOULDN'T'VE ASKED YOU TO COME ALONG.
IF I'M READING THIS RIGHT, WE SHOULD MAKE PLANETFALL IN FIVE, FOUR...
KATHOOOM
APPARENTLY, I WASN'T READING IT RIGHT.
CRACK THE HATCH.
DR. BRASHEAR SAID HE ARRANGED TO HAVE US LAND OUTSIDE THE SOURCE...

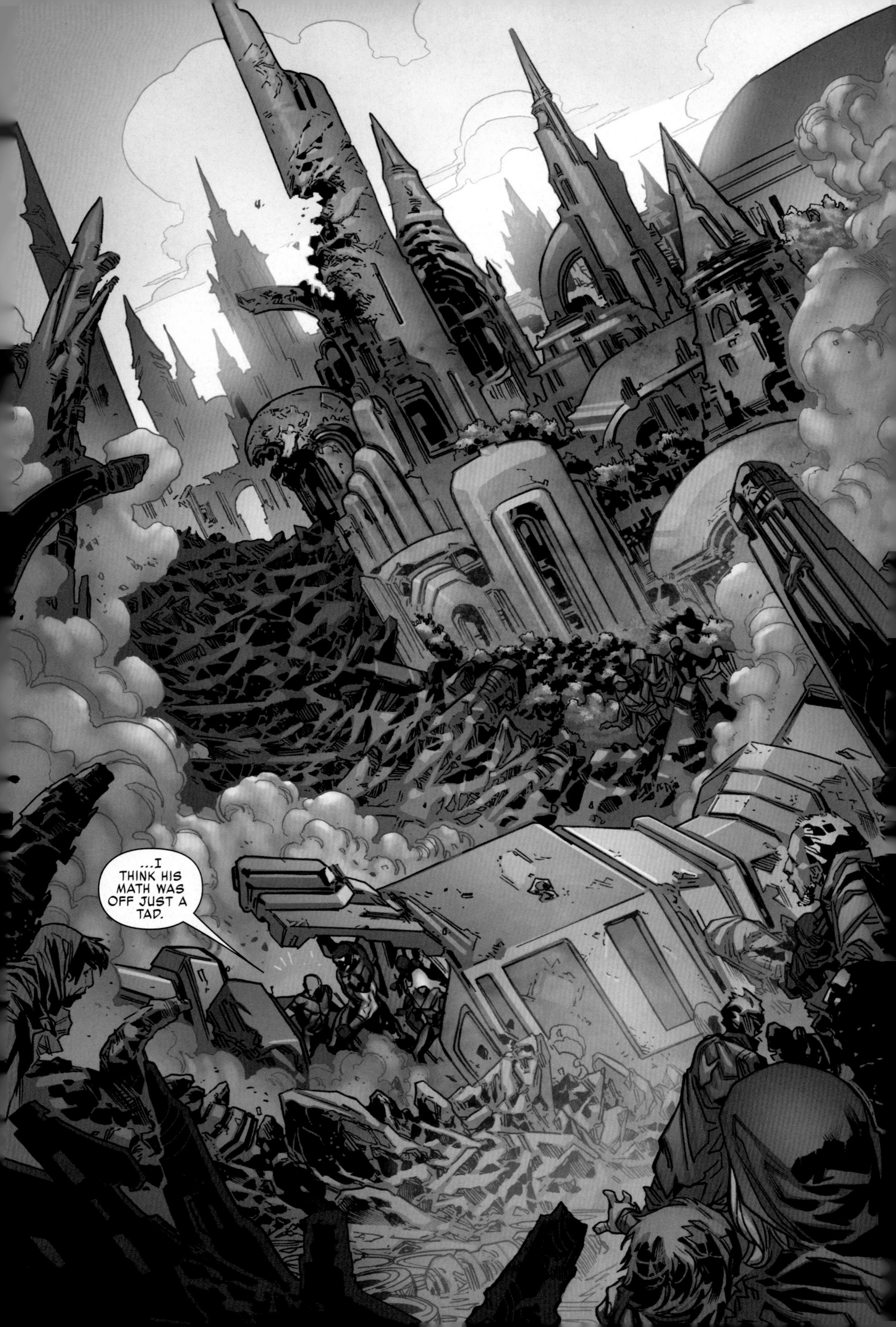
...I THINK HIS MATH WAS OFF JUST A TAD.

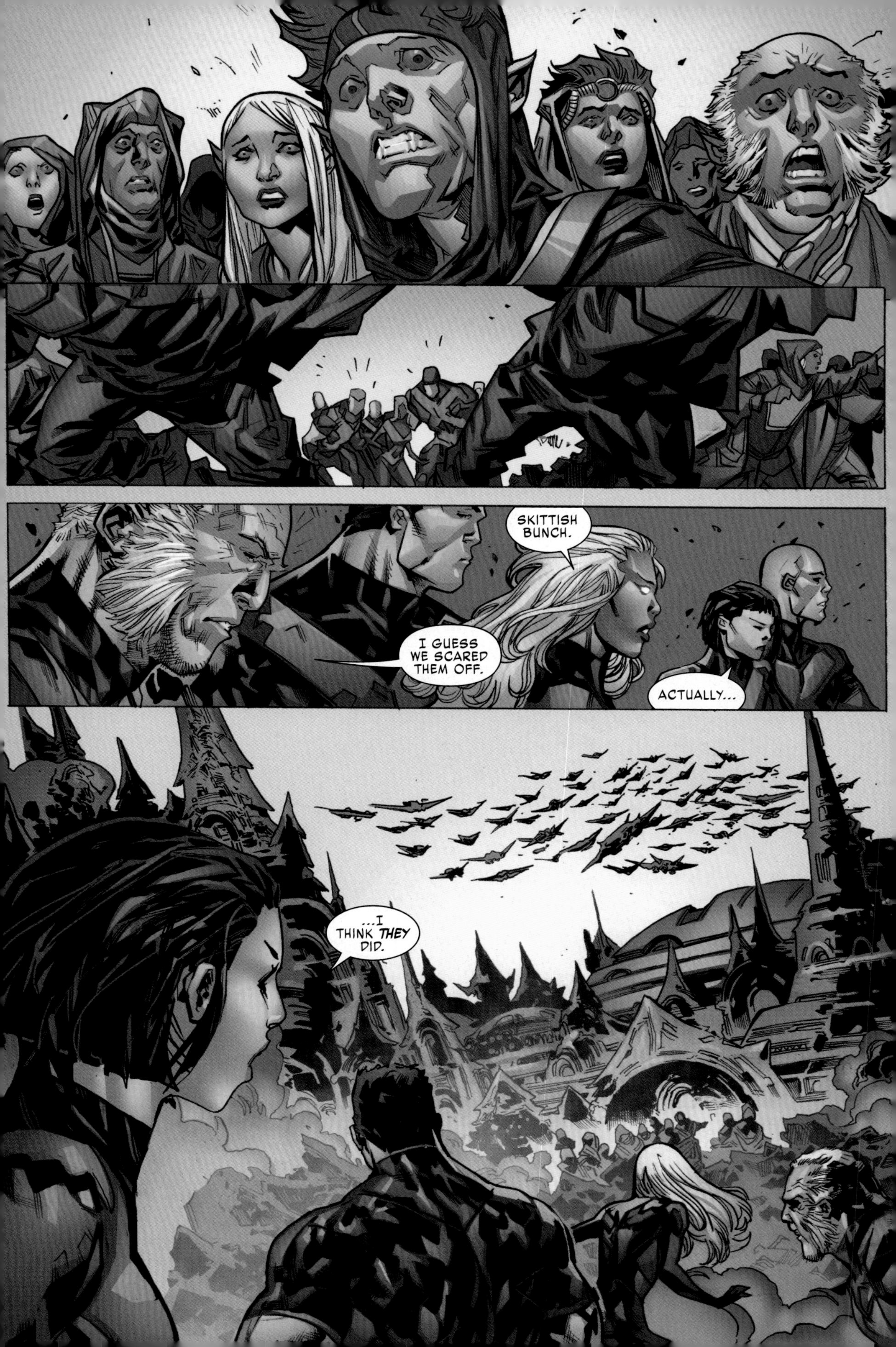
SKITTISH BUNCH.
I GUESS WE SCARED THEM OFF.
ACTUALLY...
...I THINK *THEY* DID.

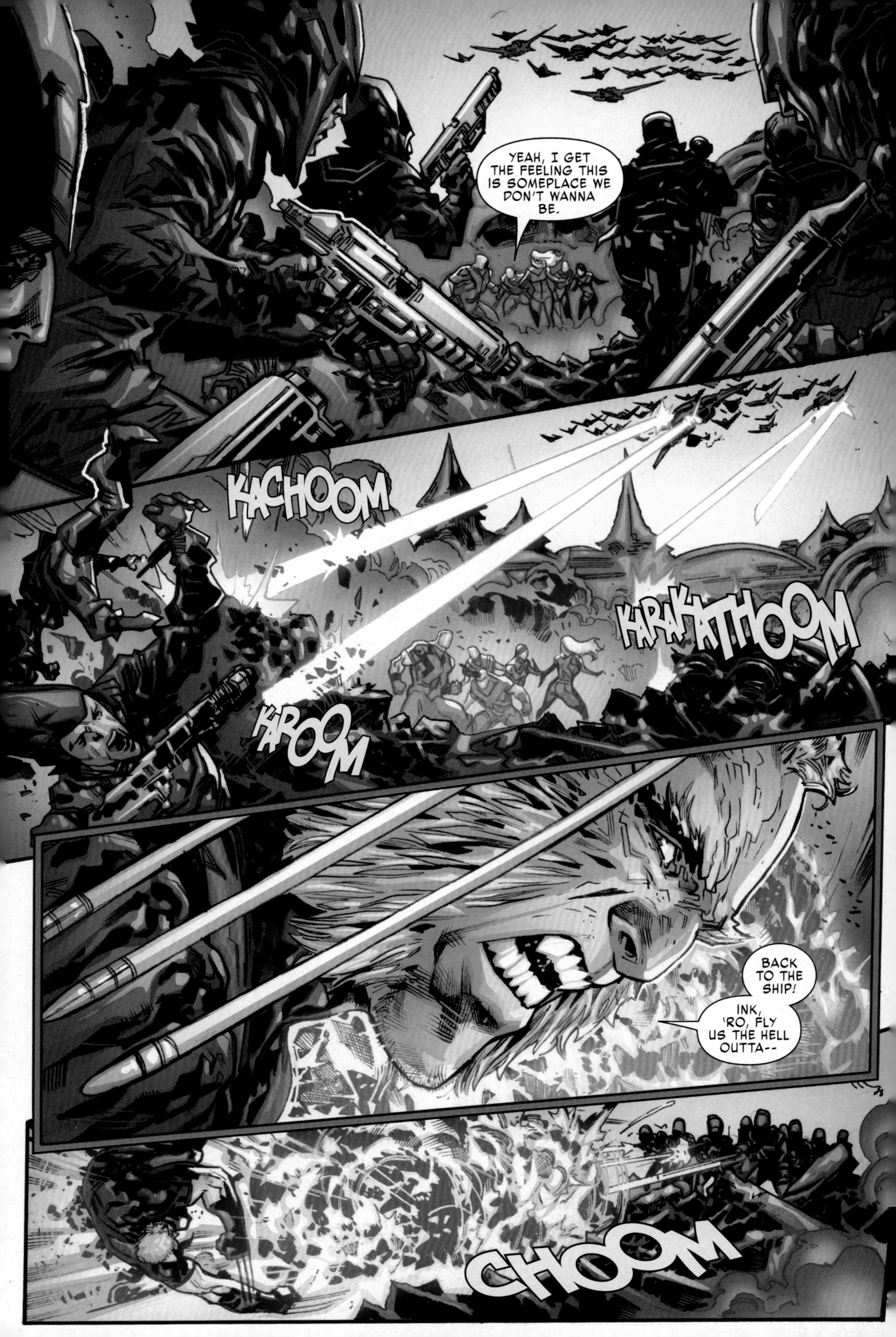
YEAH, I GET THE FEELING THIS IS SOMEPLACE WE DON'T WANNA BE.
KACHOOM
KARAKATHOOM
KAROOM
BACK TO THE SHIP!
INK, 'RO, FLY US THE HELL OUTTA--
CHOOM

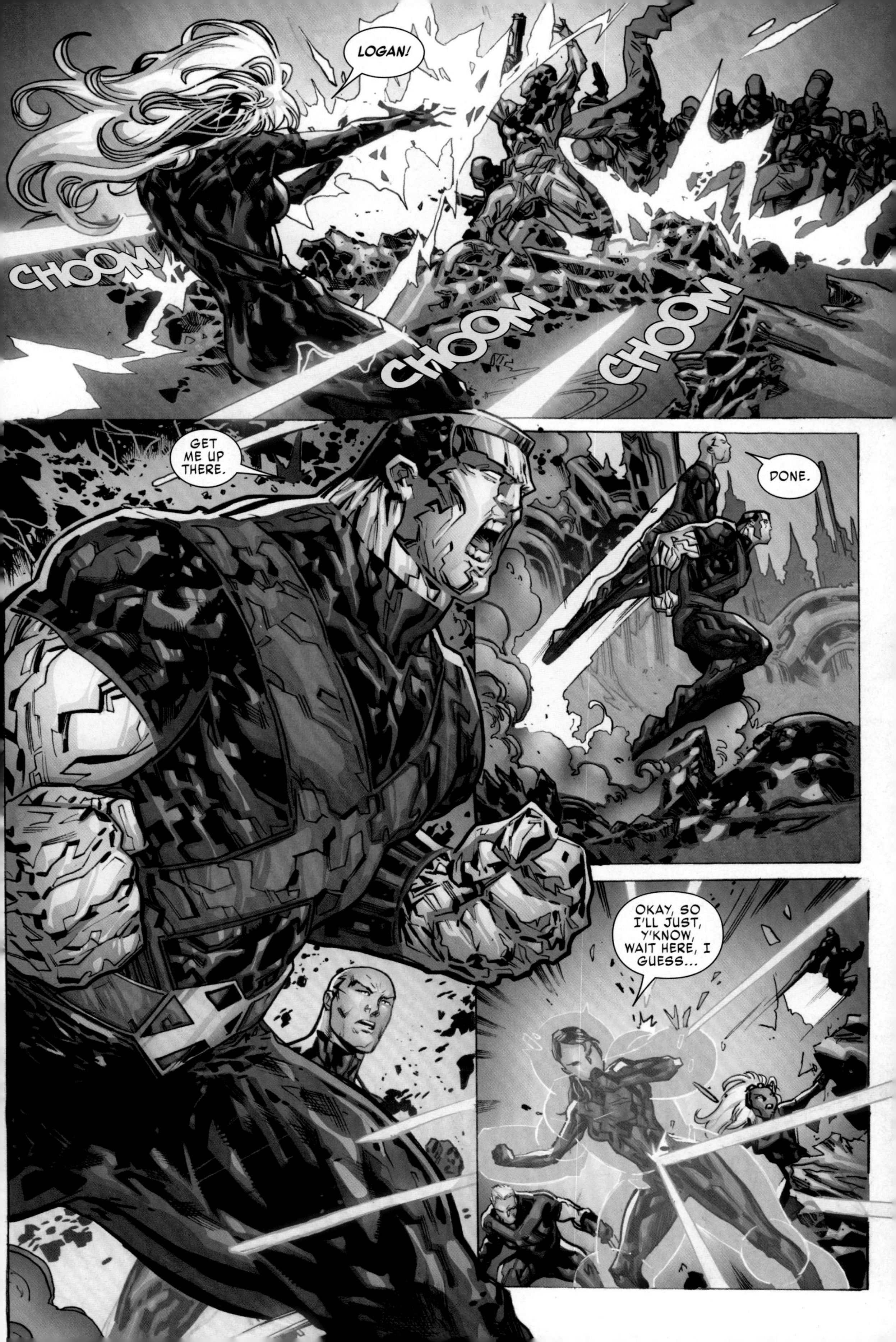
LOGAN!
CHOOM
CHOOM
CHOOM
GET ME UP THERE.
DONE.
OKAY, SO I'LL JUST, Y'KNOW, WAIT HERE, I GUESS...

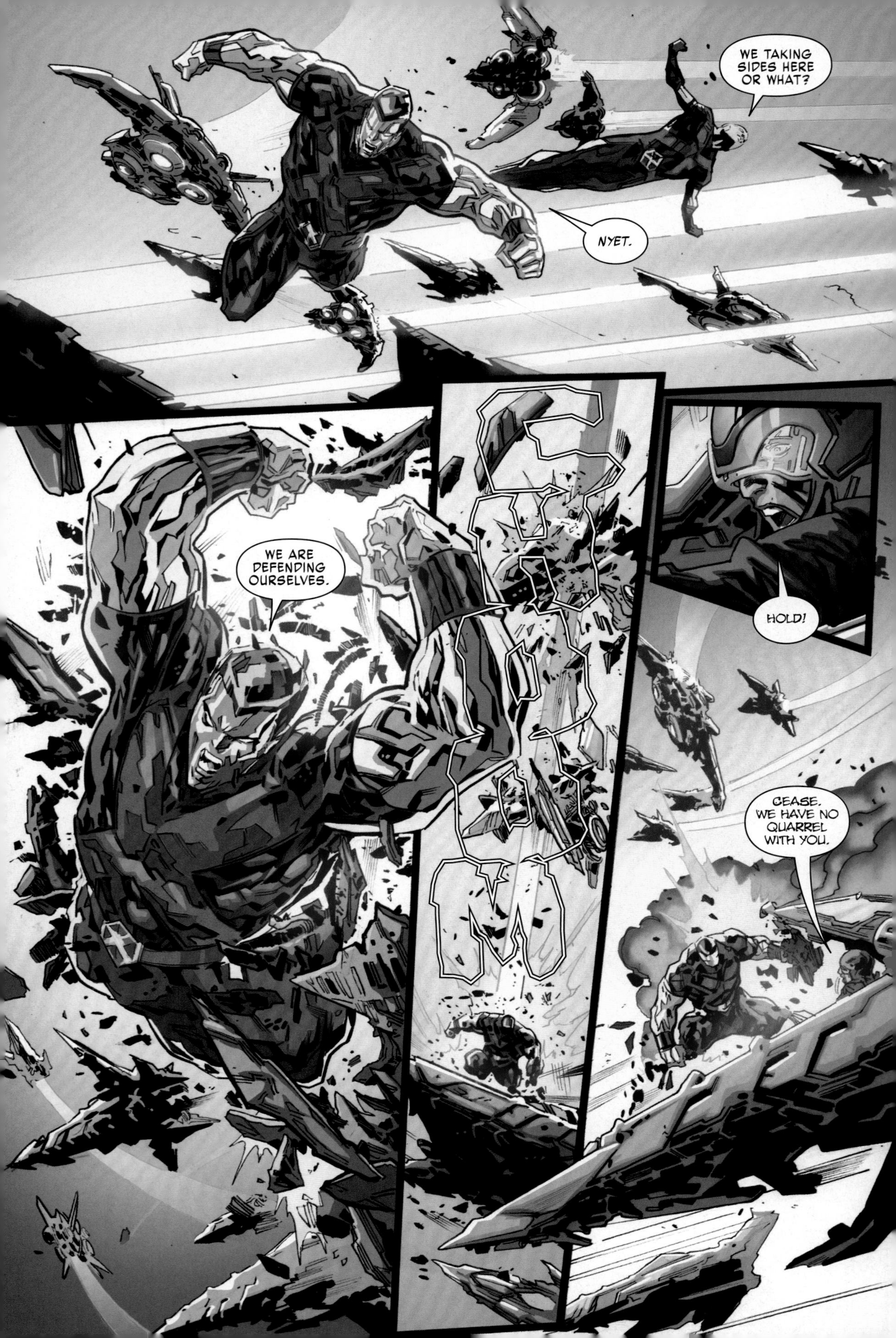
WE TAKING SIDES HERE OR WHAT?
NYET.
WE ARE DEFENDING OURSELVES.
HOLD!
CEASE. WE HAVE NO QUARREL WITH YOU.

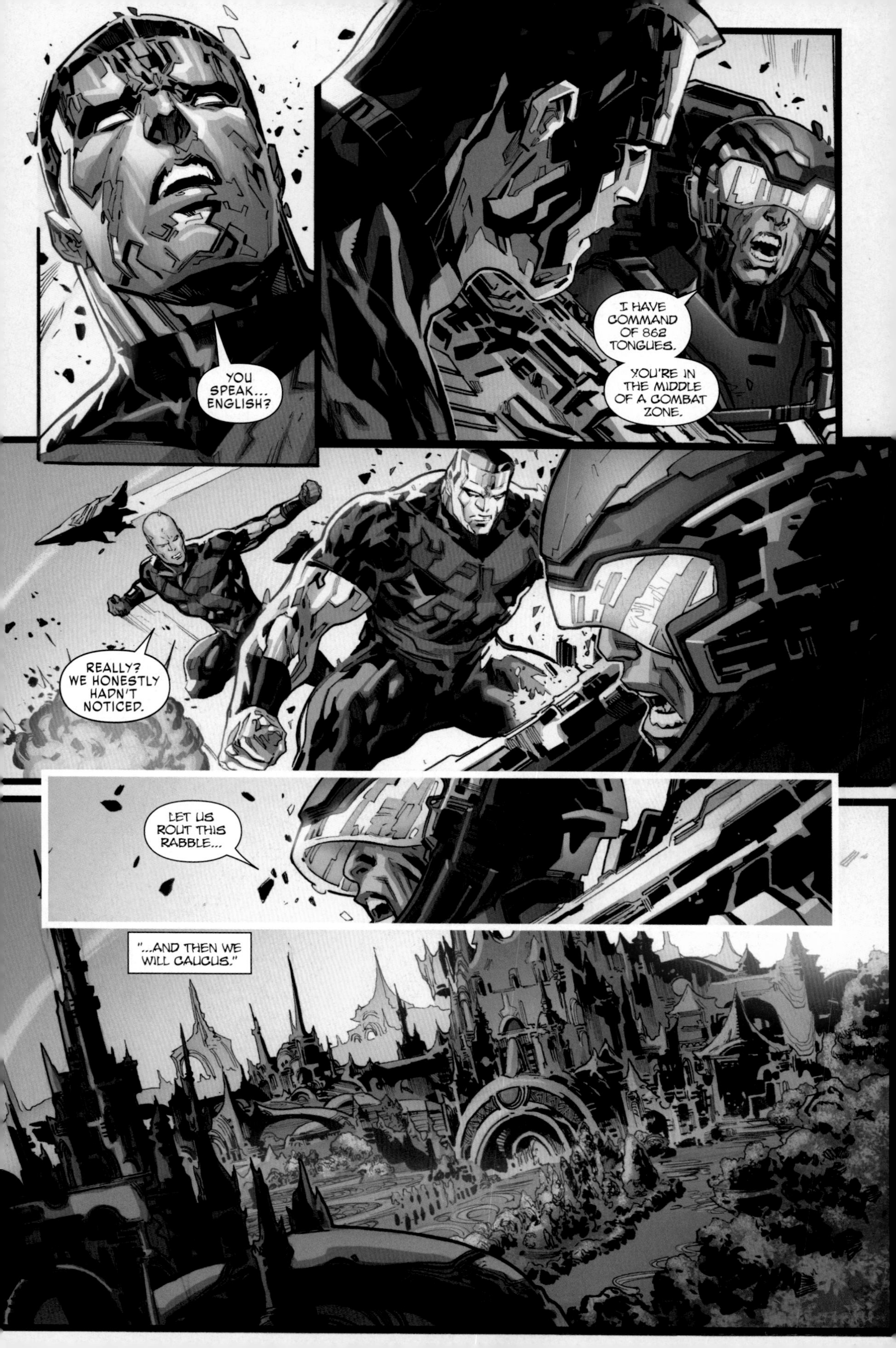
YOU SPEAK... ENGLISH?
I HAVE COMMAND OF 862 TONGUES.
YOU'RE IN THE MIDDLE OF A COMBAT ZONE.
REALLY? WE HONESTLY HADN'T NOTICED.
LET US ROUT THIS RABBLE...
"...AND THEN WE WILL CAUCUS."

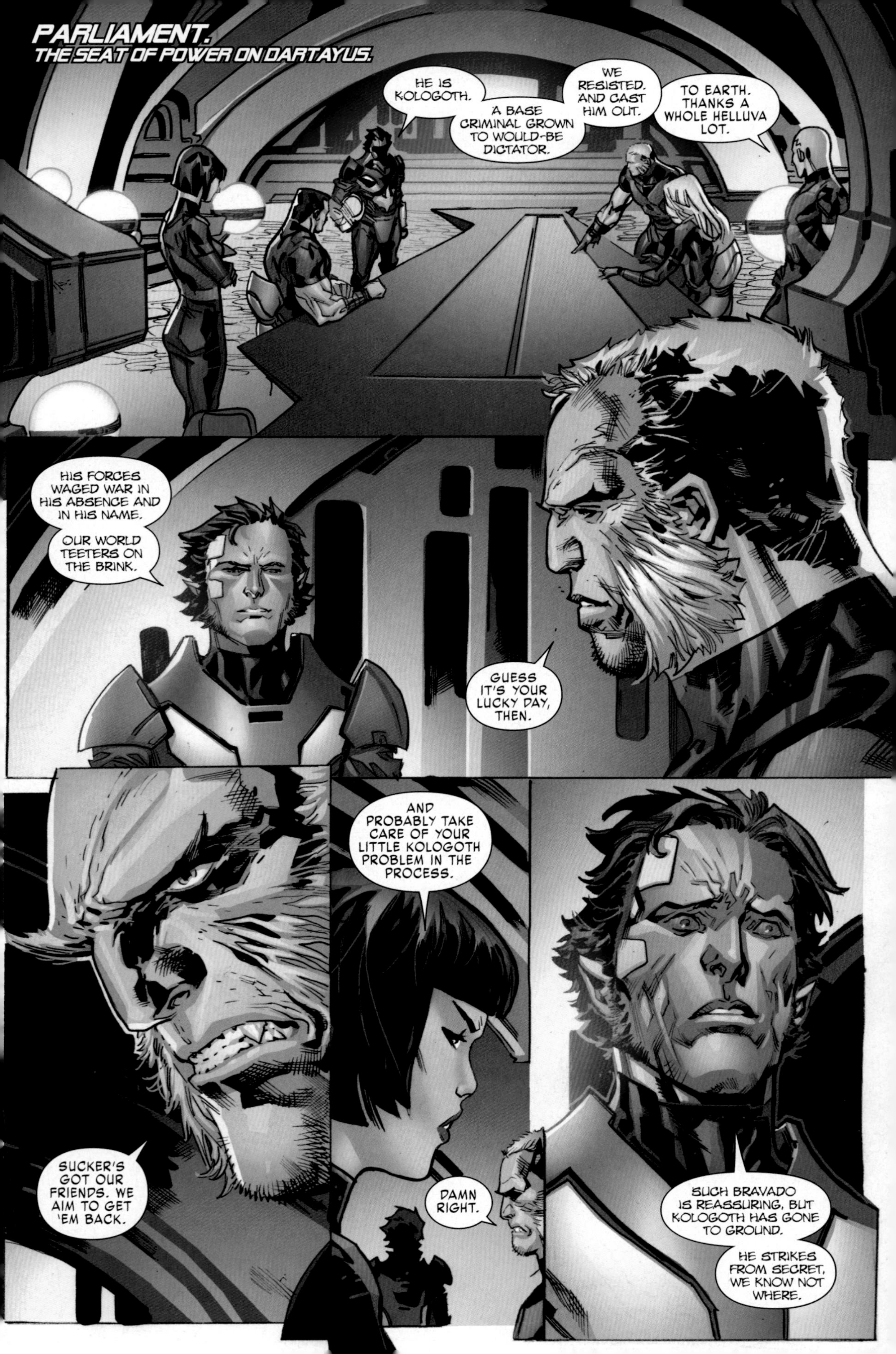
PARLIAMENT.
THE SEAT OF POWER ON DARTAYUS.
HE IS KOLOGOTH.
A BASE CRIMINAL GROWN TO WOULD-BE DICTATOR.
WE RESISTED. AND CAST HIM OUT.
TO EARTH. THANKS A WHOLE HELLUVA LOT.
HIS FORCES WAGED WAR IN HIS ABSENCE AND IN HIS NAME.
OUR WORLD TEETERS ON THE BRINK.
GUESS IT'S YOUR LUCKY DAY, THEN.
SUCKER'S GOT OUR FRIENDS. WE AIM TO GET 'EM BACK.
AND PROBABLY TAKE CARE OF YOUR LITTLE KOLOGOTH PROBLEM IN THE PROCESS.
DAMN RIGHT.
SUCH BRAVADO IS REASSURING, BUT KOLOGOTH HAS GONE TO GROUND.
HE STRIKES FROM SECRET, WE KNOW NOT WHERE.

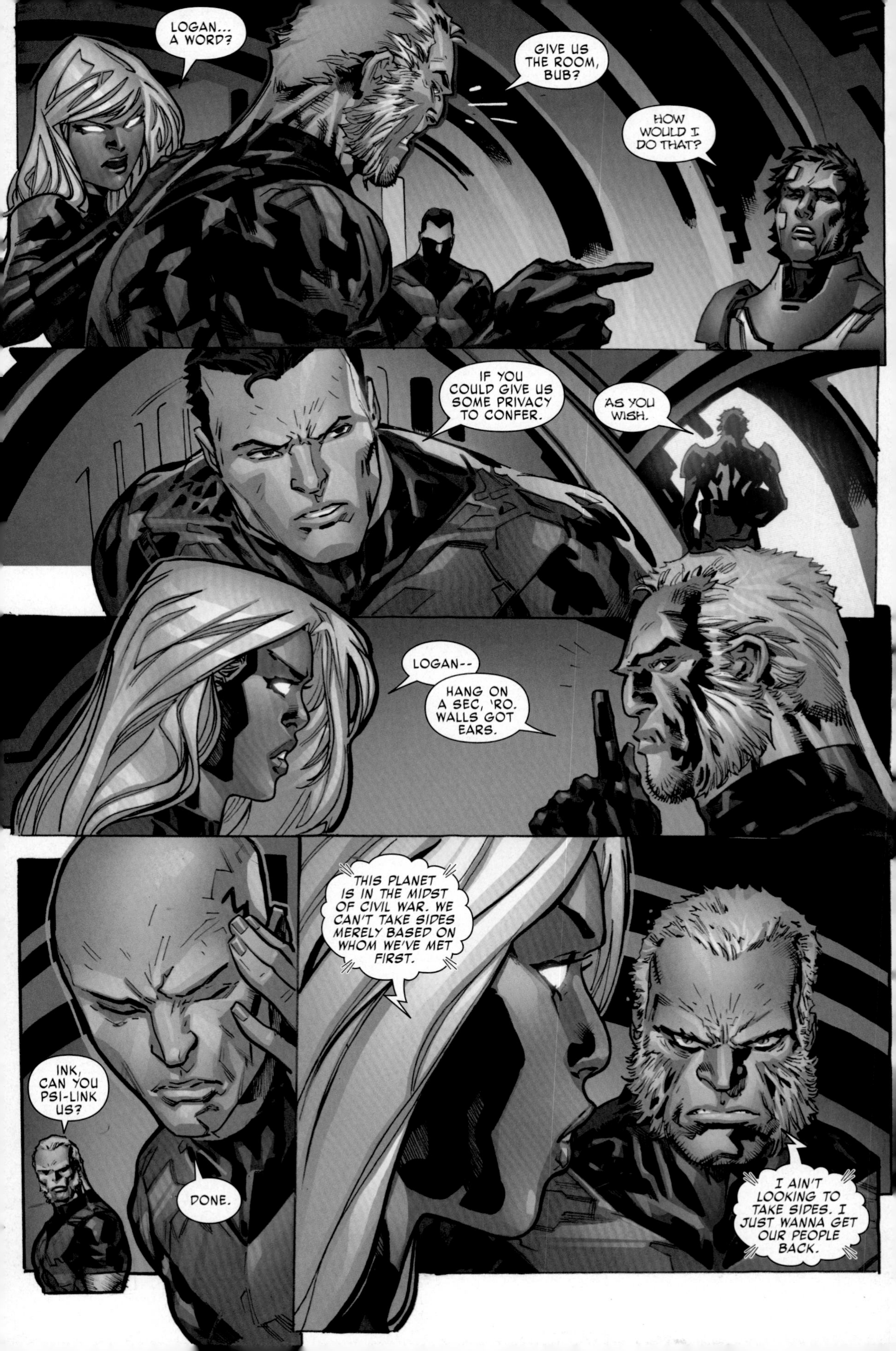
LOGAN... A WORD?
GIVE US THE ROOM, BUB?
HOW WOULD I DO THAT?
IF YOU COULD GIVE US SOME PRIVACY TO CONFER.
AS YOU WISH.
LOGAN--
HANG ON A SEC, 'RO. WALLS GOT EARS.
INK, CAN YOU PSI-LINK US?
DONE.
THIS PLANET IS IN THE MIDST OF CIVIL WAR. WE CAN'T TAKE SIDES MERELY BASED ON WHOM WE'VE MET FIRST.
I AIN'T LOOKING TO TAKE SIDES. I JUST WANNA GET OUR PEOPLE BACK.

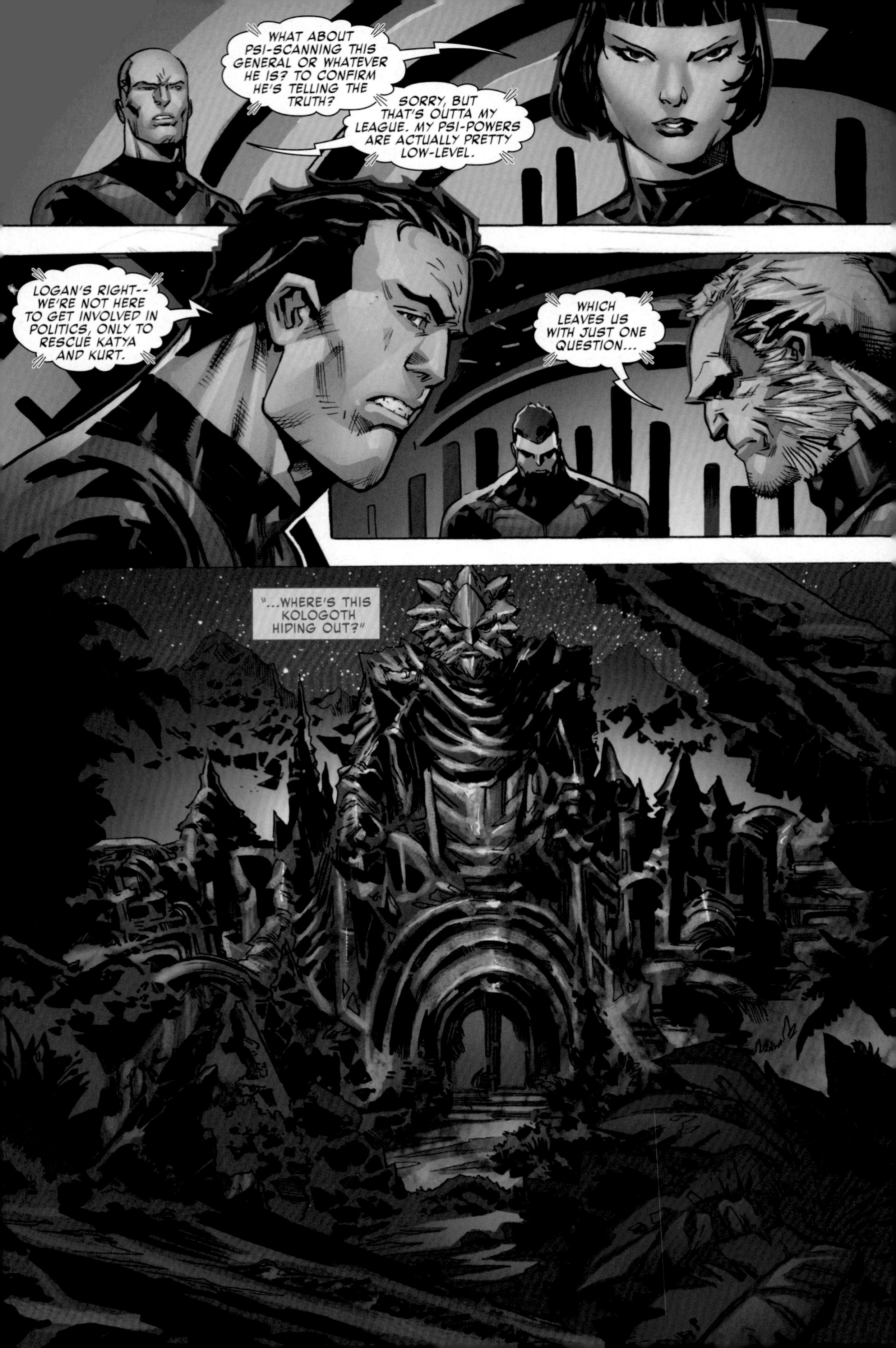
WHAT ABOUT PSI-SCANNING THIS GENERAL OR WHATEVER HE IS? TO CONFIRM HE'S TELLING THE TRUTH?
SORRY, BUT THAT'S OUTTA MY LEAGUE. MY PSI-POWERS ARE ACTUALLY PRETTY LOW-LEVEL.
LOGAN'S RIGHT-- WE'RE NOT HERE TO GET INVOLVED IN POLITICS, ONLY TO RESCUE KATYA AND KURT.
WHICH LEAVES US WITH JUST ONE QUESTION...
"...WHERE'S THIS KOLOGOTH HIDING OUT?"

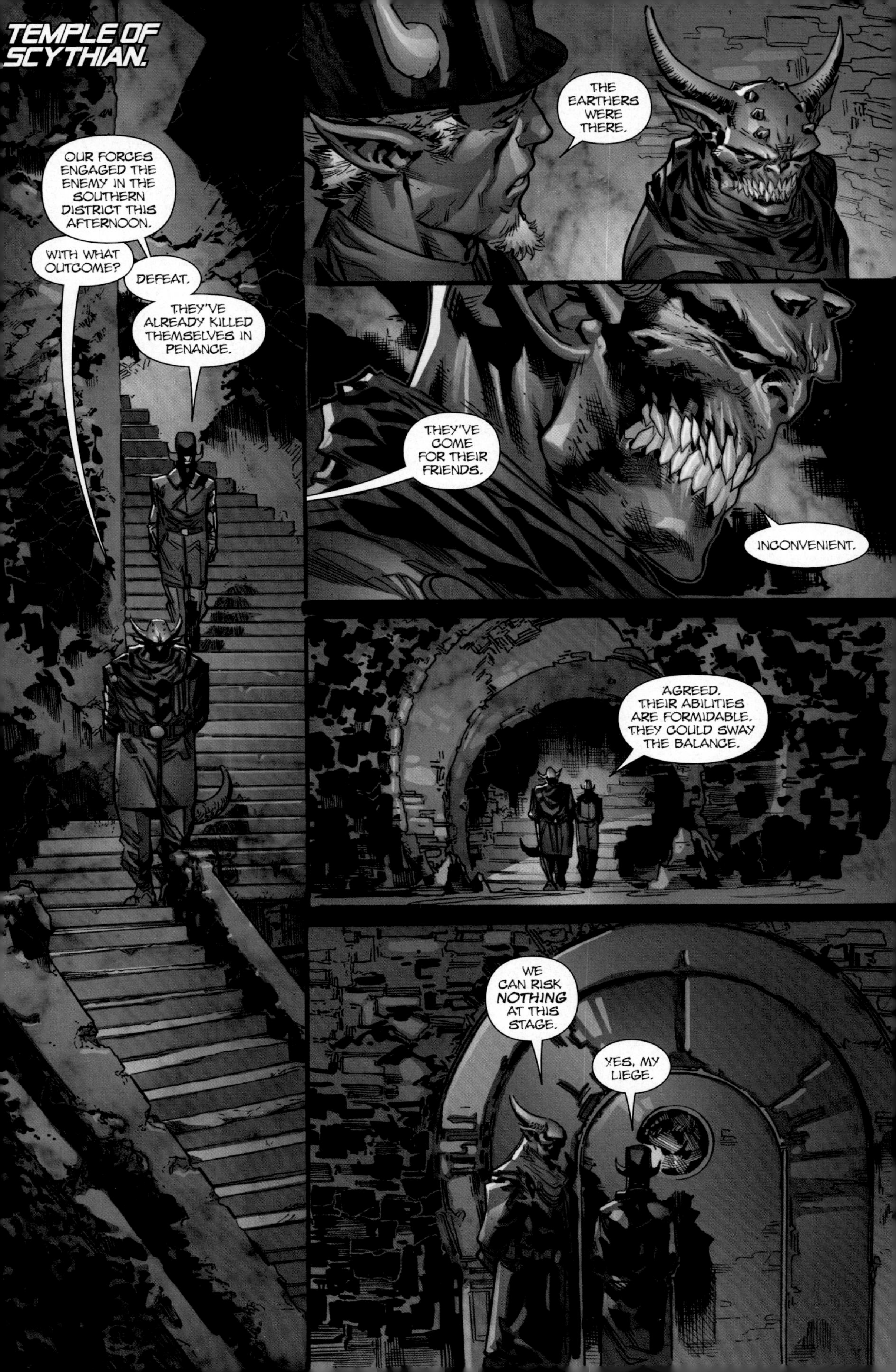
TEMPLE OF SCYTHIAN.
OUR FORCES ENGAGED THE ENEMY IN THE SOUTHERN DISTRICT THIS AFTERNOON.
WITH WHAT OUTCOME?
DEFEAT.
THEY'VE ALREADY KILLED THEMSELVES IN PENANCE.
THE EARTHERS WERE THERE.
THEY'VE COME FOR THEIR FRIENDS.
INCONVENIENT.
AGREED. THEIR ABILITIES ARE FORMIDABLE. THEY COULD SWAY THE BALANCE.
WE CAN RISK NOTHING AT THIS STAGE.
YES, MY LIEGE.

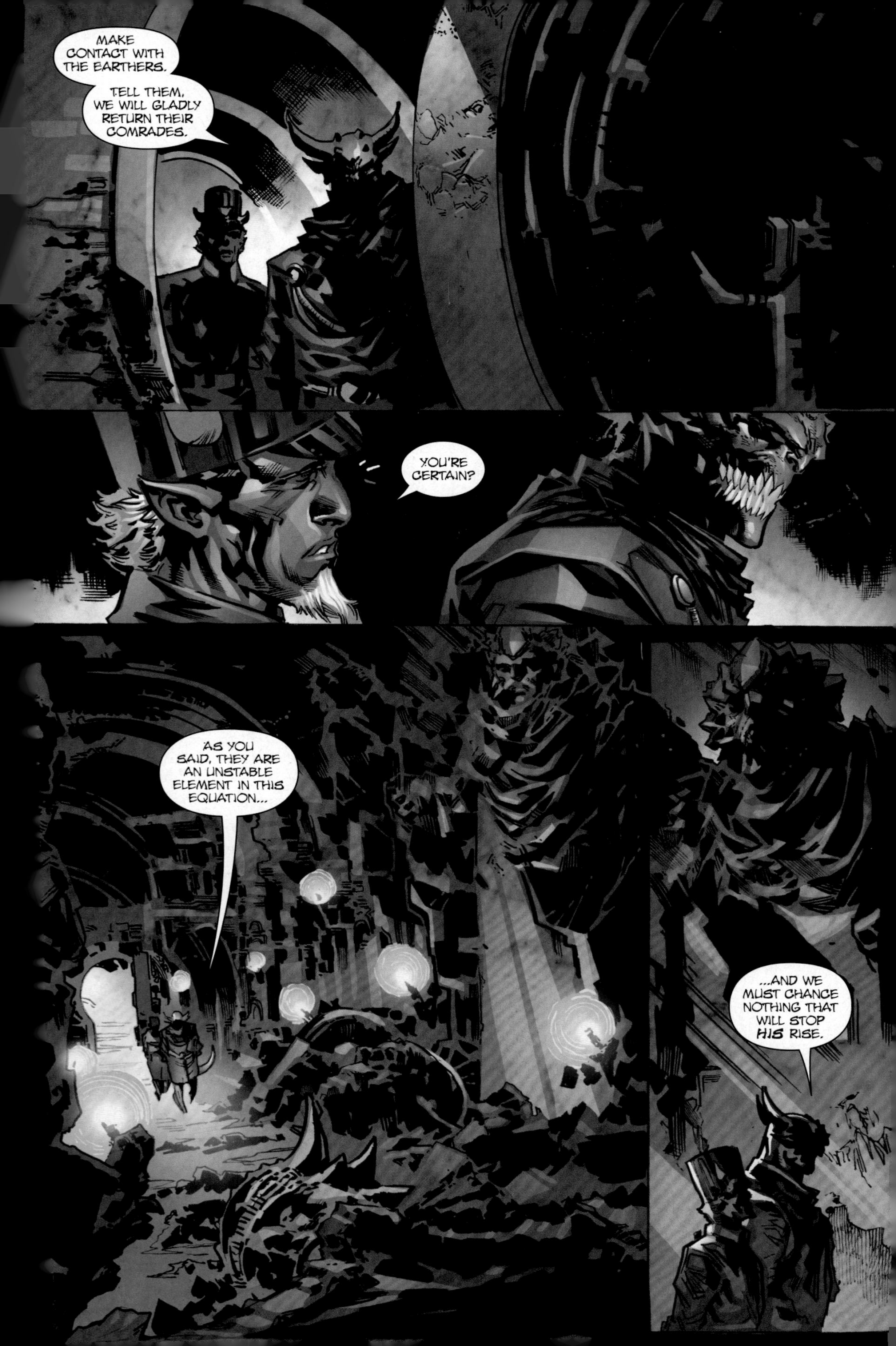
MAKE CONTACT WITH THE EARTHERS.
TELL THEM, WE WILL GLADLY RETURN THEIR COMRADES.
YOU'RE CERTAIN?
AS YOU SAID, THEY ARE AN UNSTABLE ELEMENT IN THIS EQUATION...
...AND WE MUST CHANCE NOTHING THAT WILL STOP HIS RISE.

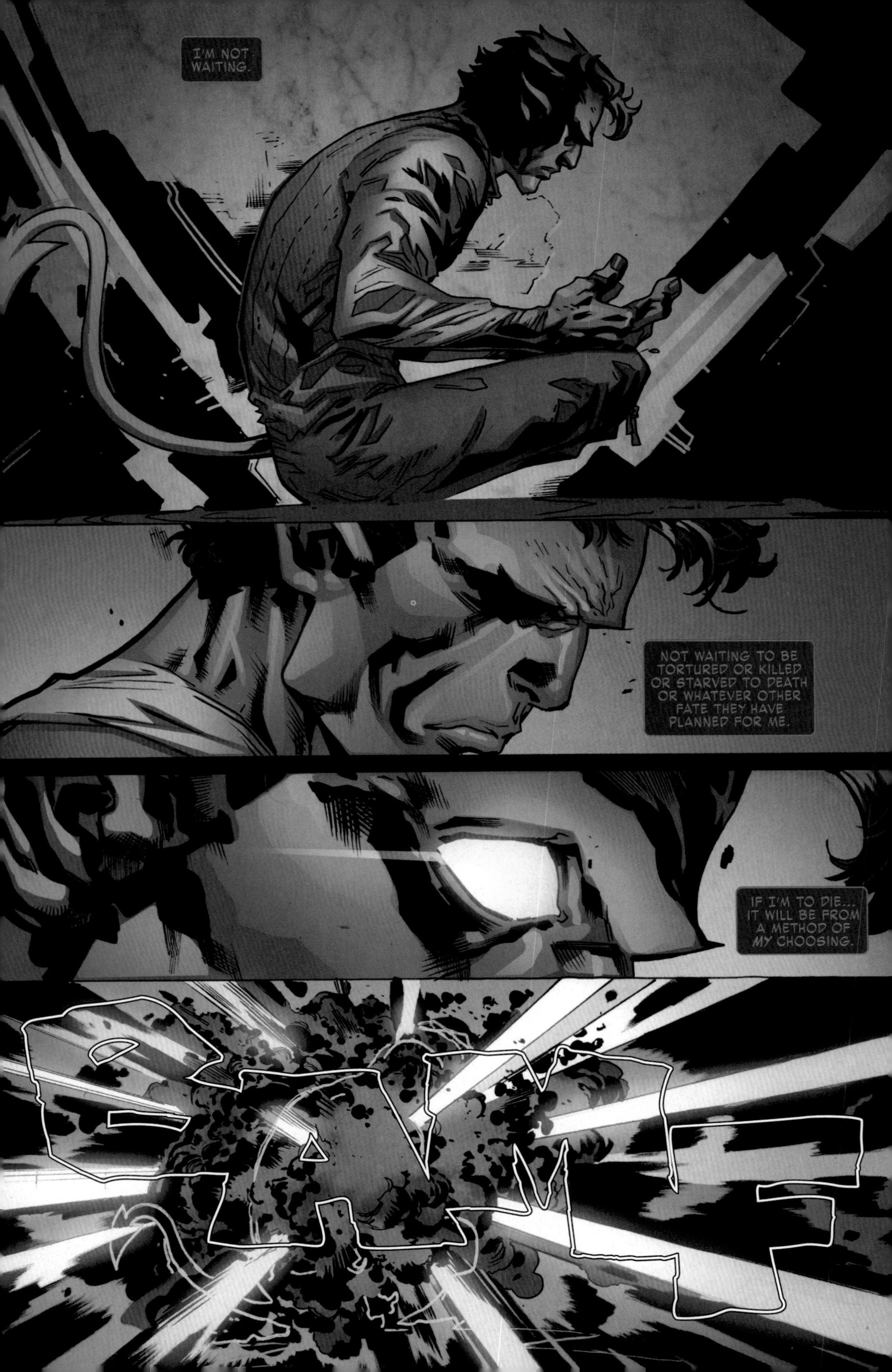
I'M NOT WAITING.
NOT WAITING TO BE TORTURED OR KILLED OR STARVED TO DEATH OR WHATEVER OTHER FATE THEY HAVE PLANNED FOR ME.
IF I'M TO DIE... IT WILL BE FROM A METHOD OF *MY* CHOOSING.
BAMF

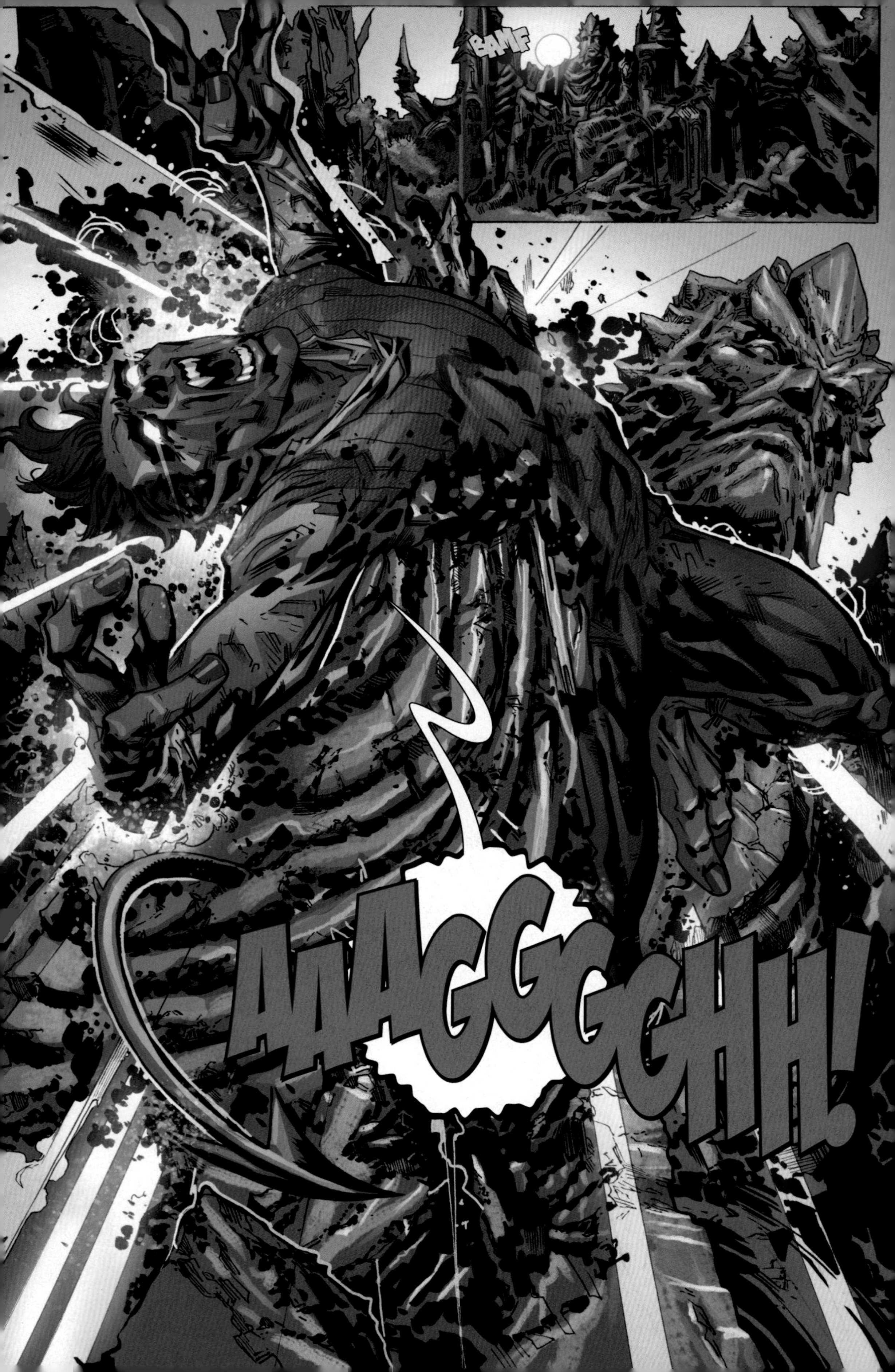
BAMF
AAAGGGGHH!

18

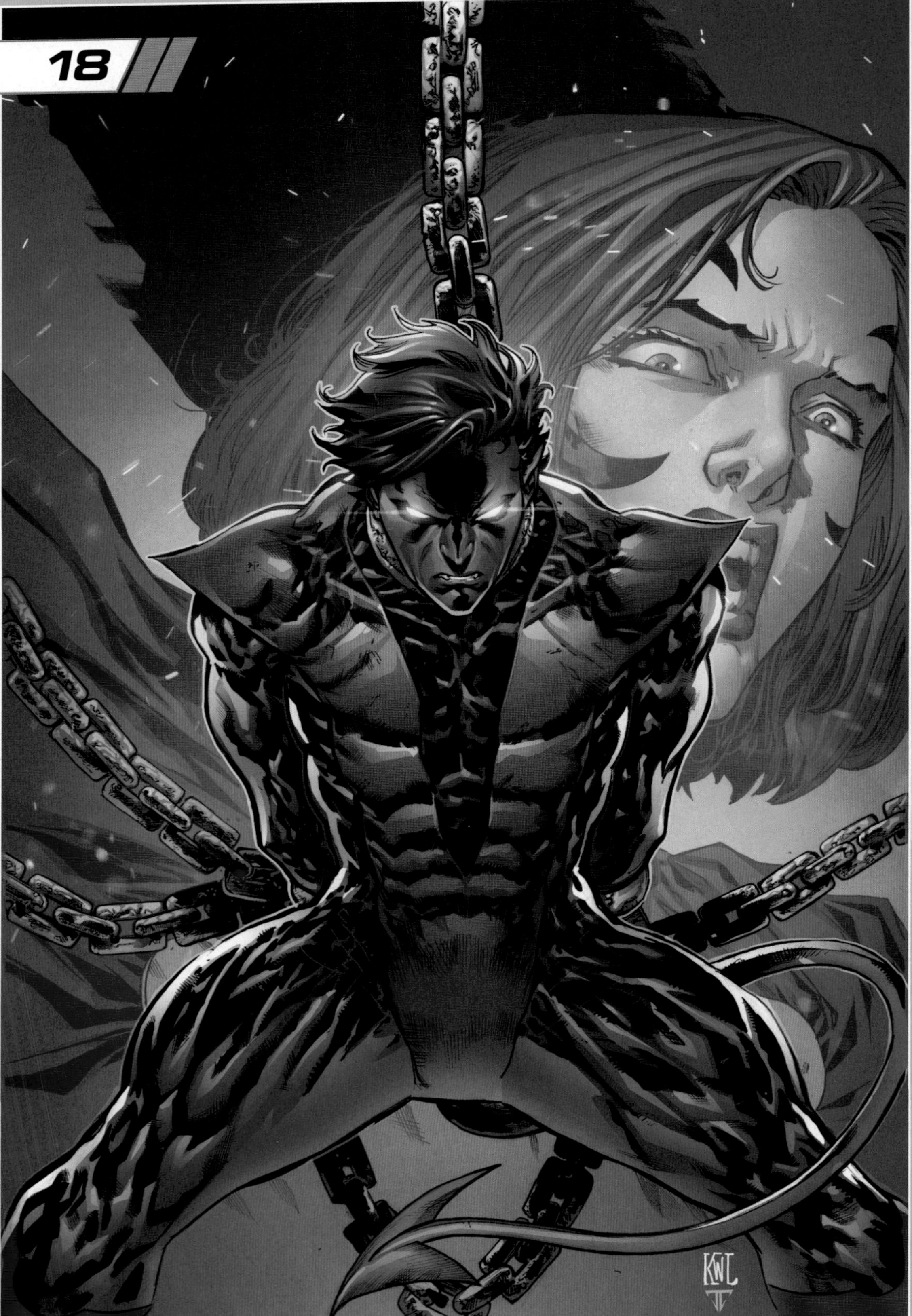

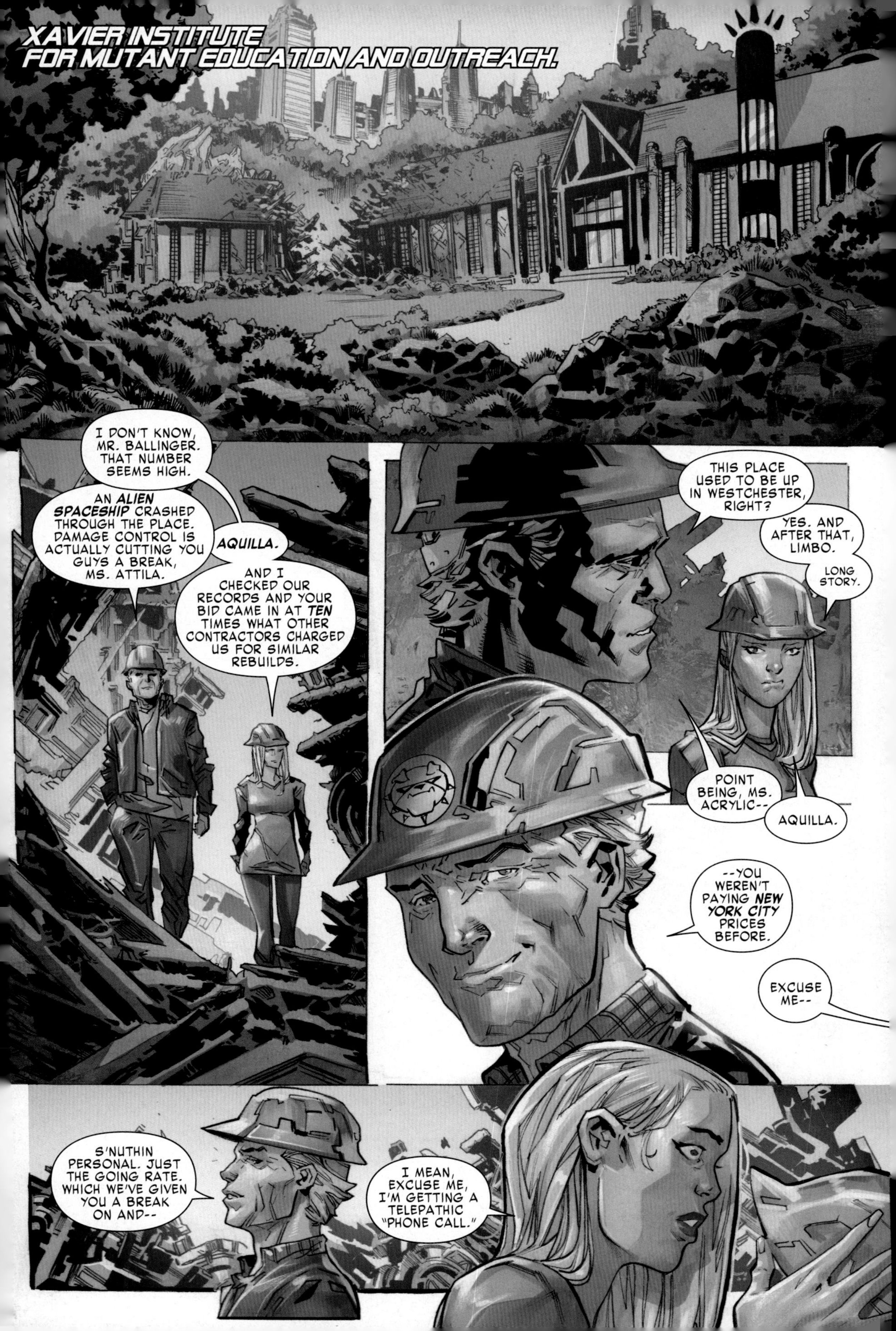
XAVIER INSTITUTE FOR MUTANT EDUCATION AND OUTREACH.
I DON'T KNOW, MR. BALLINGER. THAT NUMBER SEEMS HIGH.
AN ALIEN SPACESHIP CRASHED THROUGH THE PLACE. DAMAGE CONTROL IS ACTUALLY CUTTING YOU GUYS A BREAK, MS. ATTILA.
AQUILLA.
AND I CHECKED OUR RECORDS AND YOUR BID CAME IN AT TEN TIMES WHAT OTHER CONTRACTORS CHARGED US FOR SIMILAR REBUILDS.
THIS PLACE USED TO BE UP IN WESTCHESTER, RIGHT?
YES. AND AFTER THAT, LIMBO.
LONG STORY.
POINT BEING, MS. ACRYLIC--
AQUILLA.
--YOU WEREN'T PAYING NEW YORK CITY PRICES BEFORE.
EXCUSE ME--
S'NUTHIN PERSONAL. JUST THE GOING RATE. WHICH WE'VE GIVEN YOU A BREAK ON AND--
I MEAN, EXCUSE ME, I'M GETTING A TELEPATHIC "PHONE CALL."

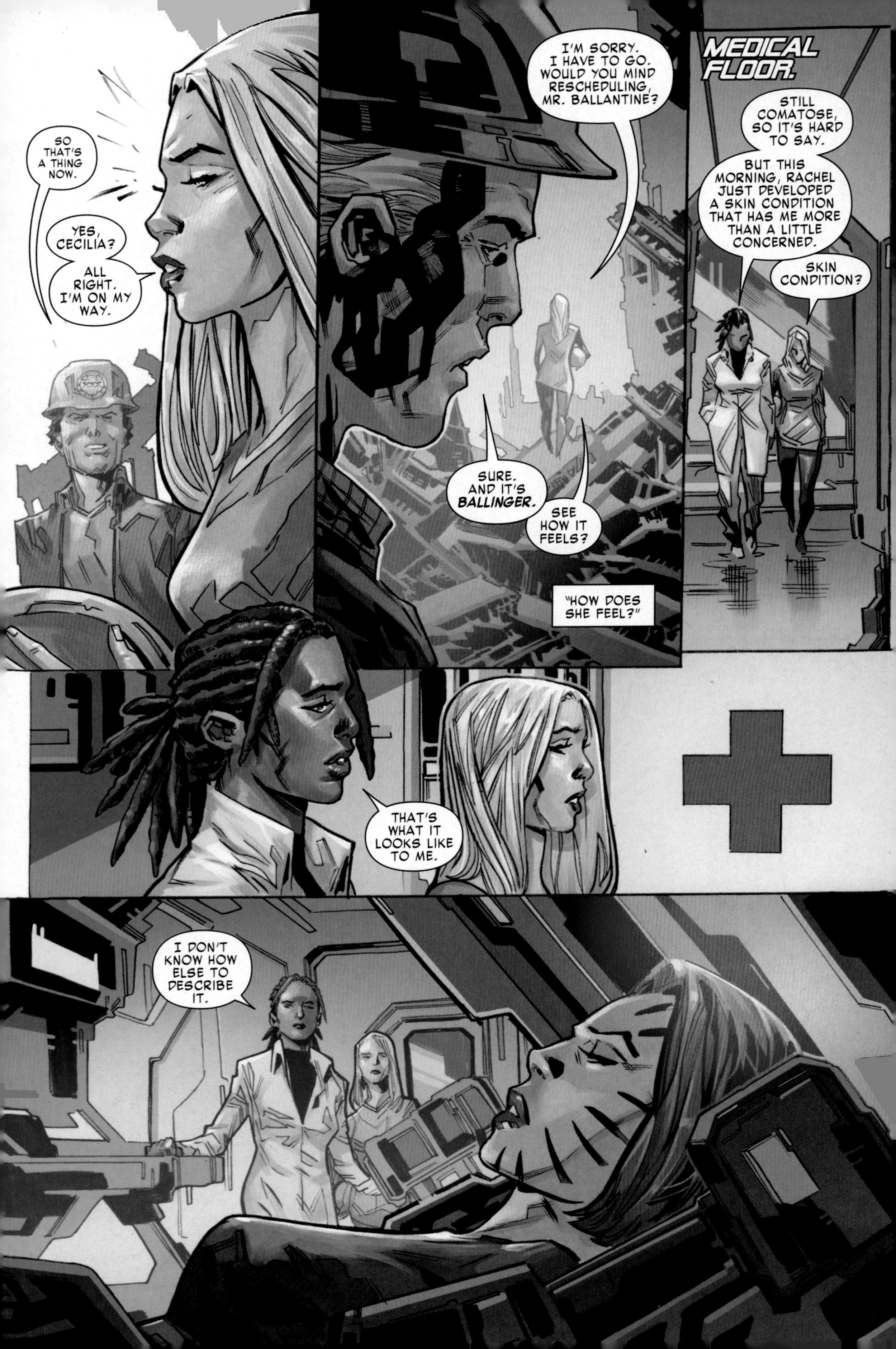
SO THAT'S A THING NOW.
YES, CECILIA?
ALL RIGHT. I'M ON MY WAY.
I'M SORRY. I HAVE TO GO. WOULD YOU MIND RESCHEDULING, MR. BALLANTINE?
SURE. AND IT'S BALLINGER.
SEE HOW IT FEELS?
MEDICAL FLOOR.
"HOW DOES SHE FEEL?"
STILL COMATOSE, SO IT'S HARD TO SAY.
BUT THIS MORNING, RACHEL JUST DEVELOPED A SKIN CONDITION THAT HAS ME MORE THAN A LITTLE CONCERNED.
SKIN CONDITION?
THAT'S WHAT IT LOOKS LIKE TO ME.
I DON'T KNOW HOW ELSE TO DESCRIBE IT.

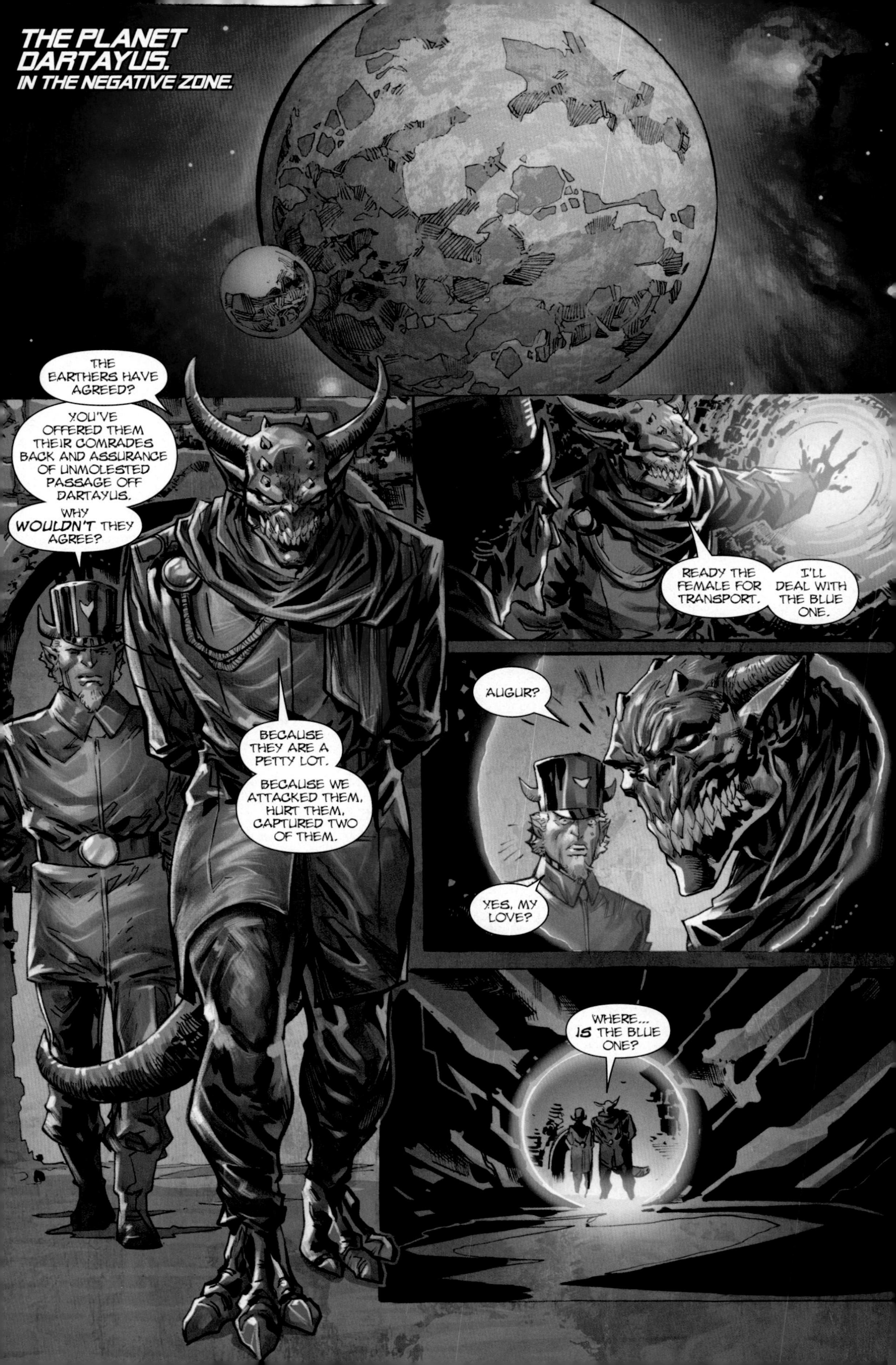
THE PLANET DARTAYUS. IN THE NEGATIVE ZONE.
THE EARTHERS HAVE AGREED?
YOU'VE OFFERED THEM THEIR COMRADES BACK AND ASSURANCE OF UNMOLESTED PASSAGE OFF DARTAYUS.
WHY WOULDN'T THEY AGREE?
BECAUSE THEY ARE A PETTY LOT.
BECAUSE WE ATTACKED THEM, HURT THEM, CAPTURED TWO OF THEM.
READY THE FEMALE FOR TRANSPORT.
I'LL DEAL WITH THE BLUE ONE.
AUGUR?
YES, MY LOVE?
WHERE... IS THE BLUE ONE?

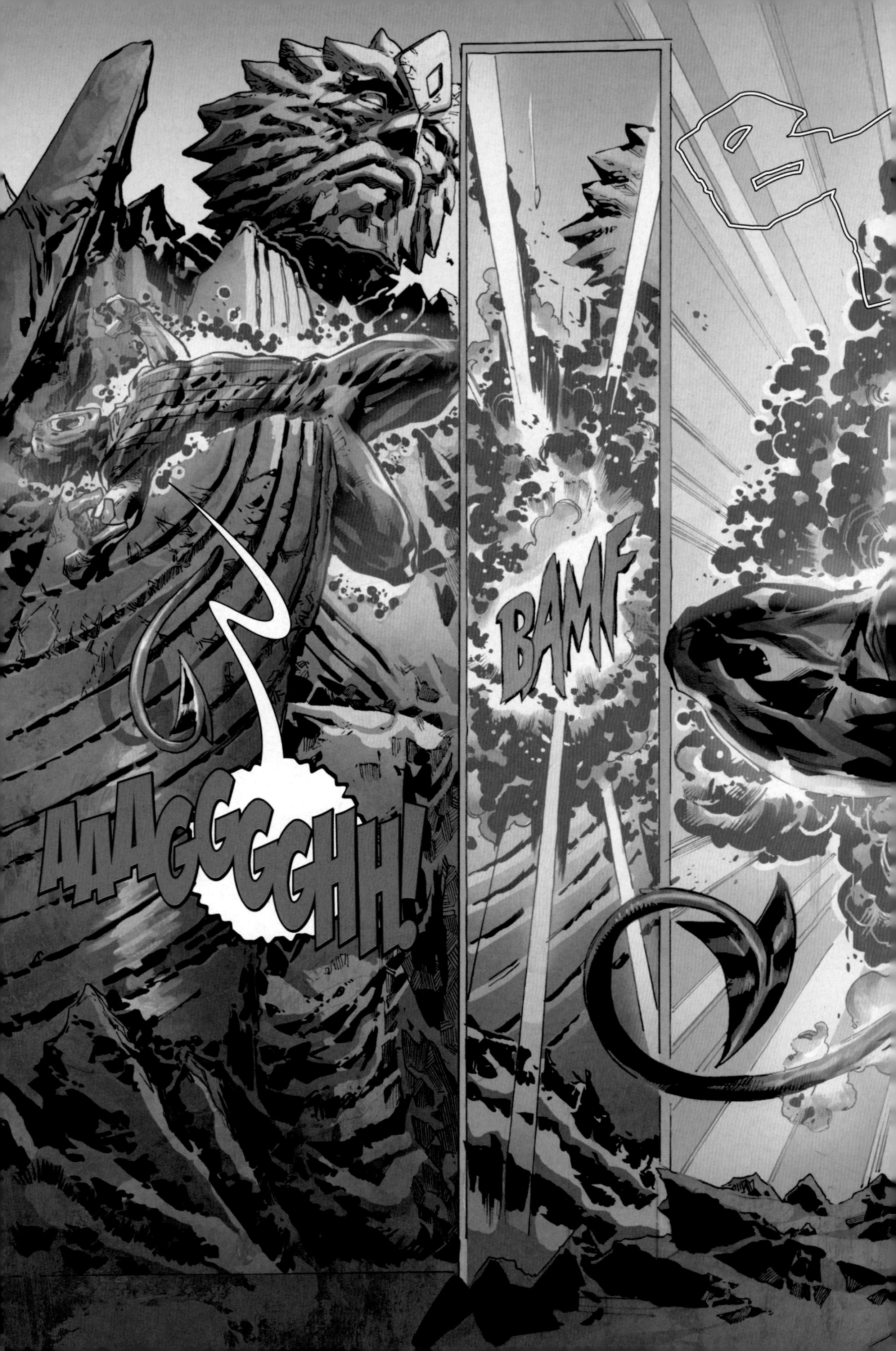
AAAGGGGHH!
BAMF

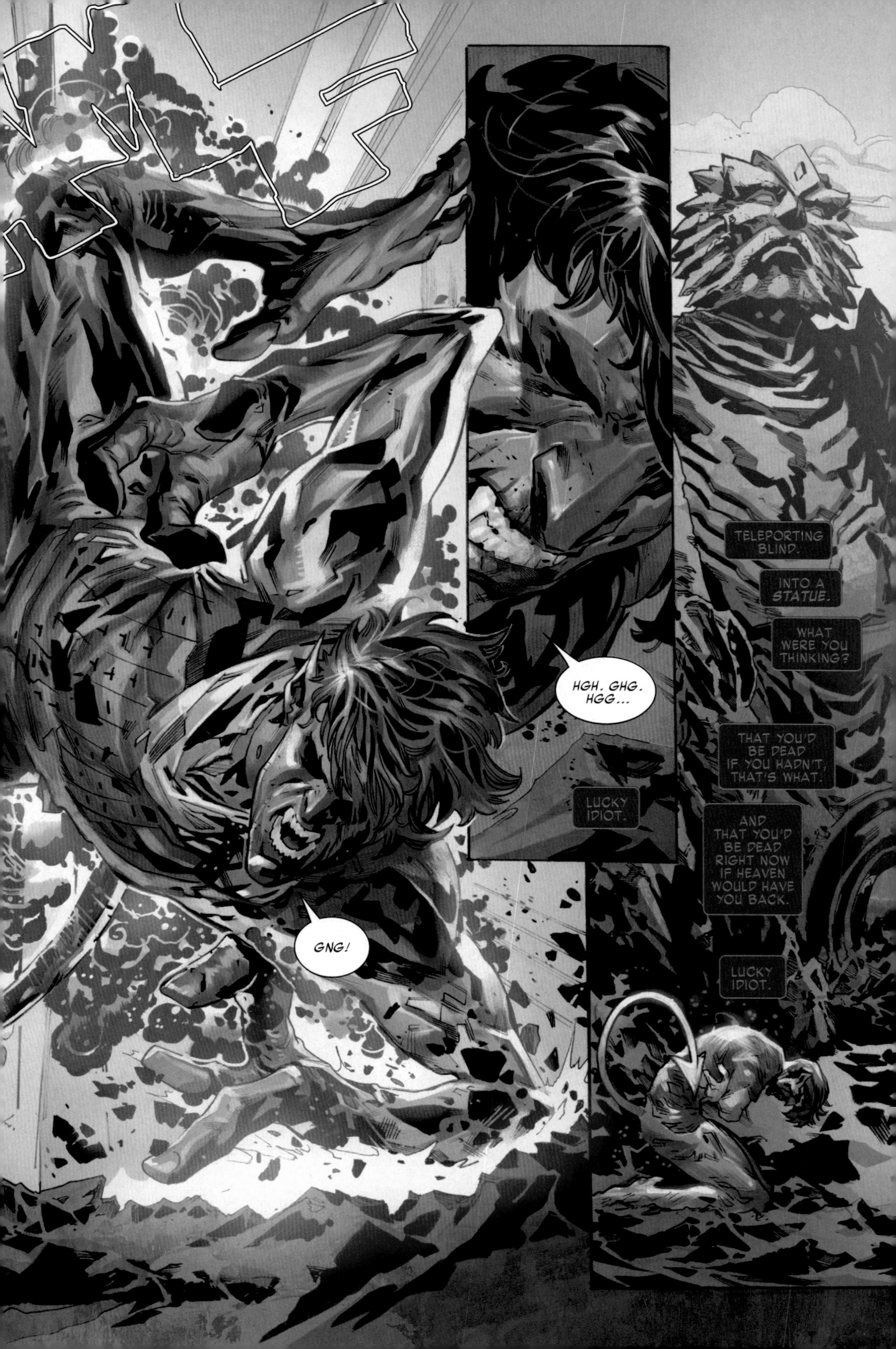
GNG!
HGH. GHG. HGG...
LUCKY IDIOT.
TELEPORTING BLIND.
INTO A STATUE.
WHAT WERE YOU THINKING?
THAT YOU'D BE DEAD IF YOU HADN'T, THAT'S WHAT.
AND THAT YOU'D BE DEAD RIGHT NOW IF HEAVEN WOULD HAVE YOU BACK.
LUCKY IDIOT.

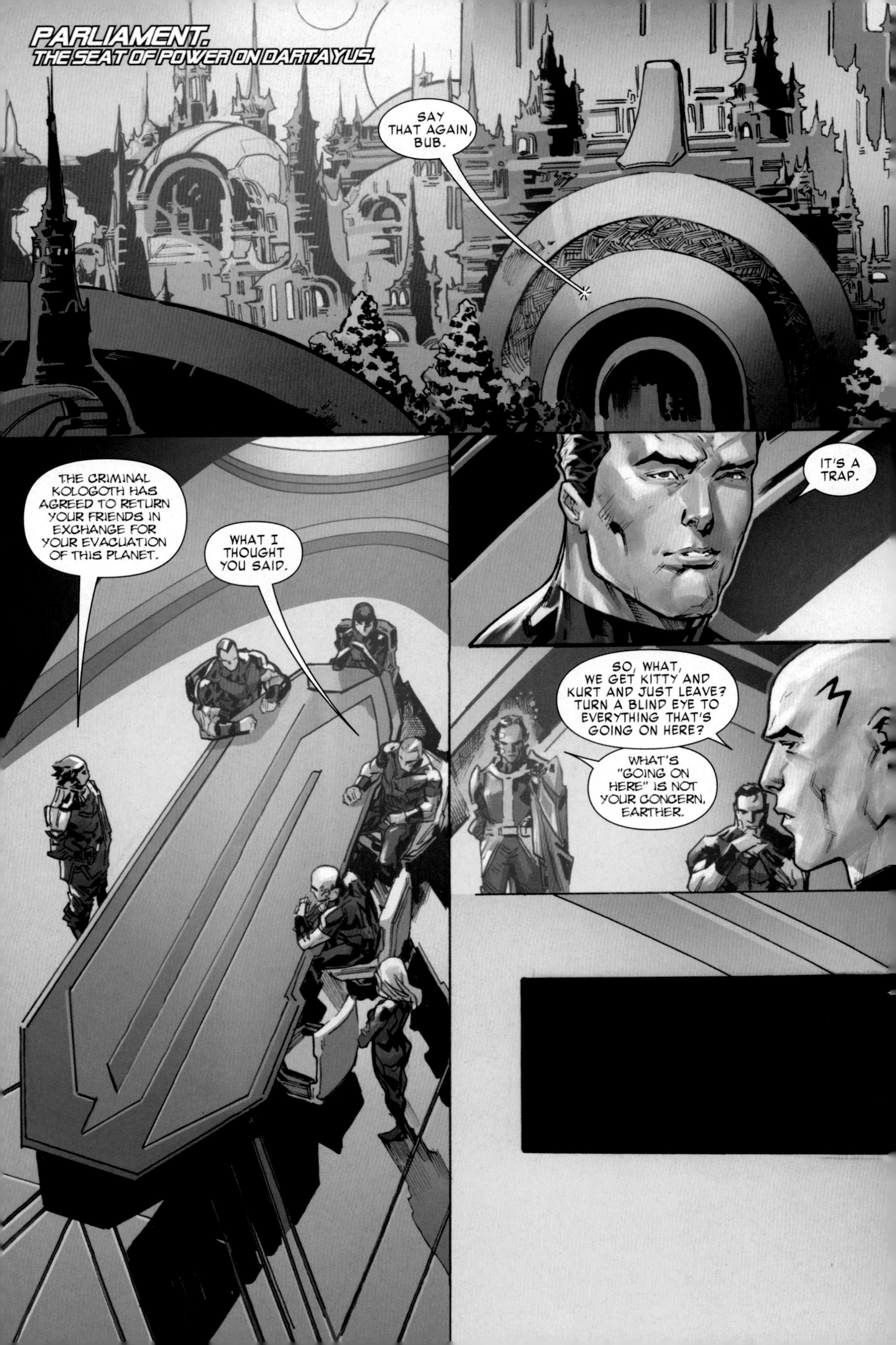
PARLIAMENT.
THE SEAT OF POWER ON DARTAYUS.
SAY THAT AGAIN, BUB.
THE CRIMINAL KOLOGOTH HAS AGREED TO RETURN YOUR FRIENDS IN EXCHANGE FOR YOUR EVACUATION OF THIS PLANET.
WHAT I THOUGHT YOU SAID.
IT'S A TRAP.
SO, WHAT, WE GET KITTY AND KURT AND JUST LEAVE? TURN A BLIND EYE TO EVERYTHING THAT'S GOING ON HERE?
WHAT'S "GOING ON HERE" IS NOT YOUR CONCERN, EARTHER.

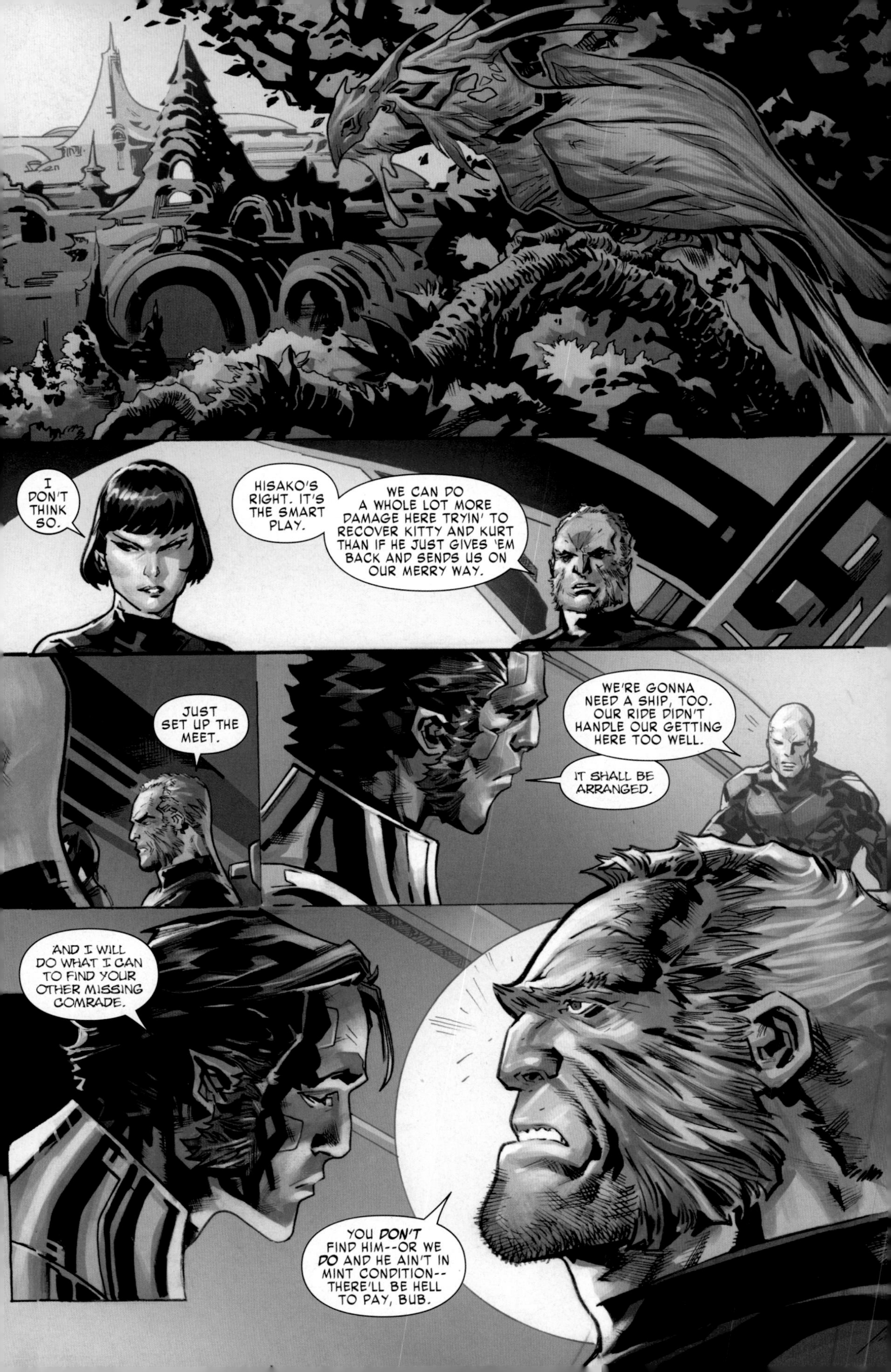
I DON'T THINK SO.
HISAKO'S RIGHT. IT'S THE SMART PLAY.
WE CAN DO A WHOLE LOT MORE DAMAGE HERE TRYIN' TO RECOVER KITTY AND KURT THAN IF HE JUST GIVES 'EM BACK AND SENDS US ON OUR MERRY WAY.
JUST SET UP THE MEET.
WE'RE GONNA NEED A SHIP, TOO. OUR RIDE DIDN'T HANDLE OUR GETTING HERE TOO WELL.
IT SHALL BE ARRANGED.
AND I WILL DO WHAT I CAN TO FIND YOUR OTHER MISSING COMRADE.
YOU **DON'T** FIND HIM--OR WE **DO** AND HE AIN'T IN MINT CONDITION--THERE'LL BE HELL TO PAY, BUB.

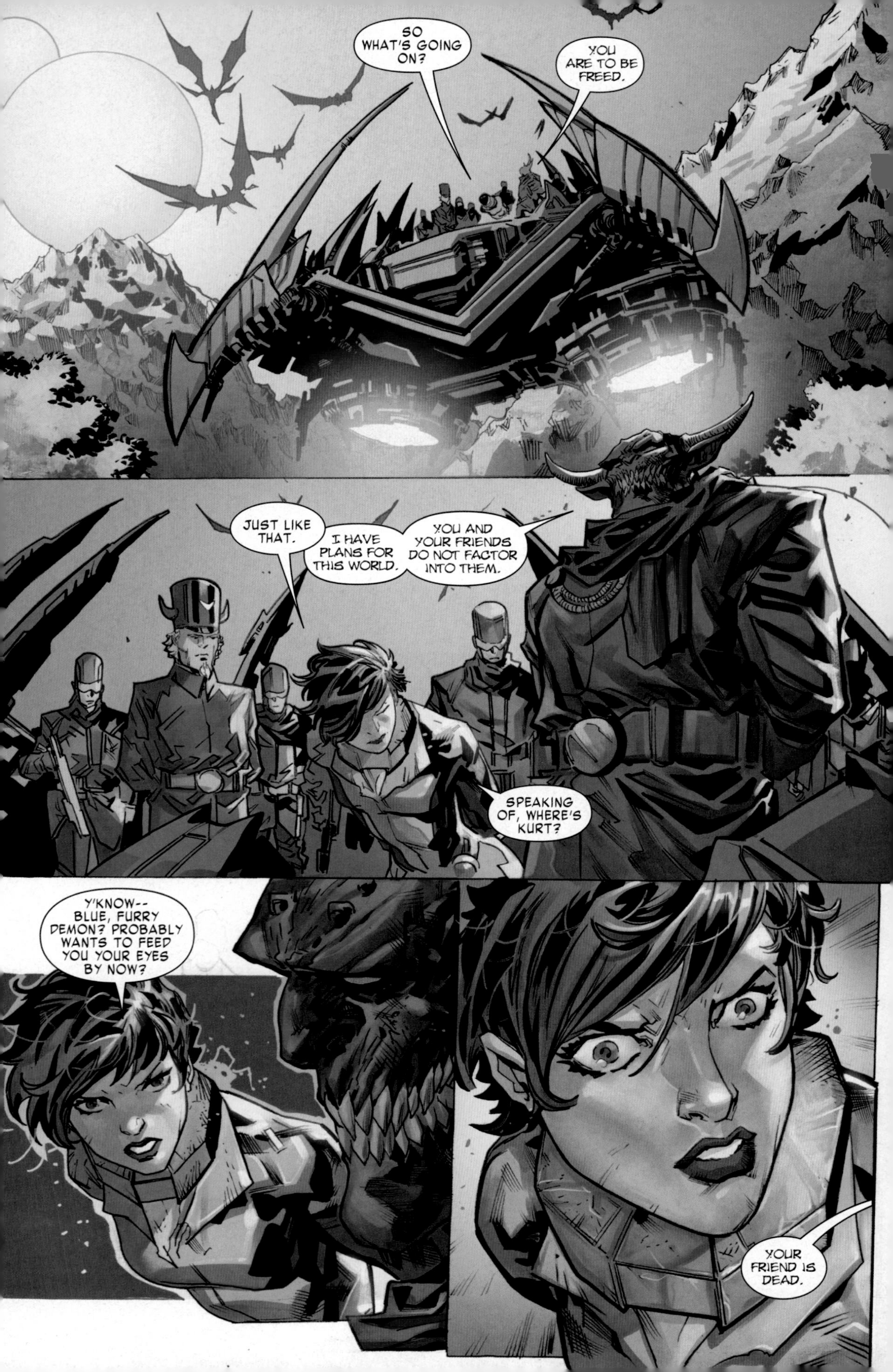
SO WHAT'S GOING ON?
YOU ARE TO BE FREED.
JUST LIKE THAT.
I HAVE PLANS FOR THIS WORLD.
YOU AND YOUR FRIENDS DO NOT FACTOR INTO THEM.
SPEAKING OF, WHERE'S KURT?
Y'KNOW-- BLUE, FURRY DEMON? PROBABLY WANTS TO FEED YOU YOUR EYES BY NOW?
YOUR FRIEND IS DEAD.

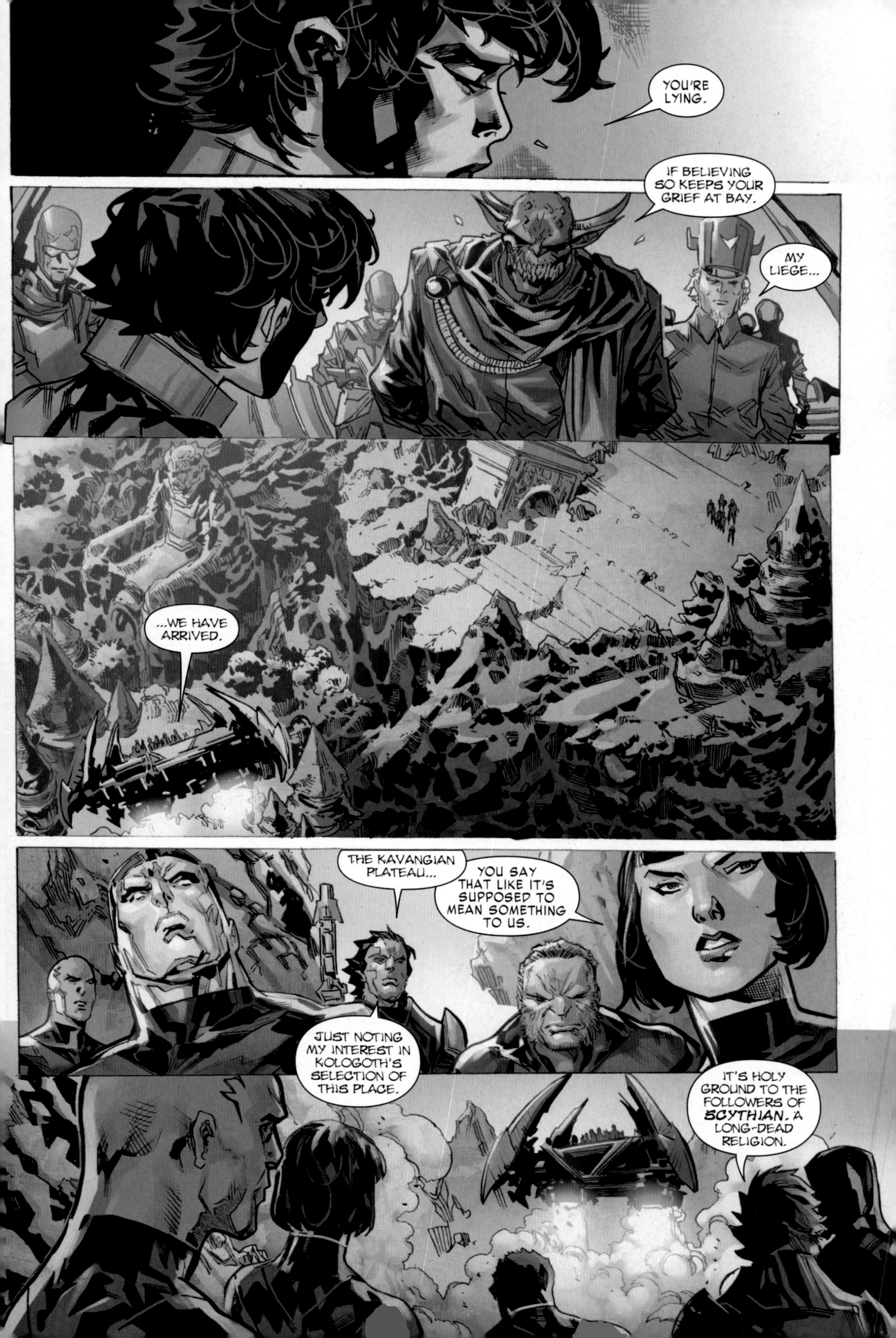
YOU'RE LYING.
IF BELIEVING SO KEEPS YOUR GRIEF AT BAY.
MY LIEGE...
...WE HAVE ARRIVED.
THE KAVANGIAN PLATEAU...
YOU SAY THAT LIKE IT'S SUPPOSED TO MEAN SOMETHING TO US.
JUST NOTING MY INTEREST IN KOLOGOTH'S SELECTION OF THIS PLACE.
IT'S HOLY GROUND TO THE FOLLOWERS OF SCYTHIAN. A LONG-DEAD RELIGION.

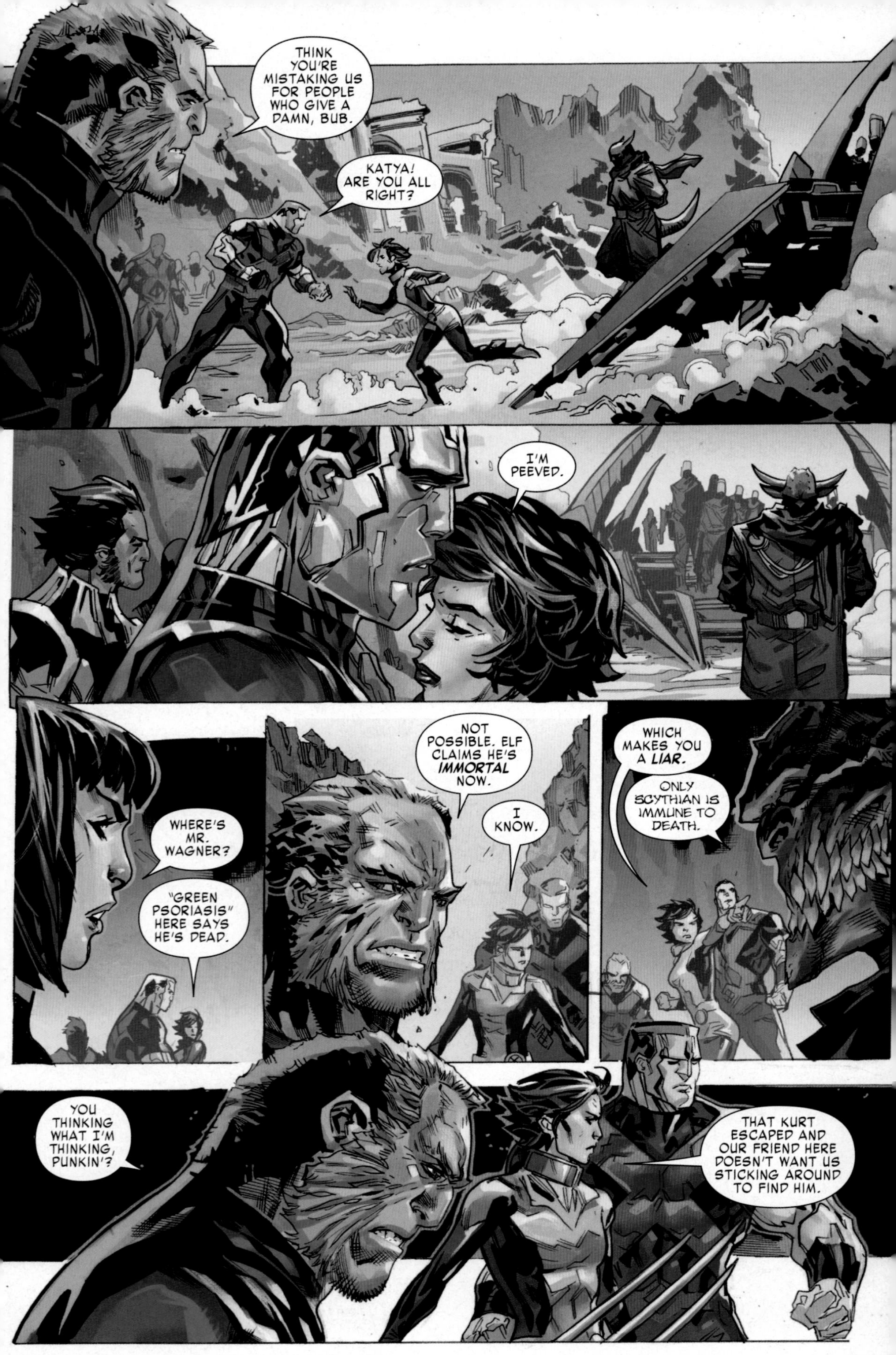
THINK YOU'RE MISTAKING US FOR PEOPLE WHO GIVE A DAMN, BUB.
KATYA! ARE YOU ALL RIGHT?
I'M PEEVED.
WHERE'S MR. WAGNER?
"GREEN PSORIASIS" HERE SAYS HE'S DEAD.
NOT POSSIBLE. ELF CLAIMS HE'S IMMORTAL NOW.
I KNOW.
WHICH MAKES YOU A LIAR.
ONLY SCYTHIAN IS IMMUNE TO DEATH.
YOU THINKING WHAT I'M THINKING, PUNKIN'?
THAT KURT ESCAPED AND OUR FRIEND HERE DOESN'T WANT US STICKING AROUND TO FIND HIM.

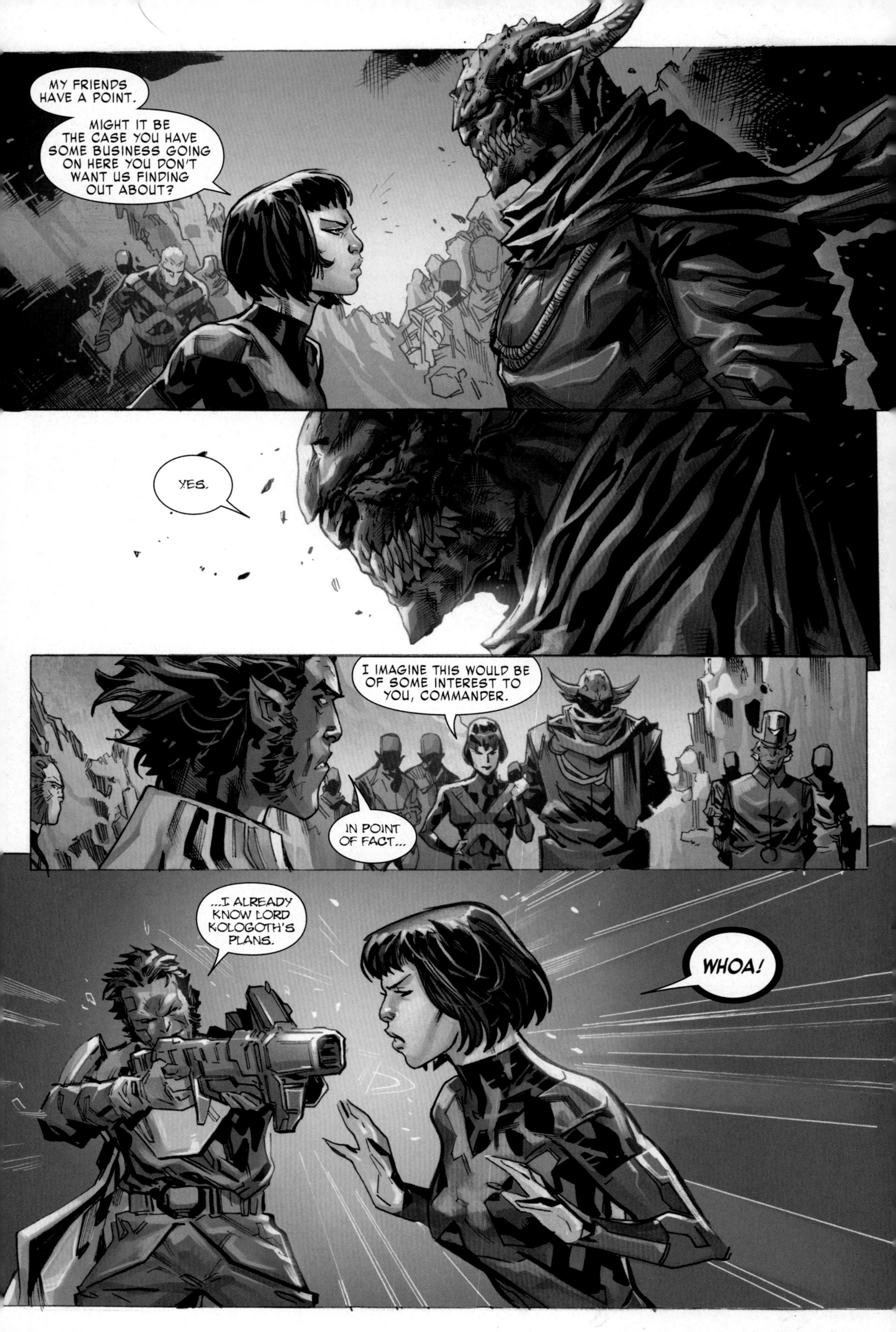
MY FRIENDS HAVE A POINT.
MIGHT IT BE THE CASE YOU HAVE SOME BUSINESS GOING ON HERE YOU DON'T WANT US FINDING OUT ABOUT?
YES.
I IMAGINE THIS WOULD BE OF SOME INTEREST TO YOU, COMMANDER.
IN POINT OF FACT...
...I ALREADY KNOW LORD KOLOGOTH'S PLANS.
WHOA!

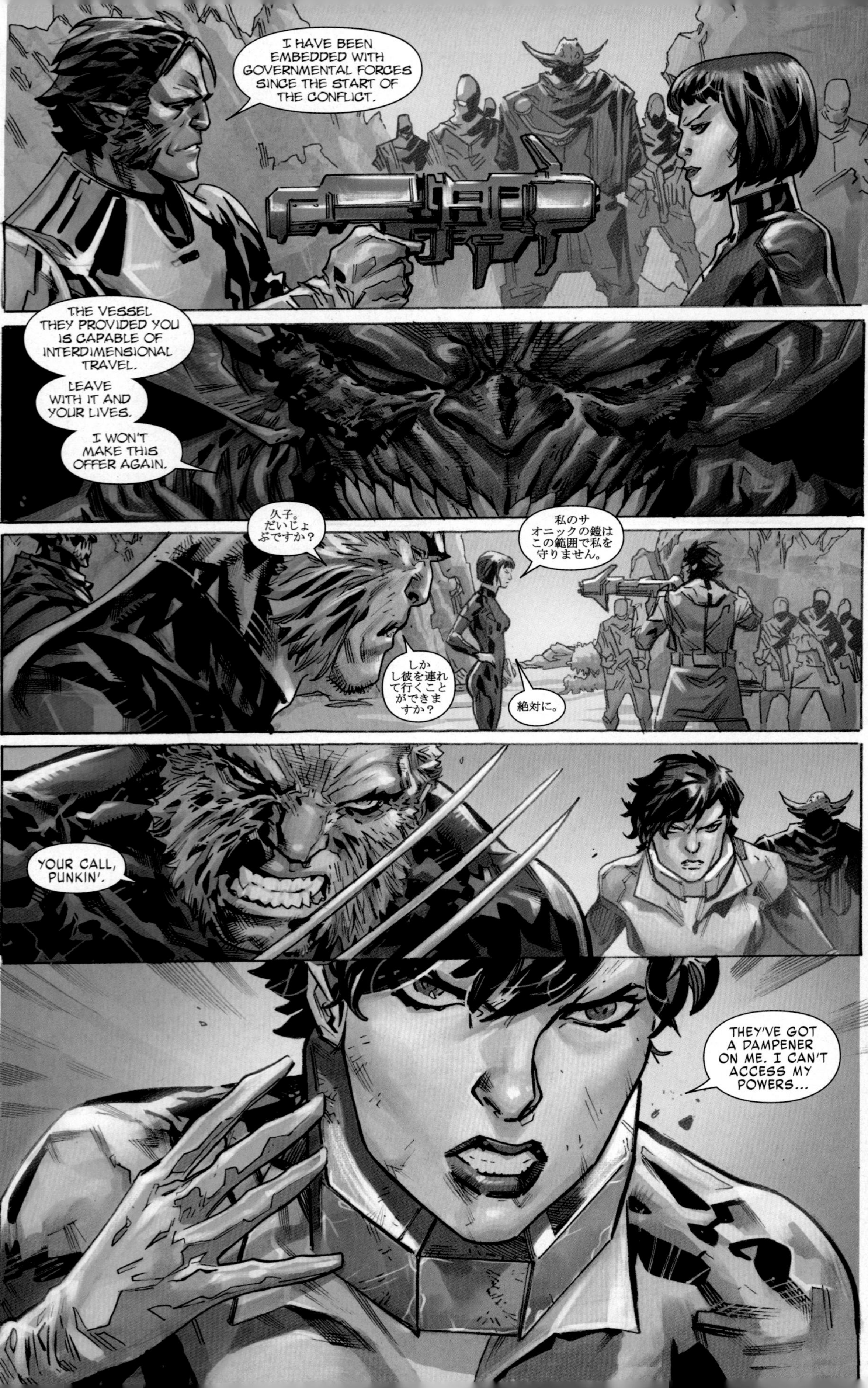
I HAVE BEEN EMBEDDED WITH GOVERNMENTAL FORCES SINCE THE START OF THE CONFLICT.
THE VESSEL THEY PROVIDED YOU IS CAPABLE OF INTERDIMENSIONAL TRAVEL.
LEAVE WITH IT AND YOUR LIVES.
I WON'T MAKE THIS OFFER AGAIN.
久子。だいじょぶですか？
私のサオニックの鎧はこの範囲で私を守りません。
しかし彼を連れて行くことができますか？
絶対に。
YOUR CALL, PUNKIN'.
THEY'VE GOT A DAMPENER ON ME. I CAN'T ACCESS MY POWERS...

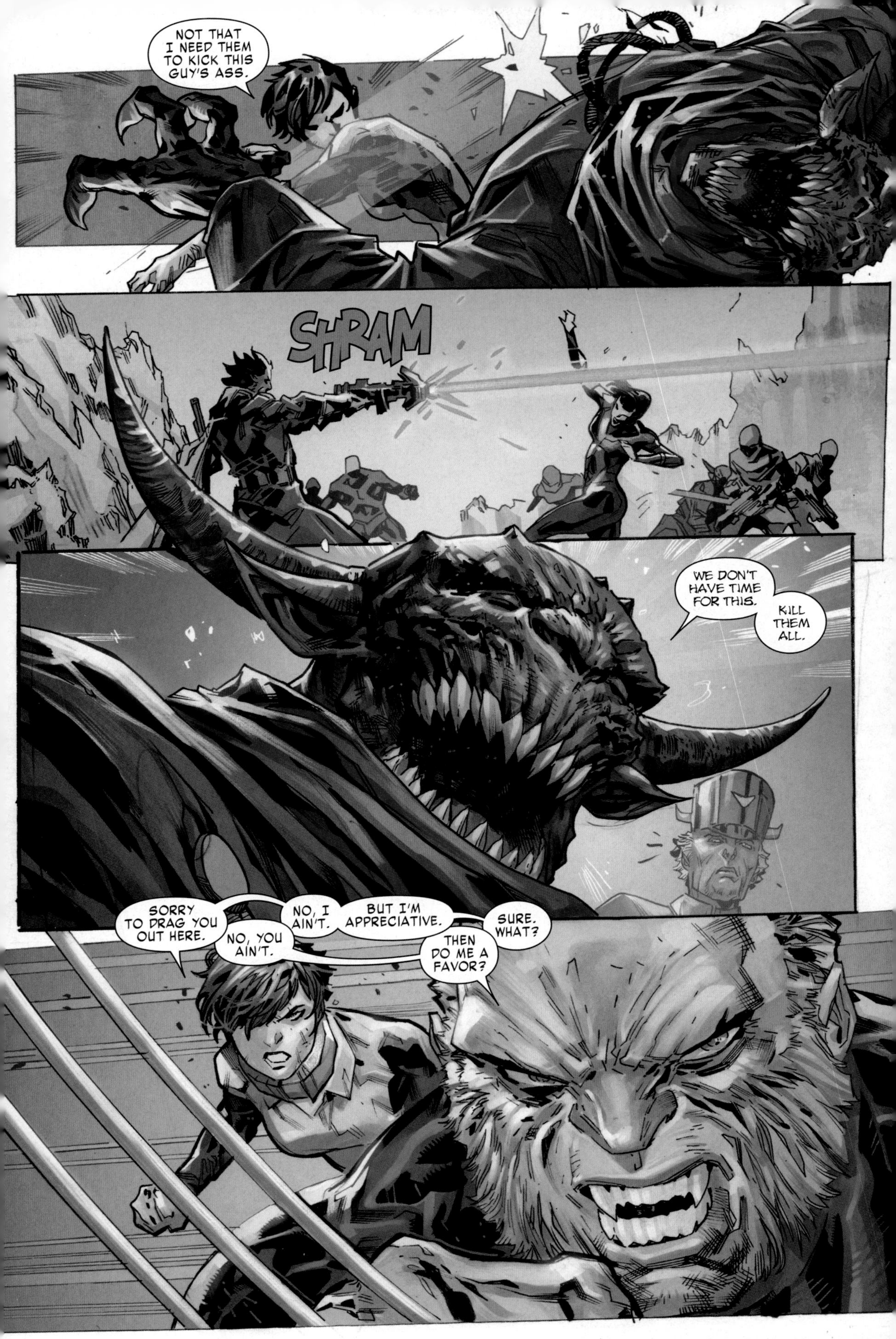
NOT THAT I NEED THEM TO KICK THIS GUY'S ASS.
SHRAM
WE DON'T HAVE TIME FOR THIS.
KILL THEM ALL.
SORRY TO DRAG YOU OUT HERE.
NO, YOU AIN'T.
NO, I AIN'T.
BUT I'M APPRECIATIVE.
THEN DO ME A FAVOR?
SURE. WHAT?

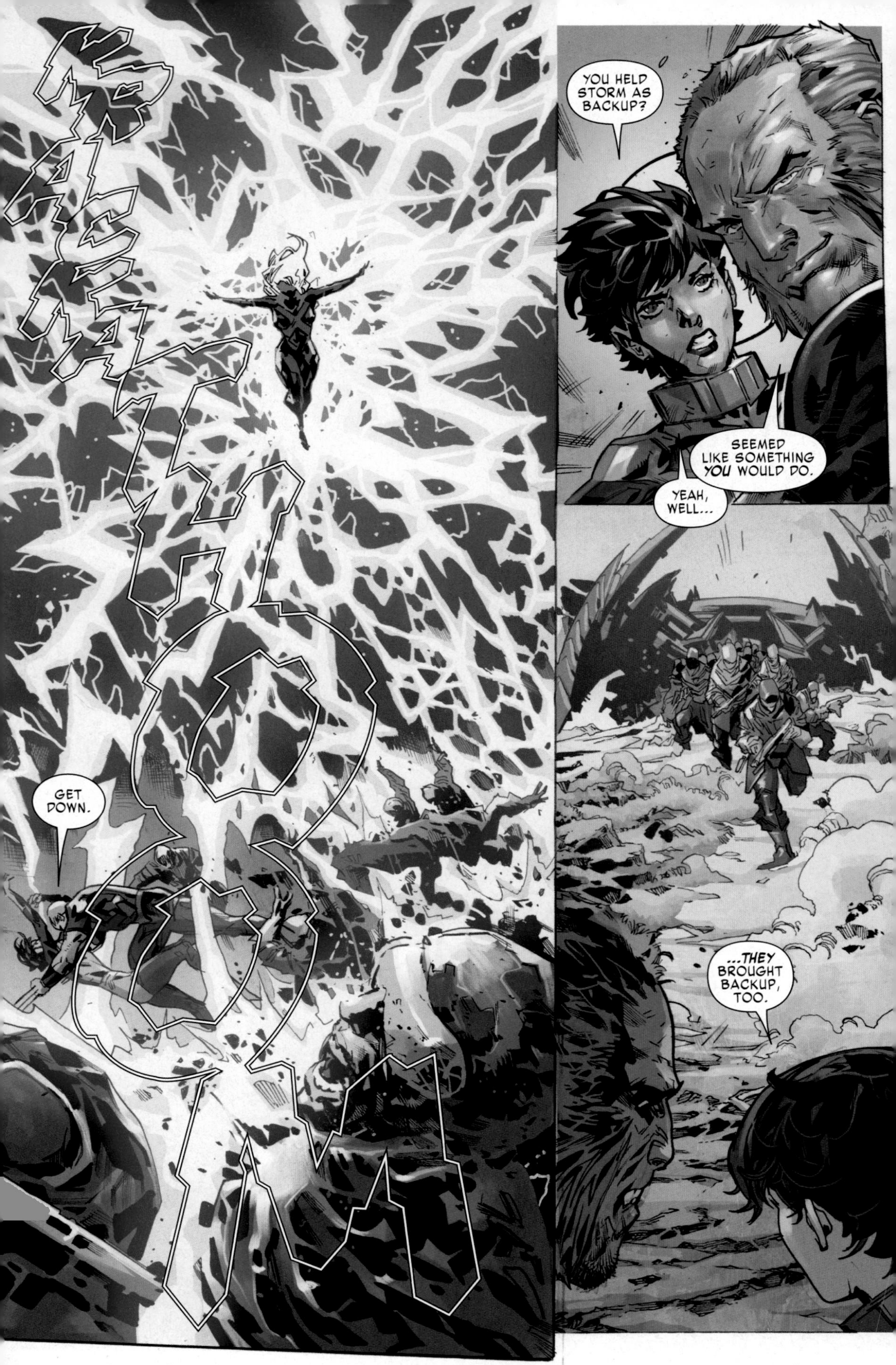

GET DOWN.
YOU HELD STORM AS BACKUP?
SEEMED LIKE SOMETHING *YOU* WOULD DO.
YEAH, WELL...
...*THEY* BROUGHT BACKUP, TOO.

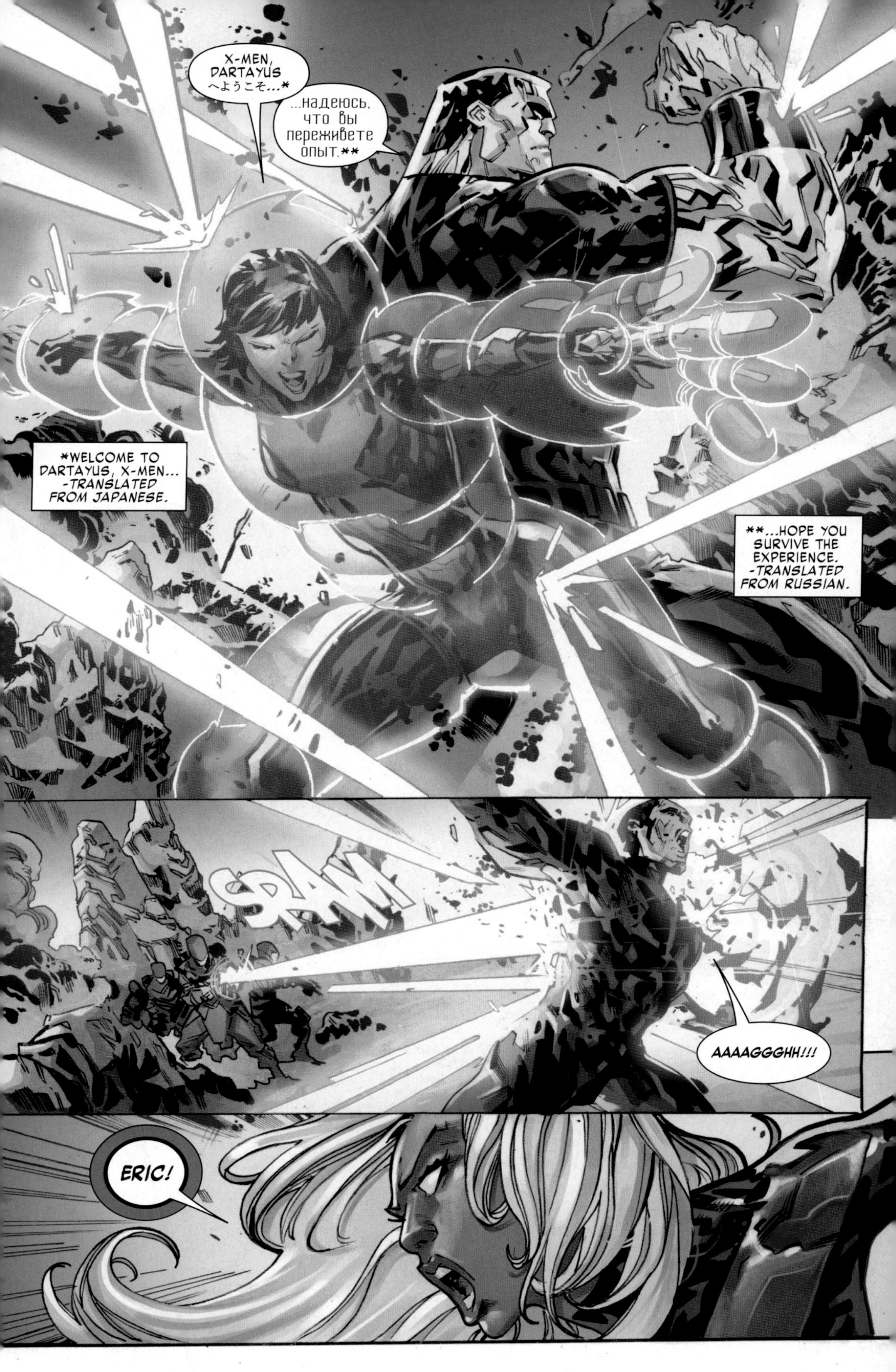
X-MEN, DARTAYUS へようこそ...*
...надеюсь, что вы переживете опыт.**
*WELCOME TO DARTAYUS, X-MEN... -TRANSLATED FROM JAPANESE.
**...HOPE YOU SURVIVE THE EXPERIENCE. -TRANSLATED FROM RUSSIAN.
SPAM
AAAAGGGHH!!!
ERIC!

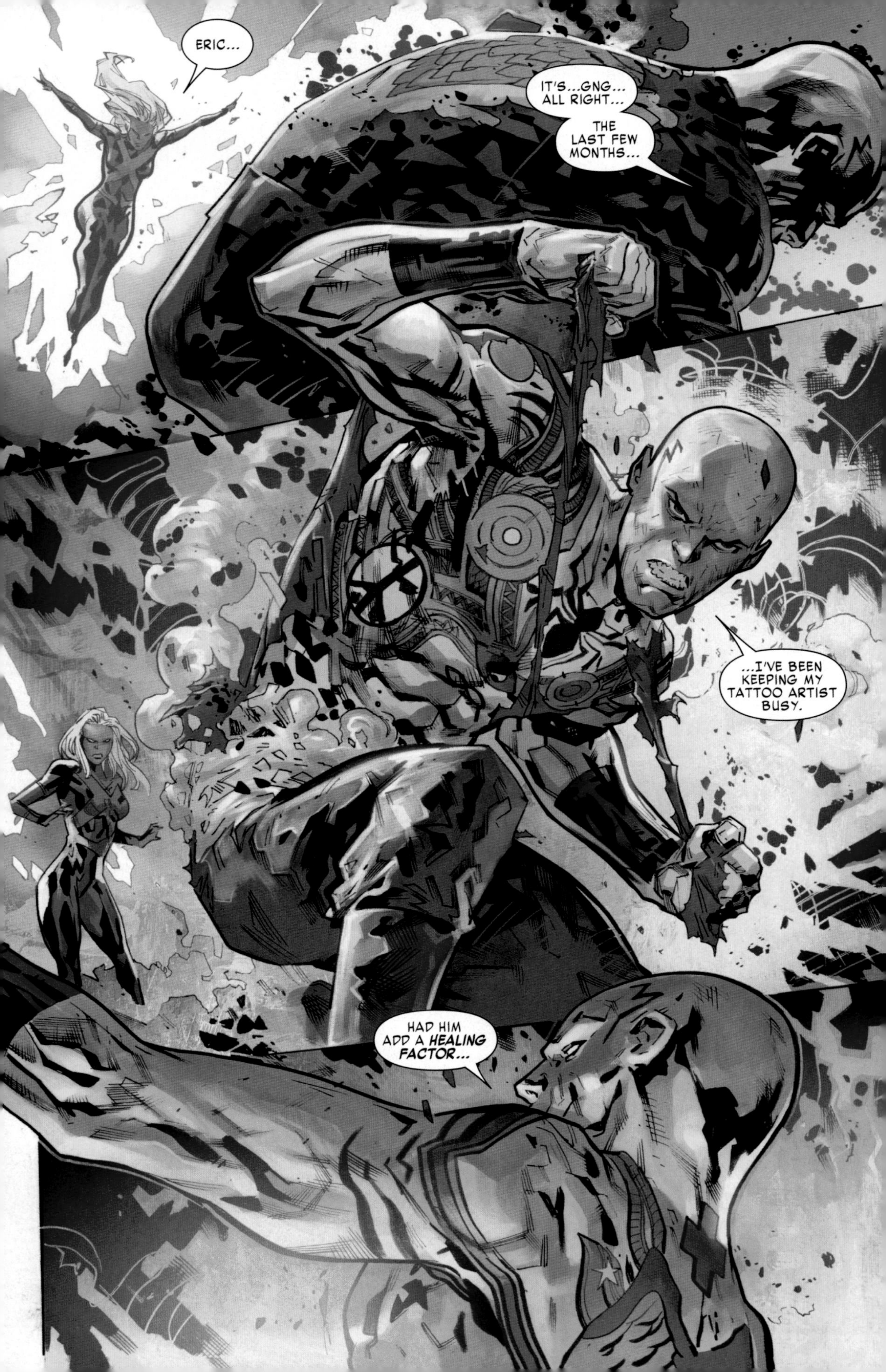
ERIC...
IT'S...GNG... ALL RIGHT...
THE LAST FEW MONTHS...
...I'VE BEEN KEEPING MY TATTOO ARTIST BUSY.
HAD HIM ADD A *HEALING FACTOR*...

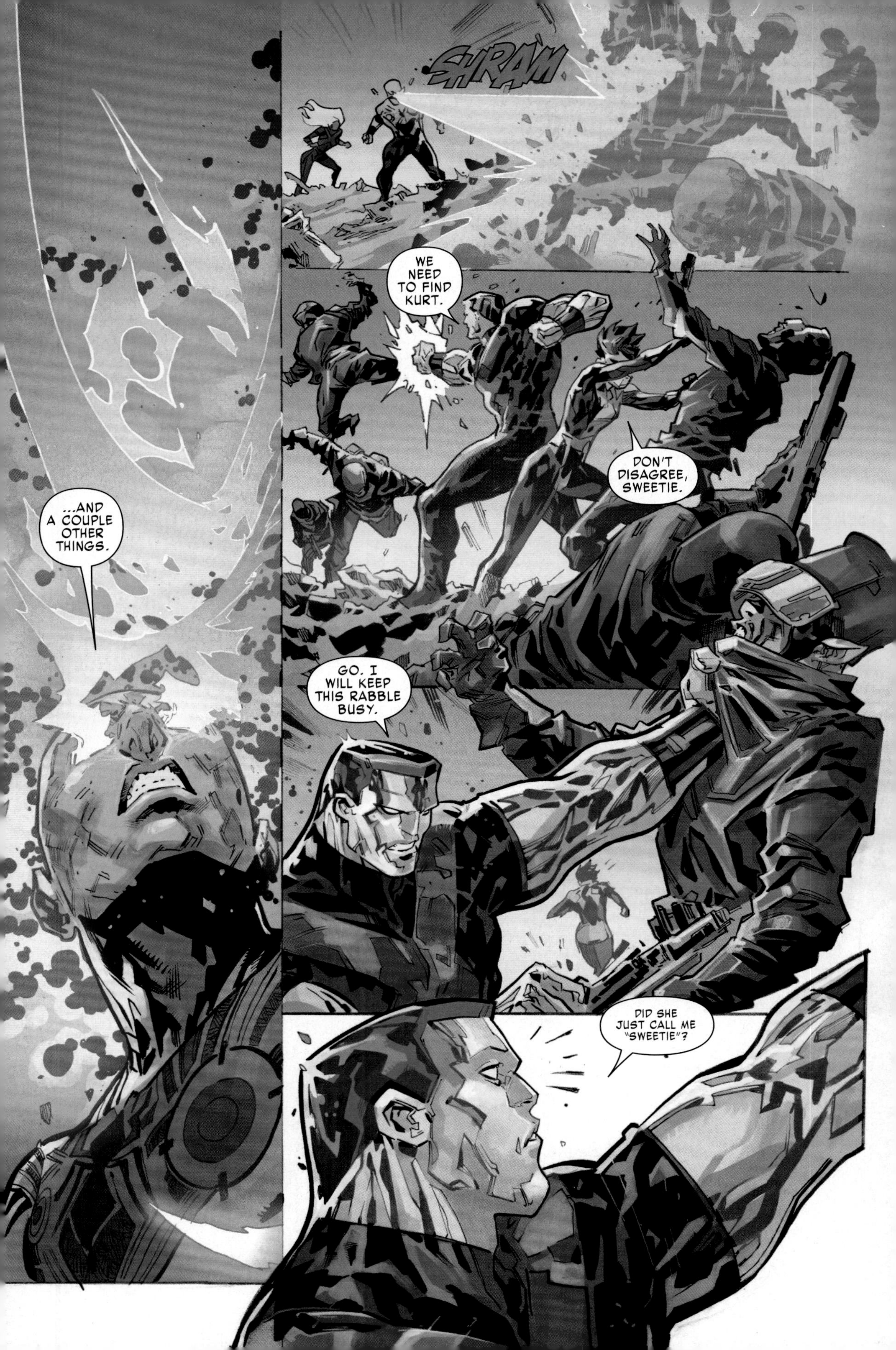

...AND A COUPLE OTHER THINGS.
SHRAM
WE NEED TO FIND KURT.
DON'T DISAGREE, SWEETIE.
GO. I WILL KEEP THIS RABBLE BUSY.
DID SHE JUST CALL ME "SWEETIE"?

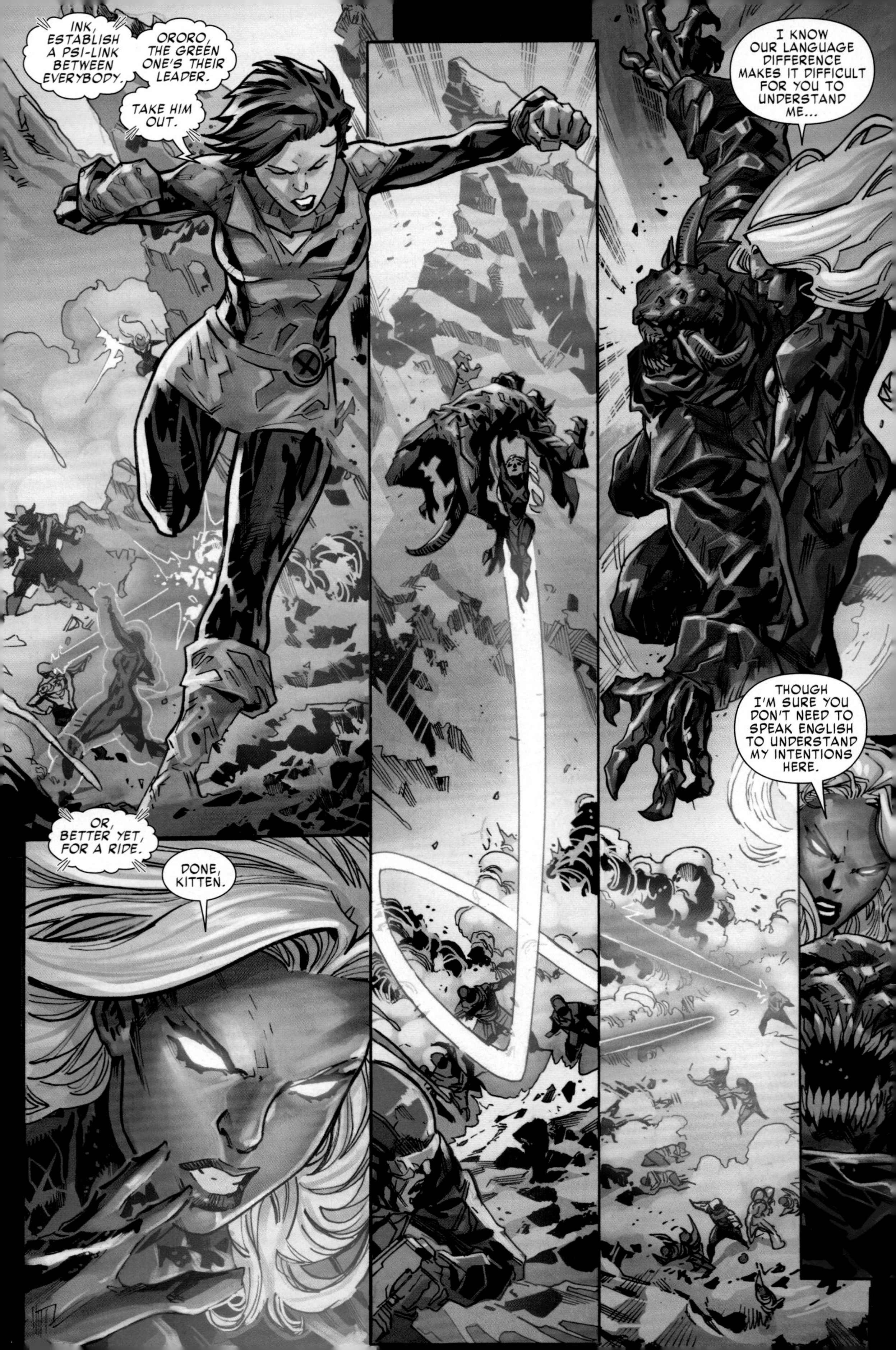
INK, ESTABLISH A PSI-LINK BETWEEN EVERYBODY.
ORORO, THE GREEN ONE'S THEIR LEADER.
TAKE HIM OUT.
OR, BETTER YET, FOR A RIDE.
DONE, KITTEN.
I KNOW OUR LANGUAGE DIFFERENCE MAKES IT DIFFICULT FOR YOU TO UNDERSTAND ME...
THOUGH I'M SURE YOU DON'T NEED TO SPEAK ENGLISH TO UNDERSTAND MY INTENTIONS HERE.

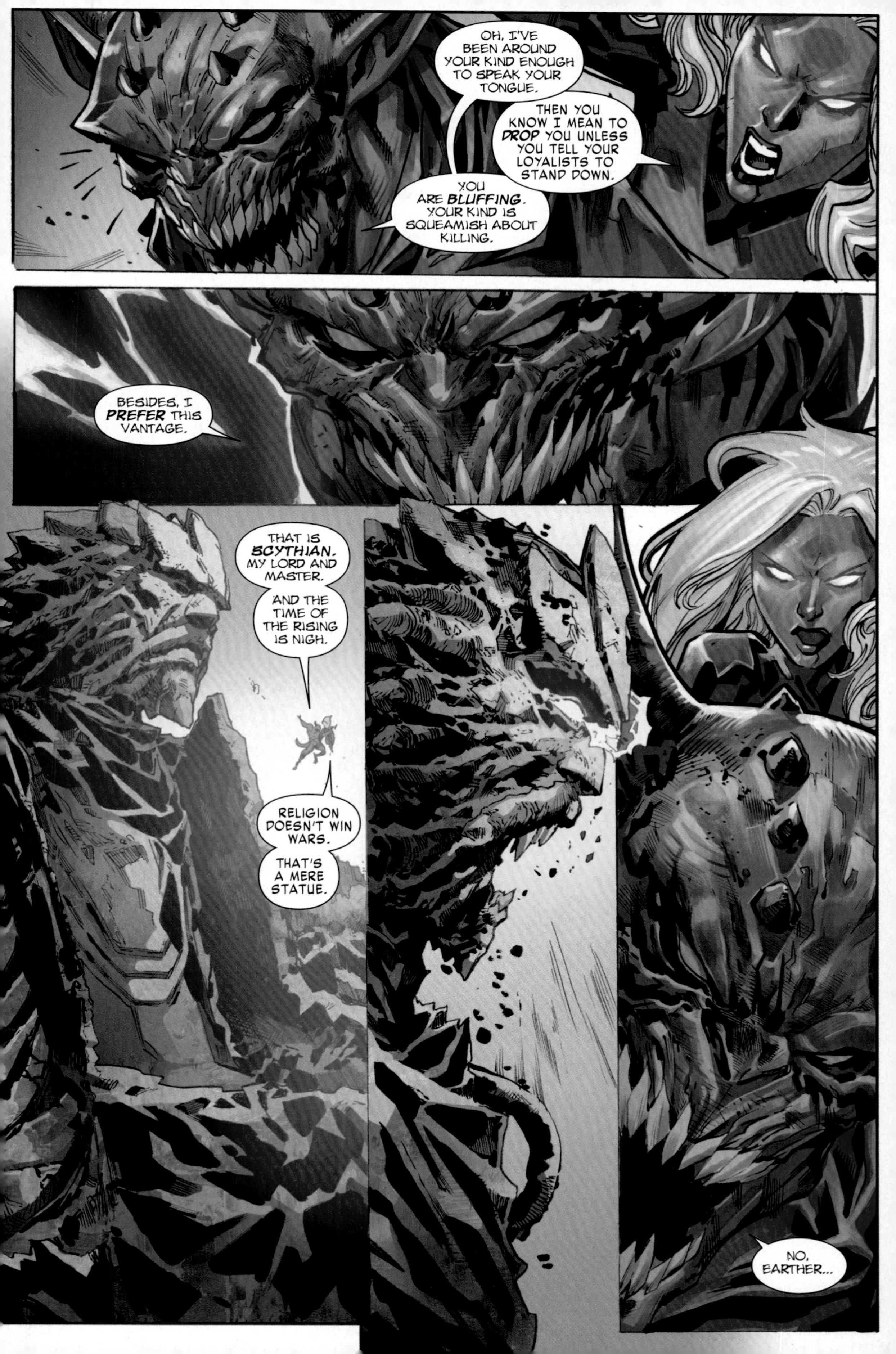
OH, I'VE BEEN AROUND YOUR KIND ENOUGH TO SPEAK YOUR TONGUE.
THEN YOU KNOW I MEAN TO DROP YOU UNLESS YOU TELL YOUR LOYALISTS TO STAND DOWN.
YOU ARE BLUFFING. YOUR KIND IS SQUEAMISH ABOUT KILLING.
BESIDES, I PREFER THIS VANTAGE.
THAT IS SCYTHIAN. MY LORD AND MASTER.
AND THE TIME OF THE RISING IS NIGH.
RELIGION DOESN'T WIN WARS.
THAT'S A MERE STATUE.
NO, EARTHER...

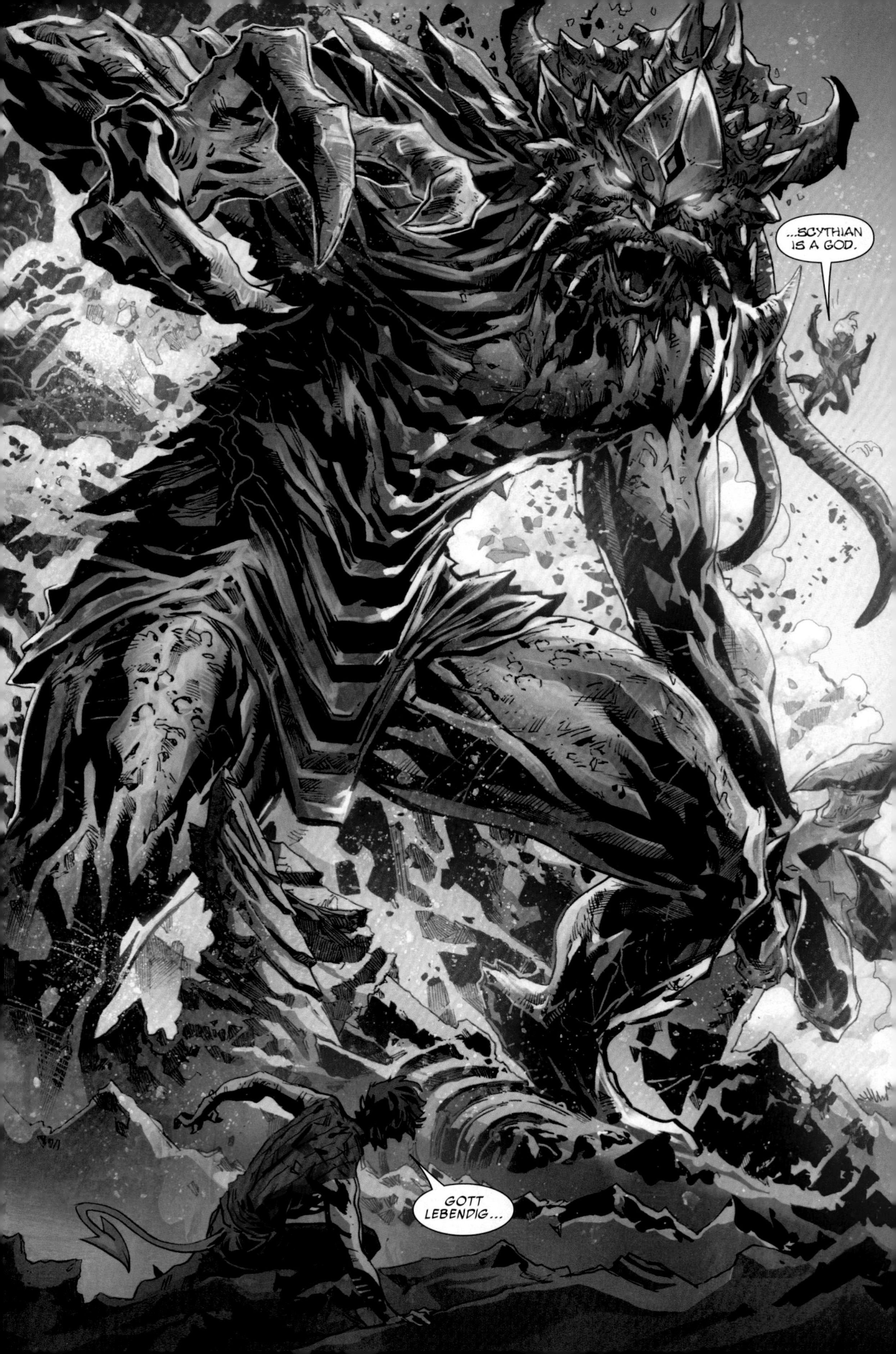
...SCYTHIAN IS A GOD.
GOTT LEBENDIG...

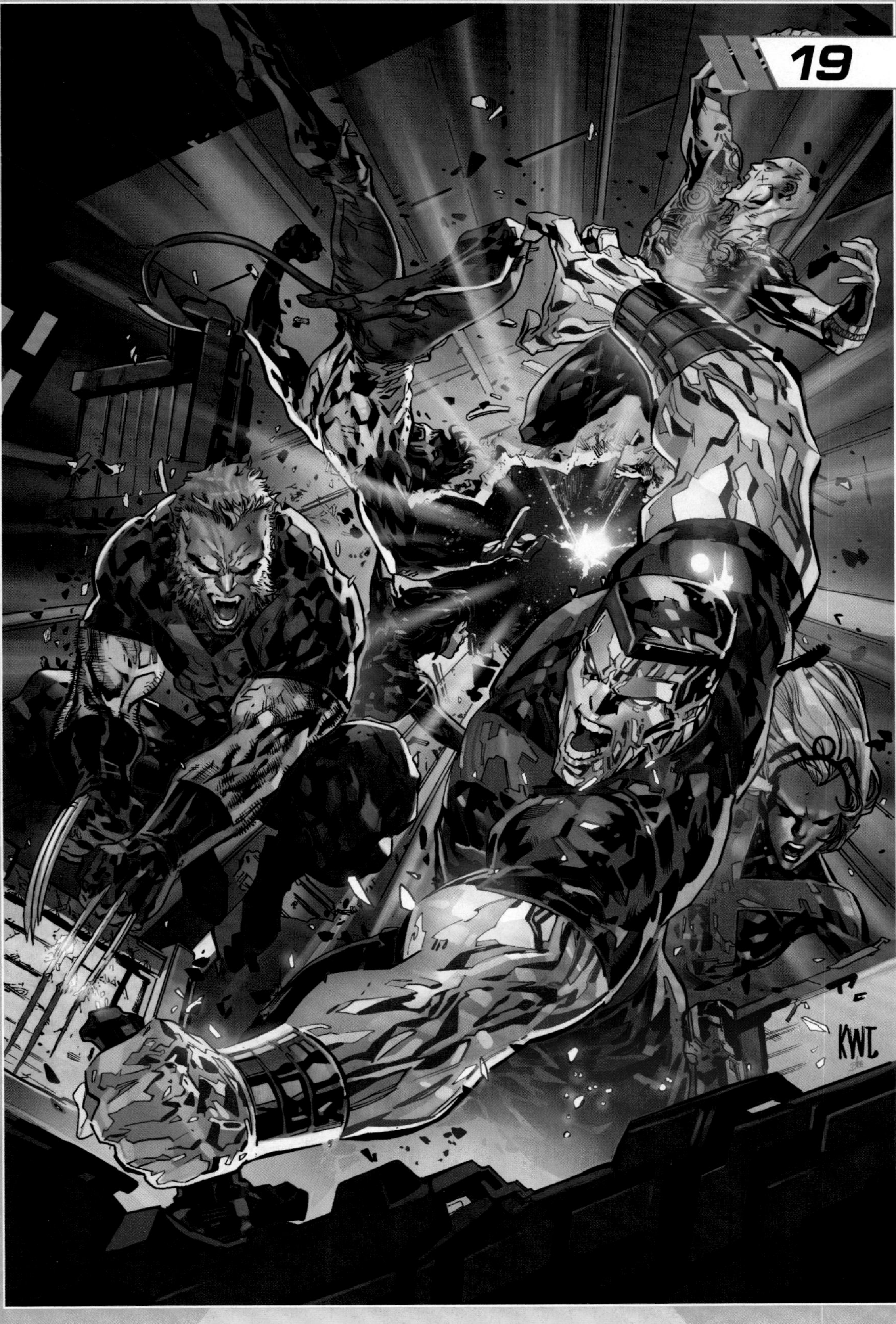

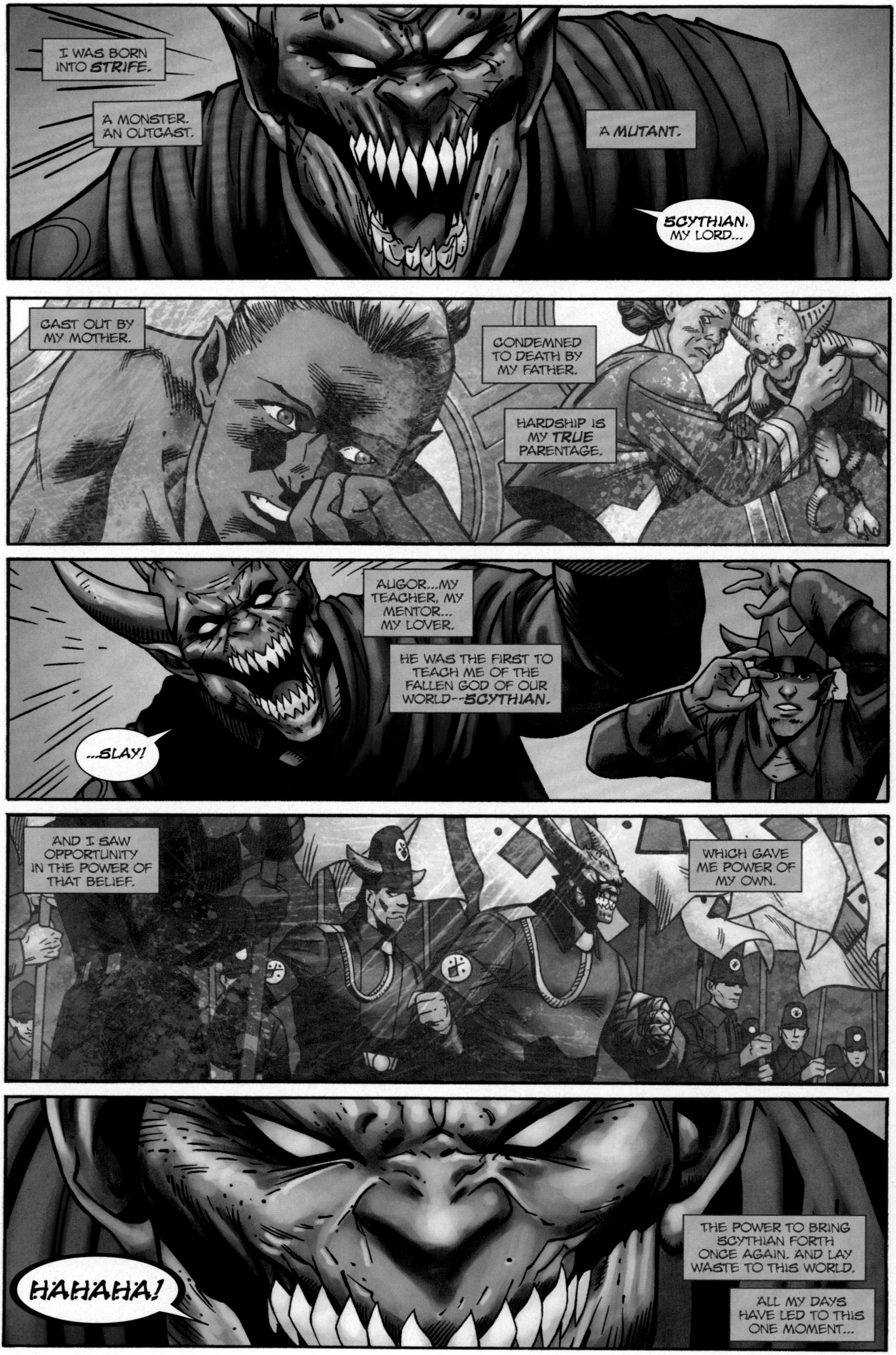
I WAS BORN INTO STRIFE.
A MONSTER. AN OUTCAST.
A MUTANT.
SCYTHIAN, MY LORD...
CAST OUT BY MY MOTHER.
CONDEMNED TO DEATH BY MY FATHER.
HARDSHIP IS MY TRUE PARENTAGE.
AUGOR...MY TEACHER, MY MENTOR... MY LOVER.
HE WAS THE FIRST TO TEACH ME OF THE FALLEN GOD OF OUR WORLD--SCYTHIAN.
...SLAY!
AND I SAW OPPORTUNITY IN THE POWER OF THAT BELIEF.
WHICH GAVE ME POWER OF MY OWN.
THE POWER TO BRING SCYTHIAN FORTH ONCE AGAIN. AND LAY WASTE TO THIS WORLD.
HAHAHA!
ALL MY DAYS HAVE LED TO THIS ONE MOMENT...

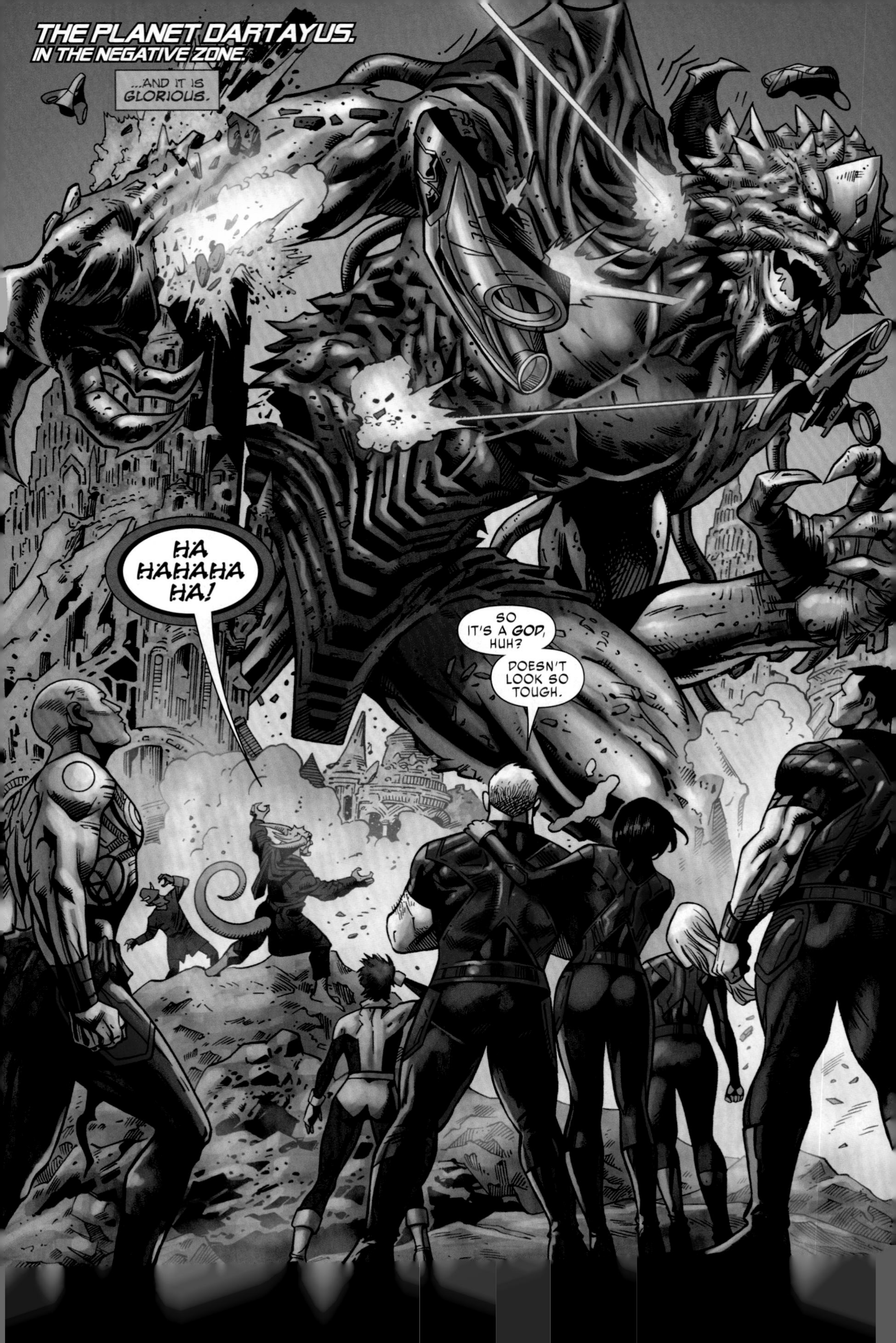
THE PLANET DARTAYUS.
IN THE NEGATIVE ZONE.
...AND IT IS GLORIOUS.
HA HAHAHA HA!
SO IT'S A GOD, HUH?
DOESN'T LOOK SO TOUGH.

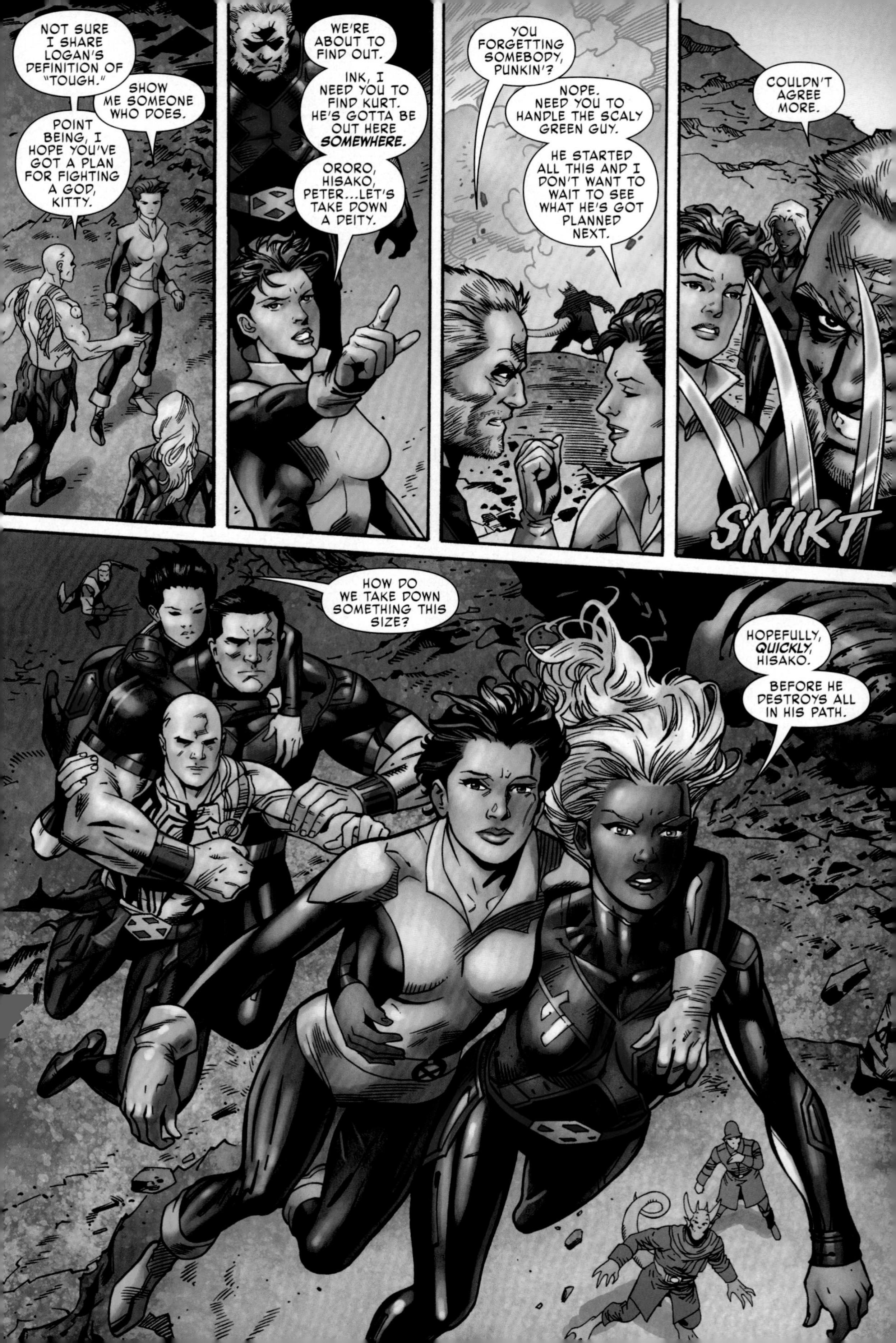
NOT SURE I SHARE LOGAN'S DEFINITION OF "TOUGH."
SHOW ME SOMEONE WHO DOES.
POINT BEING, I HOPE YOU'VE GOT A PLAN FOR FIGHTING A GOD, KITTY.
WE'RE ABOUT TO FIND OUT.
INK, I NEED YOU TO FIND KURT. HE'S GOTTA BE OUT HERE SOMEWHERE.
ORORO, HISAKO, PETER...LET'S TAKE DOWN A DEITY.
YOU FORGETTING SOMEBODY, PUNKIN'?
NOPE. NEED YOU TO HANDLE THE SCALY GREEN GUY.
HE STARTED ALL THIS AND I DON'T WANT TO WAIT TO SEE WHAT HE'S GOT PLANNED NEXT.
COULDN'T AGREE MORE.
SNIKT
HOW DO WE TAKE DOWN SOMETHING THIS SIZE?
HOPEFULLY, QUICKLY, HISAKO.
BEFORE HE DESTROYS ALL IN HIS PATH.

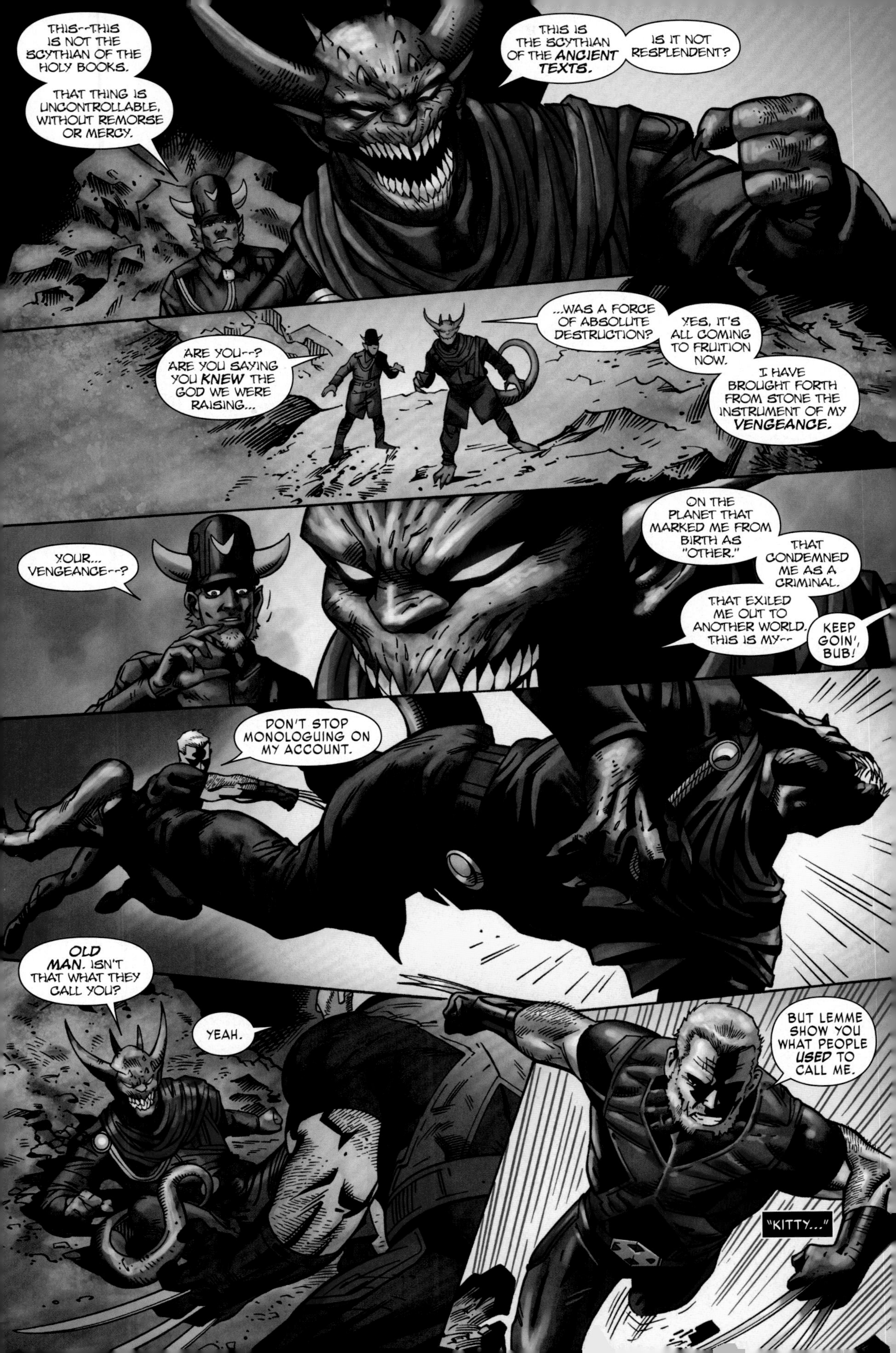

THIS--THIS IS NOT THE SCYTHIAN OF THE HOLY BOOKS.
THAT THING IS UNCONTROLLABLE, WITHOUT REMORSE OR MERCY.
THIS IS THE SCYTHIAN OF THE ANCIENT TEXTS.
IS IT NOT RESPLENDENT?
ARE YOU--? ARE YOU SAYING YOU KNEW THE GOD WE WERE RAISING...
...WAS A FORCE OF ABSOLUTE DESTRUCTION?
YES, IT'S ALL COMING TO FRUITION NOW.
I HAVE BROUGHT FORTH FROM STONE THE INSTRUMENT OF MY VENGEANCE.
YOUR... VENGEANCE--?
ON THE PLANET THAT MARKED ME FROM BIRTH AS "OTHER."
THAT CONDEMNED ME AS A CRIMINAL.
THAT EXILED ME OUT TO ANOTHER WORLD. THIS IS MY--
KEEP GOIN', BUB!
DON'T STOP MONOLOGUING ON MY ACCOUNT.
OLD MAN. ISN'T THAT WHAT THEY CALL YOU?
YEAH.
BUT LEMME SHOW YOU WHAT PEOPLE USED TO CALL ME.
"KITTY..."

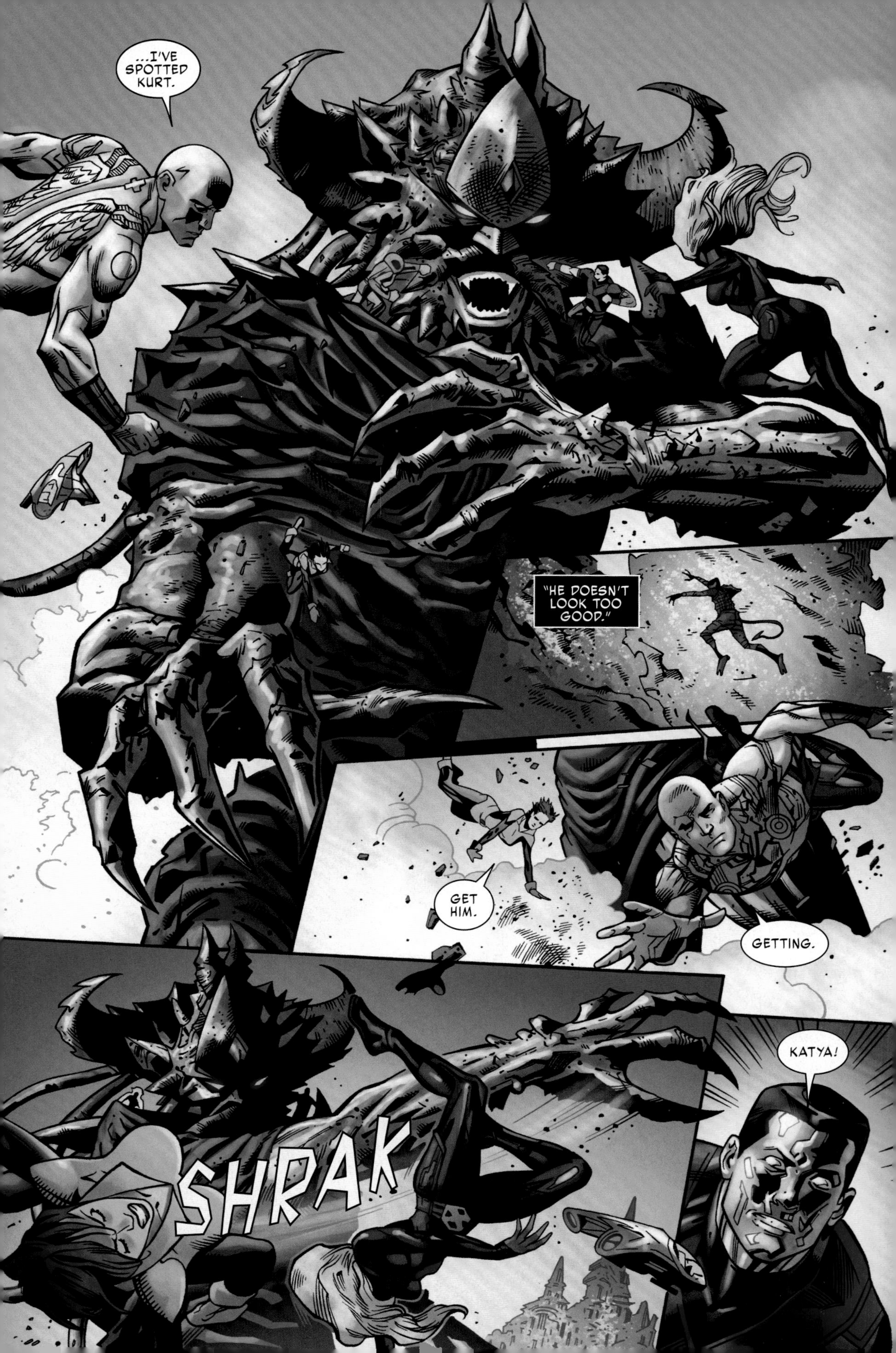
...I'VE SPOTTED KURT.
"HE DOESN'T LOOK TOO GOOD."
GET HIM.
GETTING.
KATYA!
SHRAK

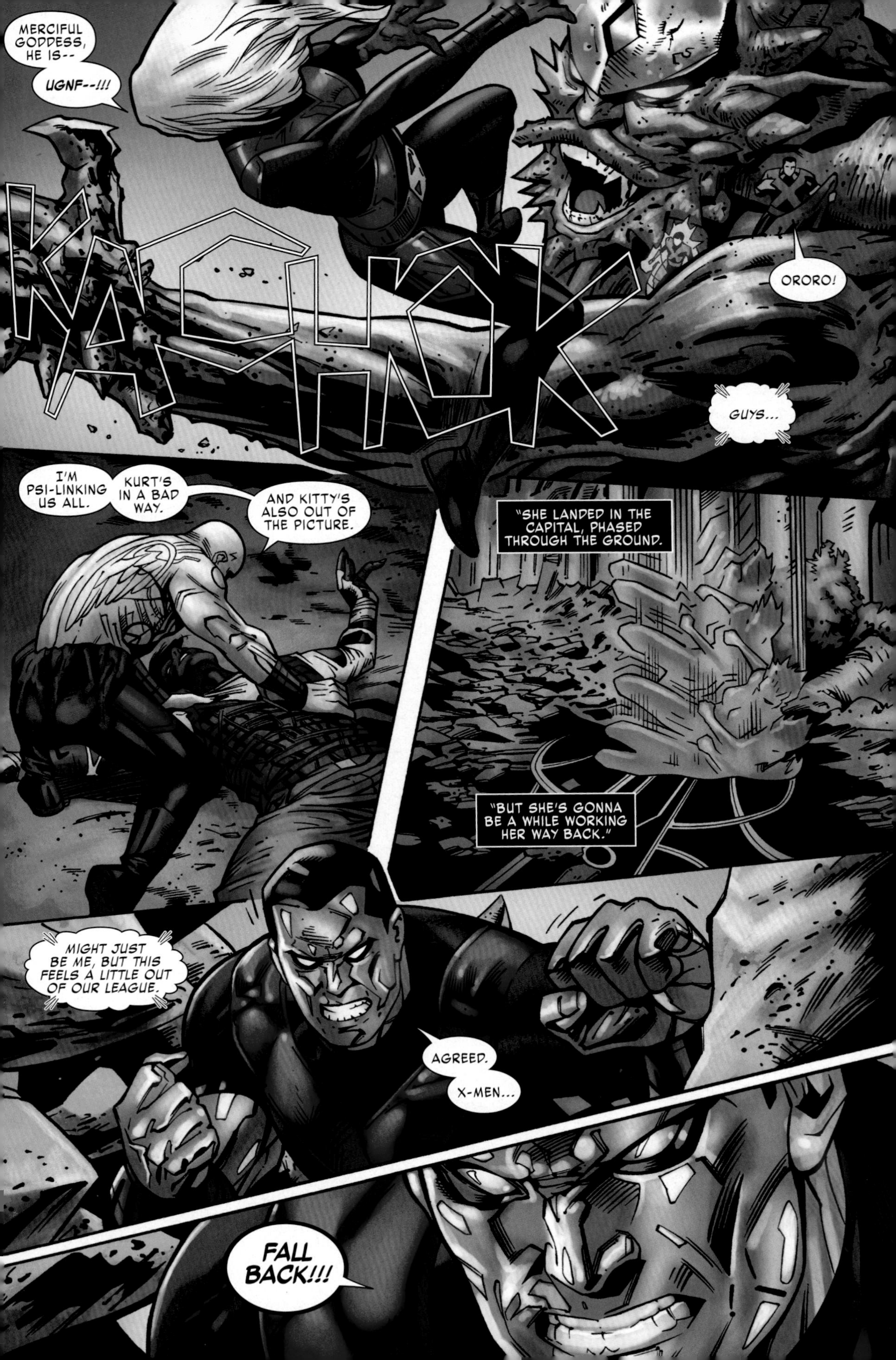
MERCIFUL GODDESS, HE IS--
UGNF--!!!
KA-CHOK
ORORO!
GUYS...
I'M PSI-LINKING US ALL.
KURT'S IN A BAD WAY.
AND KITTY'S ALSO OUT OF THE PICTURE.
"SHE LANDED IN THE CAPITAL, PHASED THROUGH THE GROUND.
"BUT SHE'S GONNA BE A WHILE WORKING HER WAY BACK."
MIGHT JUST BE ME, BUT THIS FEELS A LITTLE OUT OF OUR LEAGUE.
AGREED.
X-MEN...
FALL BACK!!!

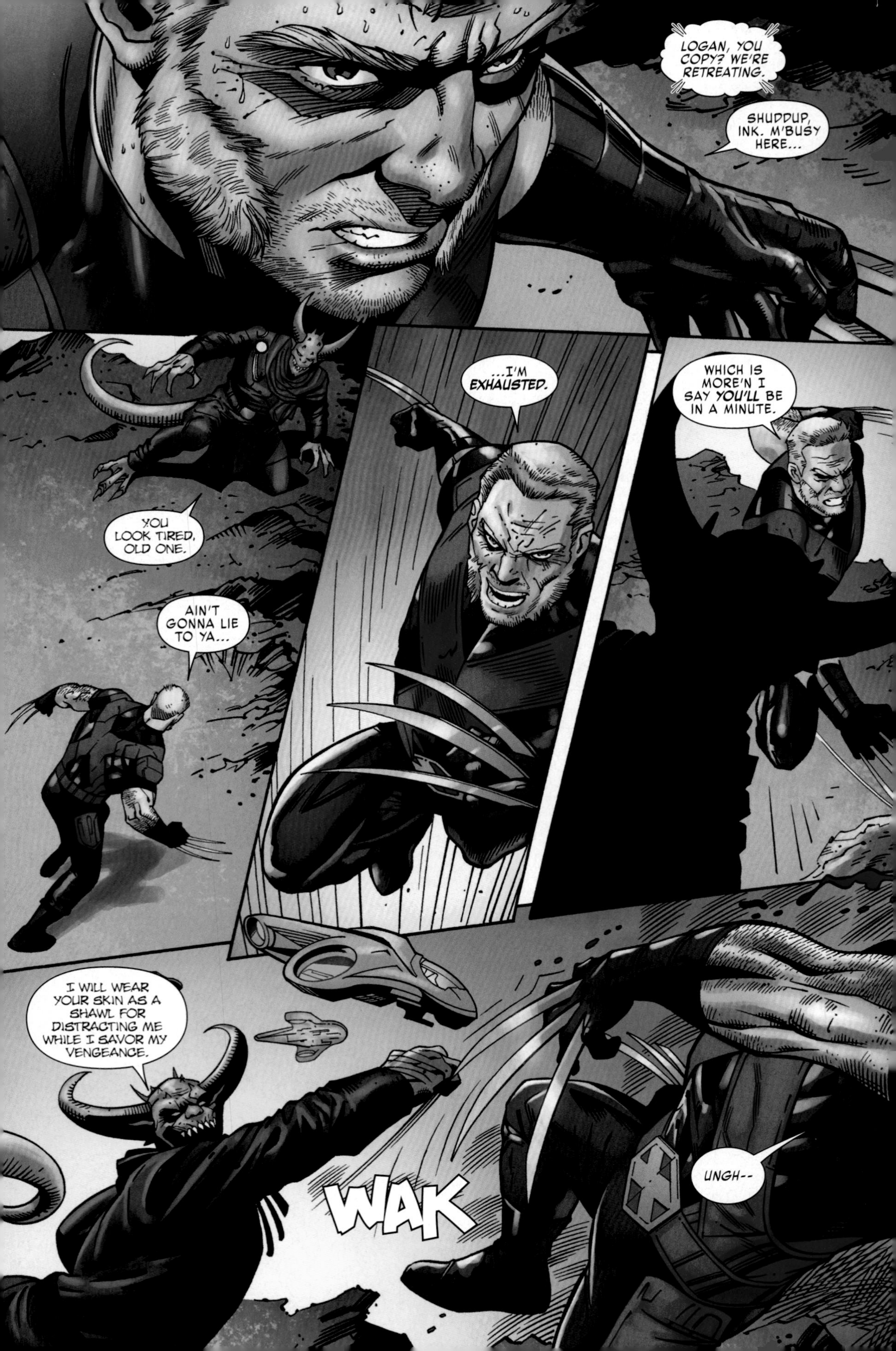
LOGAN, YOU COPY? WE'RE RETREATING.
SHUDDUP, INK. M'BUSY HERE...
YOU LOOK TIRED, OLD ONE.
AIN'T GONNA LIE TO YA...
...I'M EXHAUSTED.
WHICH IS MORE'N I SAY YOU'LL BE IN A MINUTE.
I WILL WEAR YOUR SKIN AS A SHAWL FOR DISTRACTING ME WHILE I SAVOR MY VENGEANCE.
WAK
UNGH--

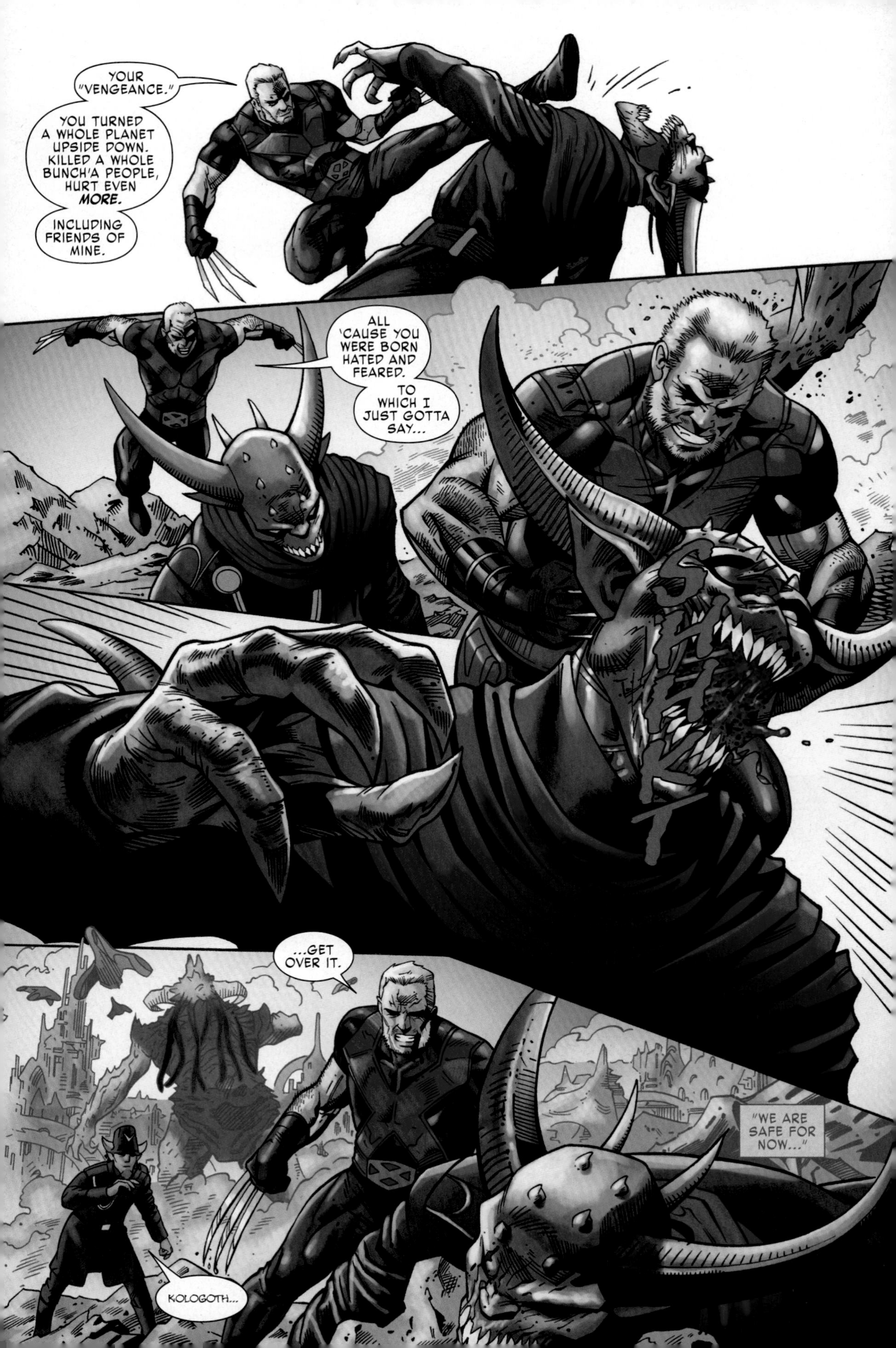
YOUR "VENGEANCE."
YOU TURNED A WHOLE PLANET UPSIDE DOWN. KILLED A WHOLE BUNCH'A PEOPLE, HURT EVEN **MORE.**
INCLUDING FRIENDS OF MINE.
ALL 'CAUSE YOU WERE BORN HATED AND FEARED.
TO WHICH I JUST GOTTA SAY...
SHHKT
...GET OVER IT.
"WE ARE SAFE FOR NOW..."
KOLOGOTH...

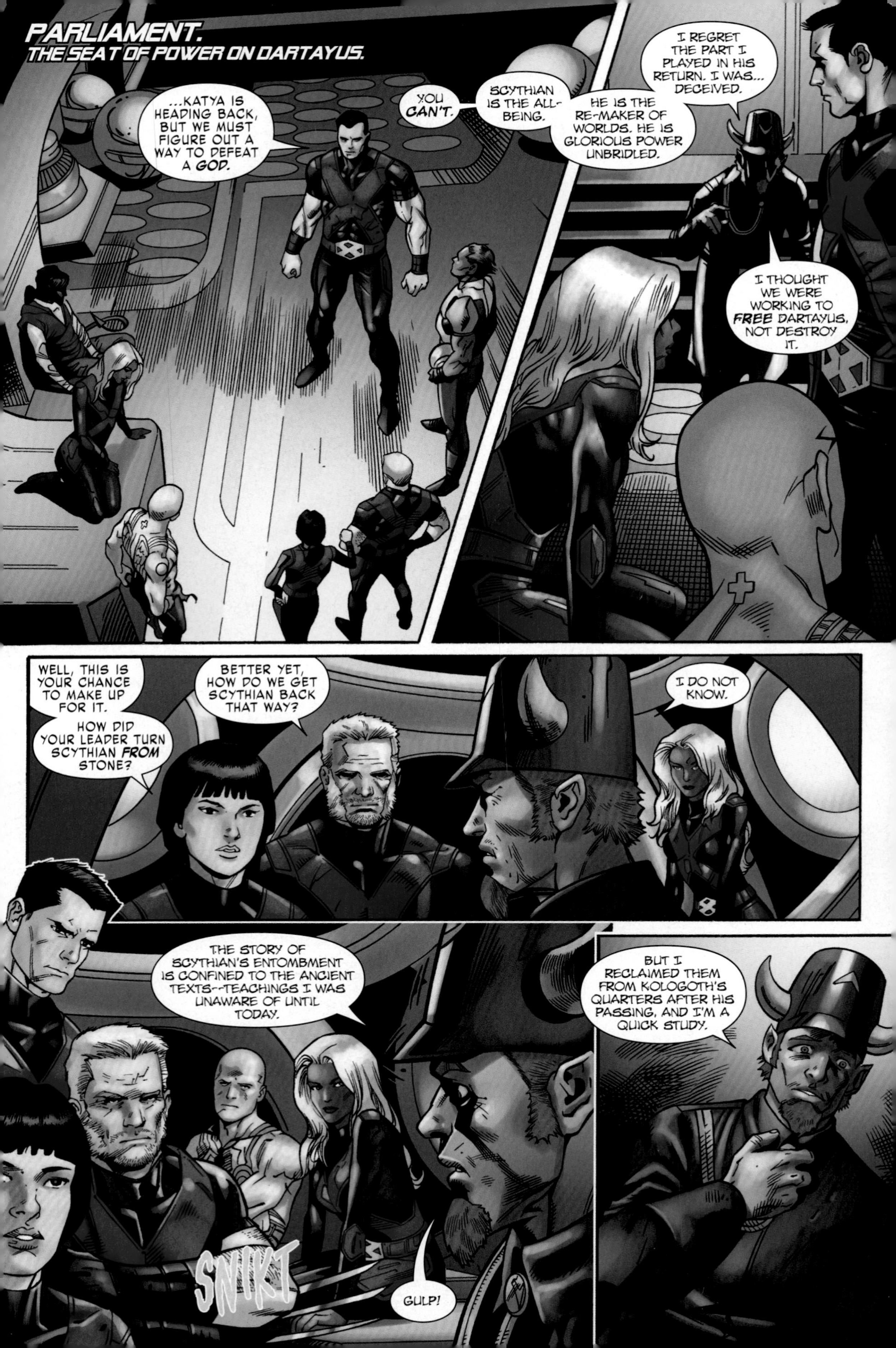
PARLIAMENT.
THE SEAT OF POWER ON DARTAYUS.
...KATYA IS HEADING BACK, BUT WE MUST FIGURE OUT A WAY TO DEFEAT A GOD.
YOU CAN'T.
SCYTHIAN IS THE ALL-BEING.
HE IS THE RE-MAKER OF WORLDS. HE IS GLORIOUS POWER UNBRIDLED.
I REGRET THE PART I PLAYED IN HIS RETURN. I WAS... DECEIVED.
I THOUGHT WE WERE WORKING TO FREE DARTAYUS, NOT DESTROY IT.
WELL, THIS IS YOUR CHANCE TO MAKE UP FOR IT.
HOW DID YOUR LEADER TURN SCYTHIAN FROM STONE?
BETTER YET, HOW DO WE GET SCYTHIAN BACK THAT WAY?
I DO NOT KNOW.
THE STORY OF SCYTHIAN'S ENTOMBMENT IS CONFINED TO THE ANCIENT TEXTS--TEACHINGS I WAS UNAWARE OF UNTIL TODAY.
SNIKT
GULP!
BUT I RECLAIMED THEM FROM KOLOGOTH'S QUARTERS AFTER HIS PASSING, AND I'M A QUICK STUDY.

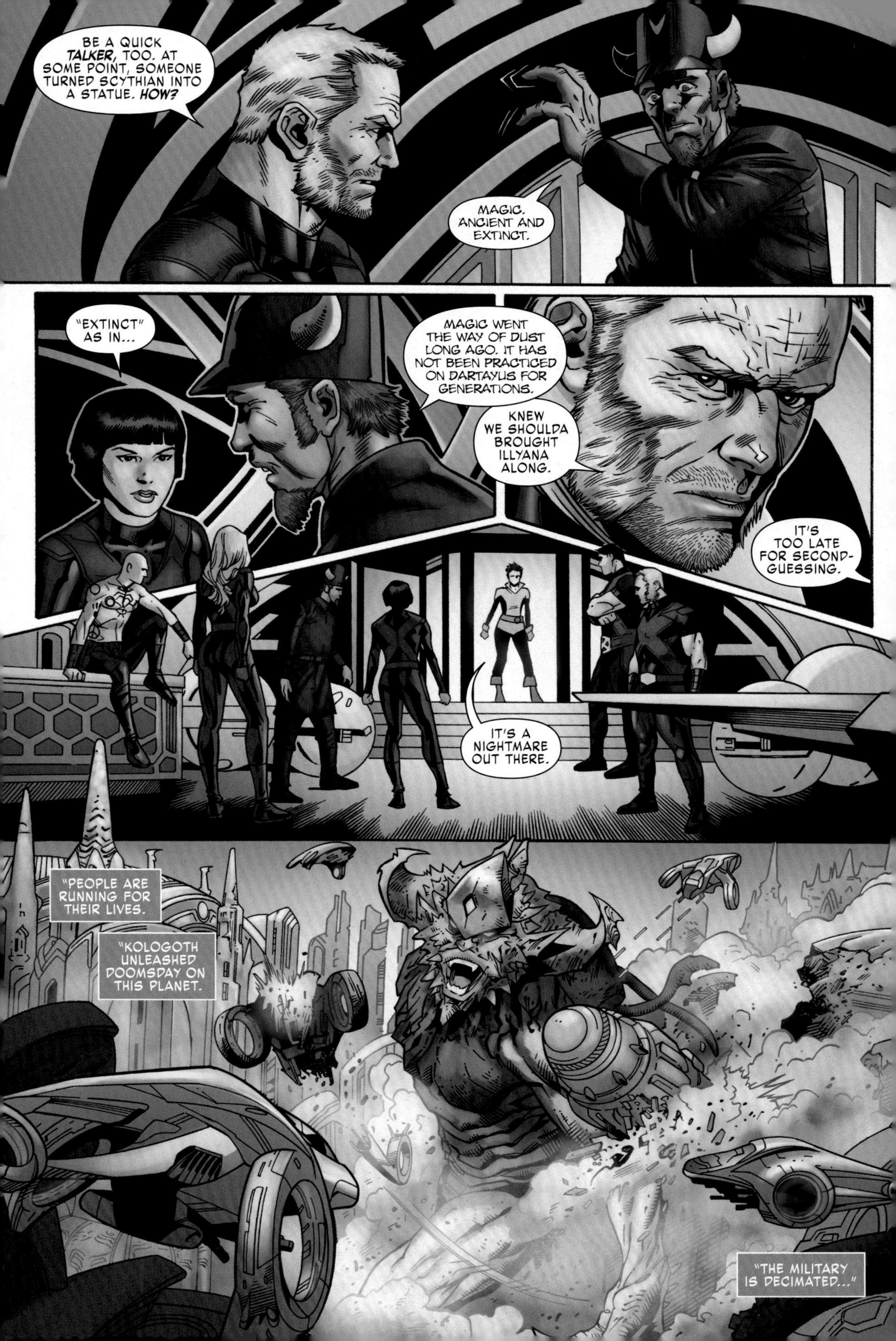
BE A QUICK TALKER, TOO. AT SOME POINT, SOMEONE TURNED SCYTHIAN INTO A STATUE. HOW?
MAGIC. ANCIENT AND EXTINCT.
"EXTINCT" AS IN...
MAGIC WENT THE WAY OF DUST LONG AGO. IT HAS NOT BEEN PRACTICED ON DARTAYUS FOR GENERATIONS.
KNEW WE SHOULDA BROUGHT ILLYANA ALONG.
IT'S TOO LATE FOR SECOND-GUESSING.
IT'S A NIGHTMARE OUT THERE.
"PEOPLE ARE RUNNING FOR THEIR LIVES.
"KOLOGOTH UNLEASHED DOOMSDAY ON THIS PLANET.
"THE MILITARY IS DECIMATED..."

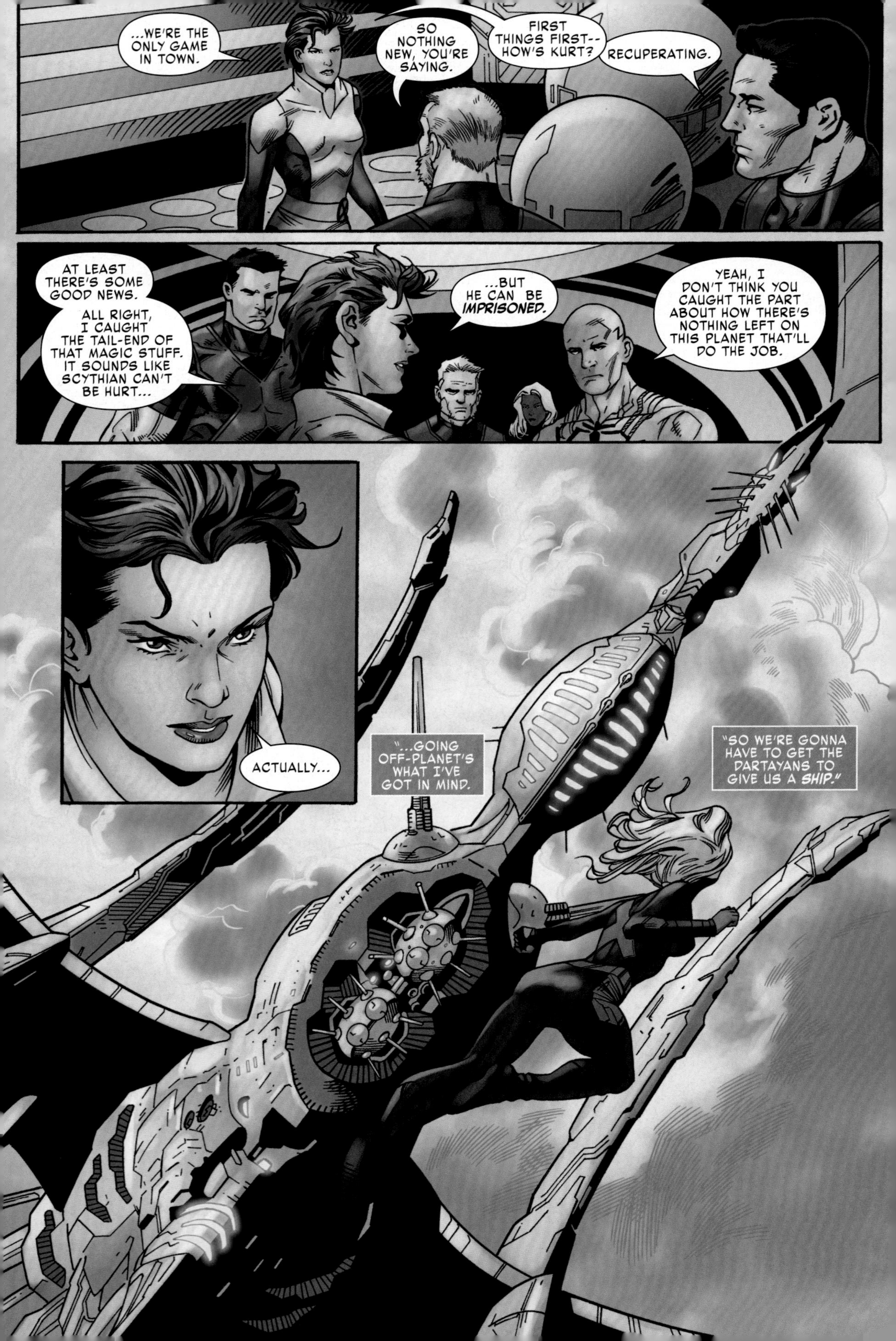
...WE'RE THE ONLY GAME IN TOWN.
SO NOTHING NEW, YOU'RE SAYING.
FIRST THINGS FIRST-- HOW'S KURT?
RECUPERATING.
AT LEAST THERE'S SOME GOOD NEWS.
ALL RIGHT, I CAUGHT THE TAIL-END OF THAT MAGIC STUFF. IT SOUNDS LIKE SCYTHIAN CAN'T BE HURT...
...BUT HE CAN BE *IMPRISONED.*
YEAH, I DON'T THINK YOU CAUGHT THE PART ABOUT HOW THERE'S NOTHING LEFT ON THIS PLANET THAT'LL DO THE JOB.
ACTUALLY...
"...GOING OFF-PLANET'S WHAT I'VE GOT IN MIND.
"SO WE'RE GONNA HAVE TO GET THE DARTAYANS TO GIVE US A *SHIP.*"

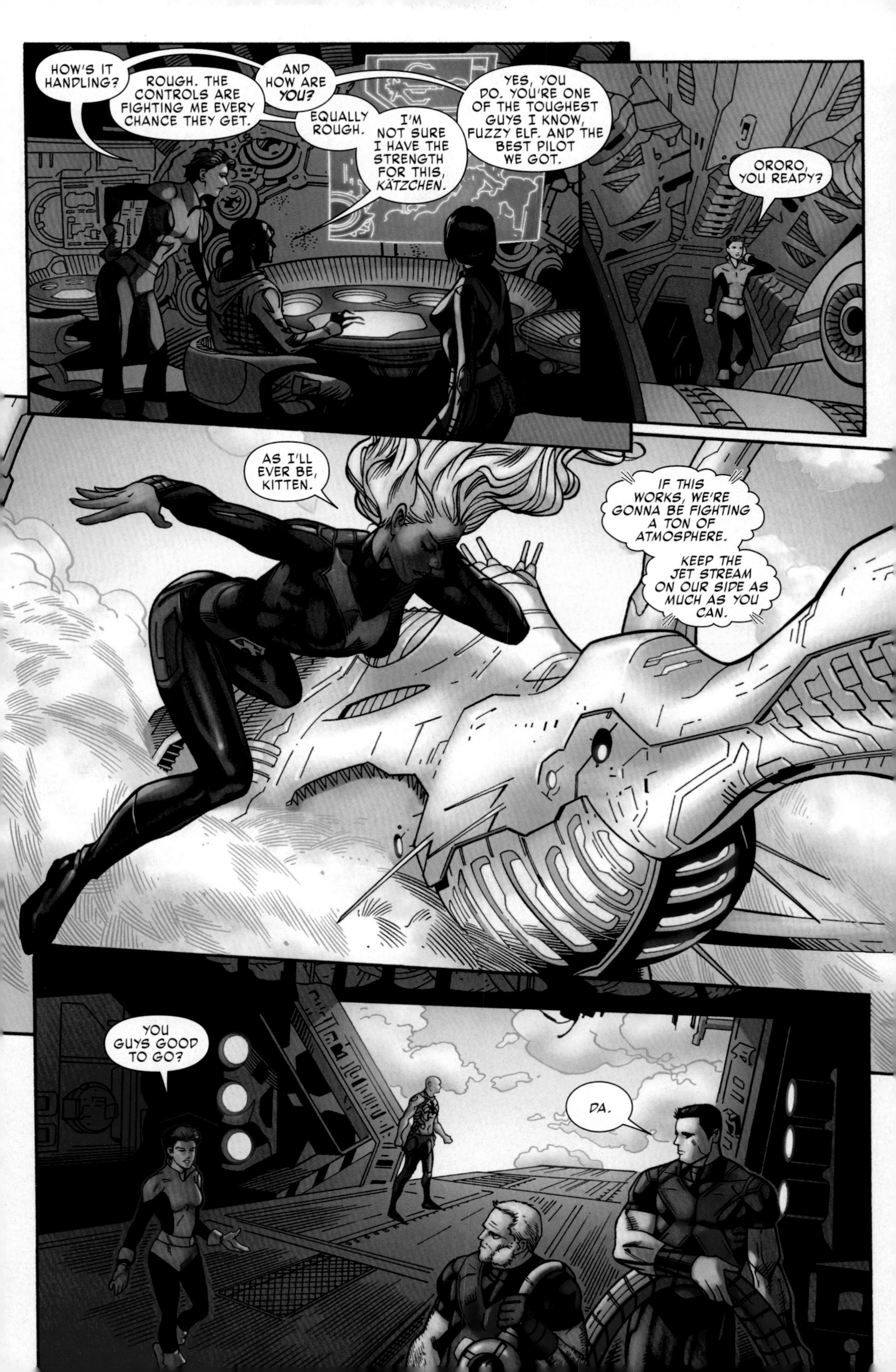

HOW'S IT HANDLING?
ROUGH. THE CONTROLS ARE FIGHTING ME EVERY CHANCE THEY GET.
AND HOW ARE YOU?
EQUALLY ROUGH.
I'M NOT SURE I HAVE THE STRENGTH FOR THIS, KÄTZCHEN.
YES, YOU DO. YOU'RE ONE OF THE TOUGHEST GUYS I KNOW, FUZZY ELF. AND THE BEST PILOT WE GOT.
ORORO, YOU READY?
AS I'LL EVER BE, KITTEN.
IF THIS WORKS, WE'RE GONNA BE FIGHTING A TON OF ATMOSPHERE.
KEEP THE JET STREAM ON OUR SIDE AS MUCH AS YOU CAN.
YOU GUYS GOOD TO GO?
DA.

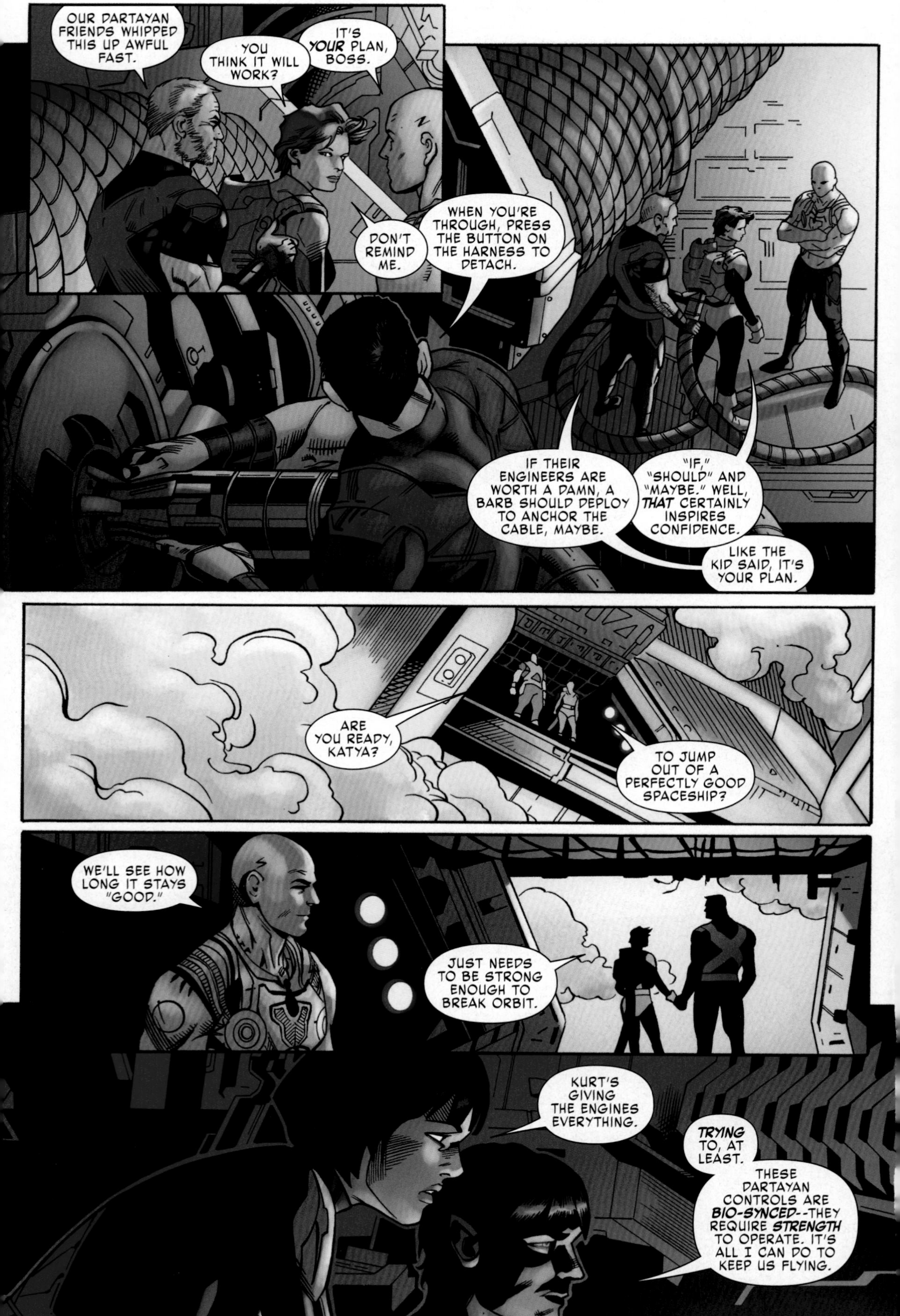
OUR DARTAYAN FRIENDS WHIPPED THIS UP AWFUL FAST.
YOU THINK IT WILL WORK?
IT'S YOUR PLAN, BOSS.
DON'T REMIND ME.
WHEN YOU'RE THROUGH, PRESS THE BUTTON ON THE HARNESS TO DETACH.
IF THEIR ENGINEERS ARE WORTH A DAMN, A BARB SHOULD DEPLOY TO ANCHOR THE CABLE, MAYBE.
"IF," "SHOULD" AND "MAYBE." WELL, THAT CERTAINLY INSPIRES CONFIDENCE.
LIKE THE KID SAID, IT'S YOUR PLAN.
ARE YOU READY, KATYA?
TO JUMP OUT OF A PERFECTLY GOOD SPACESHIP?
WE'LL SEE HOW LONG IT STAYS "GOOD."
JUST NEEDS TO BE STRONG ENOUGH TO BREAK ORBIT.
KURT'S GIVING THE ENGINES EVERYTHING.
TRYING TO, AT LEAST.
THESE DARTAYAN CONTROLS ARE BIO-SYNCED--THEY REQUIRE STRENGTH TO OPERATE. IT'S ALL I CAN DO TO KEEP US FLYING.

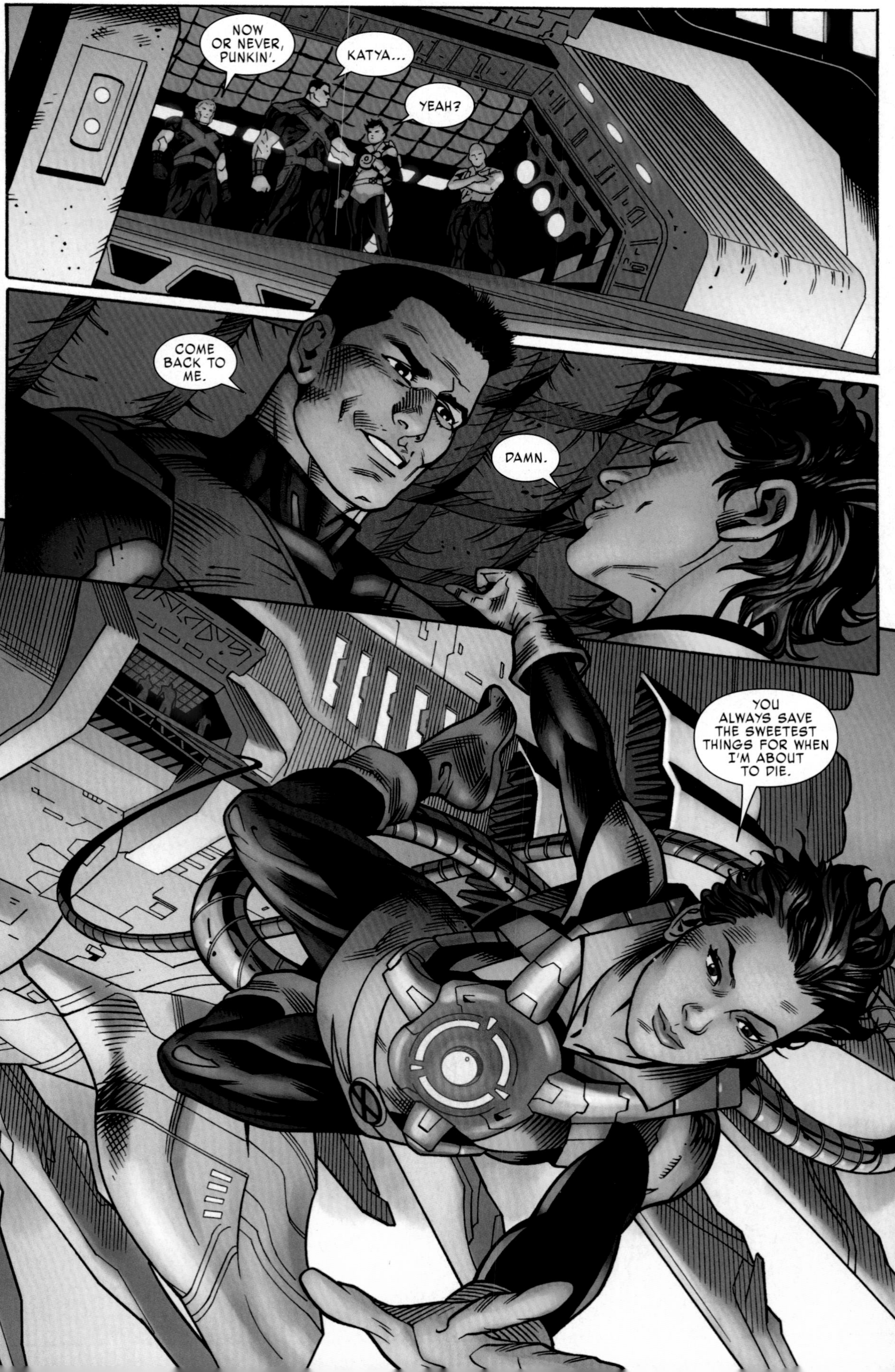
NOW OR NEVER, PUNKIN'.
KATYA...
YEAH?
COME BACK TO ME.
DAMN.
YOU ALWAYS SAVE THE SWEETEST THINGS FOR WHEN I'M ABOUT TO DIE.

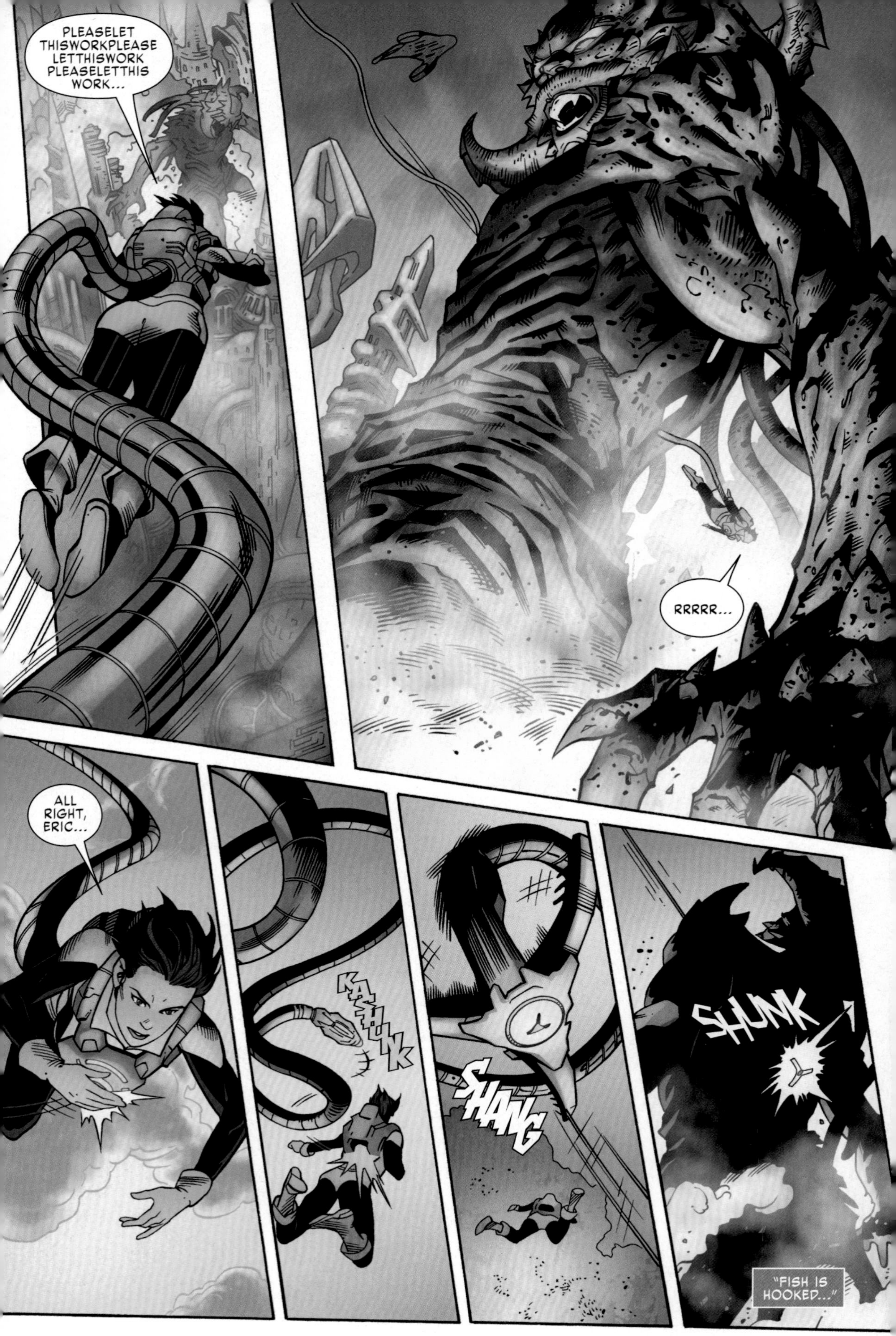
PLEASELET THISWORKPLEASE LETTHISWORK PLEASELETTHIS WORK...
RRRRR...
ALL RIGHT, ERIC...
KASHUNK
SHANG
SHUNK
"FISH IS HOOKED..."

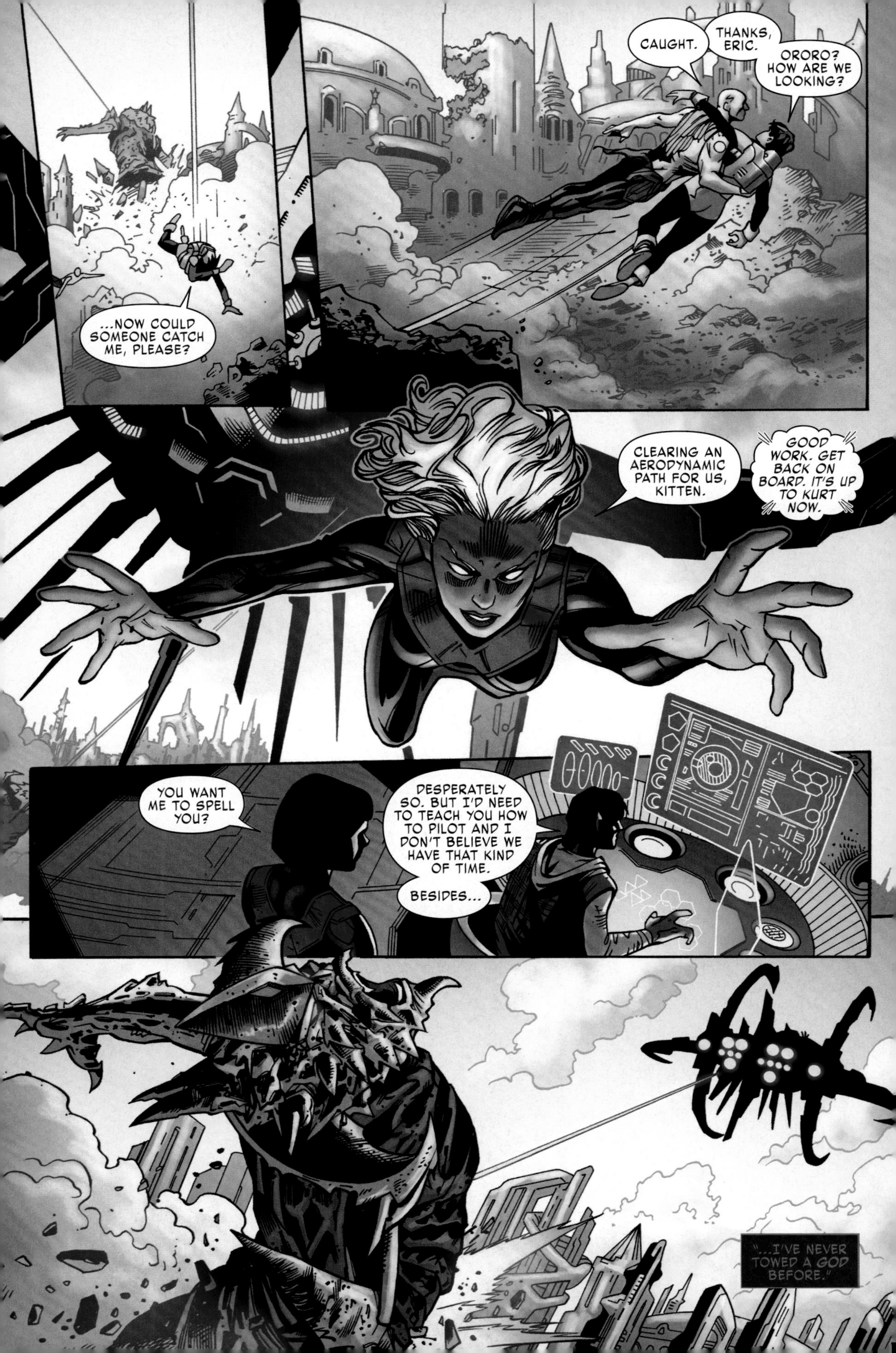
...NOW COULD SOMEONE CATCH ME, PLEASE?
CAUGHT.
THANKS, ERIC.
ORORO? HOW ARE WE LOOKING?
CLEARING AN AERODYNAMIC PATH FOR US, KITTEN.
GOOD WORK. GET BACK ON BOARD. IT'S UP TO KURT NOW.
YOU WANT ME TO SPELL YOU?
DESPERATELY SO. BUT I'D NEED TO TEACH YOU HOW TO PILOT AND I DON'T BELIEVE WE HAVE THAT KIND OF TIME.
BESIDES...
"...I'VE NEVER TOWED A GOD BEFORE."

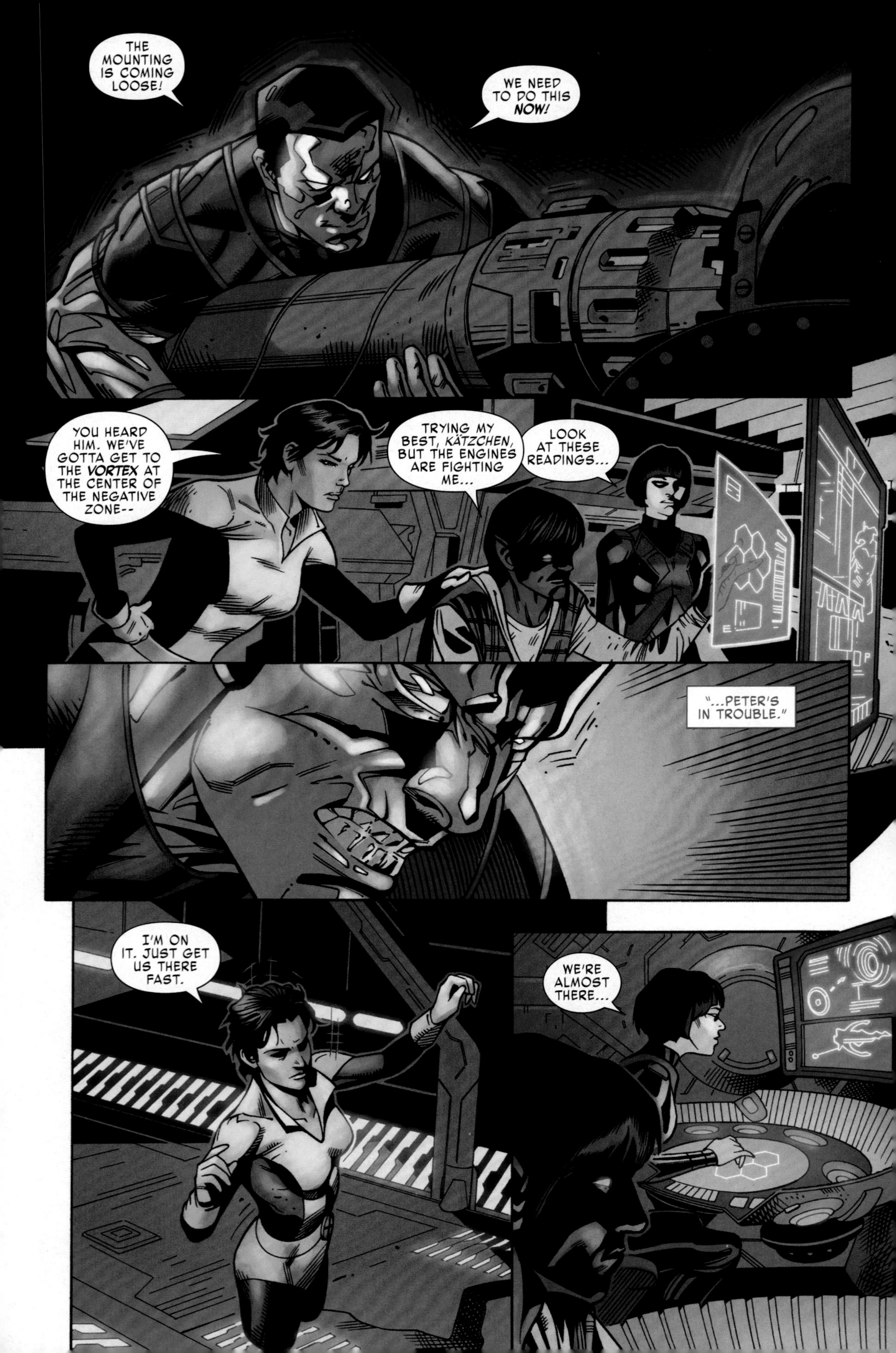

THE MOUNTING IS COMING LOOSE!
WE NEED TO DO THIS *NOW!*
YOU HEARD HIM. WE'VE GOTTA GET TO THE *VORTEX* AT THE CENTER OF THE NEGATIVE ZONE--
TRYING MY BEST, *KÄTZCHEN,* BUT THE ENGINES ARE FIGHTING ME...
LOOK AT THESE READINGS...
"...PETER'S IN TROUBLE."
I'M ON IT. JUST GET US THERE FAST.
WE'RE ALMOST THERE...

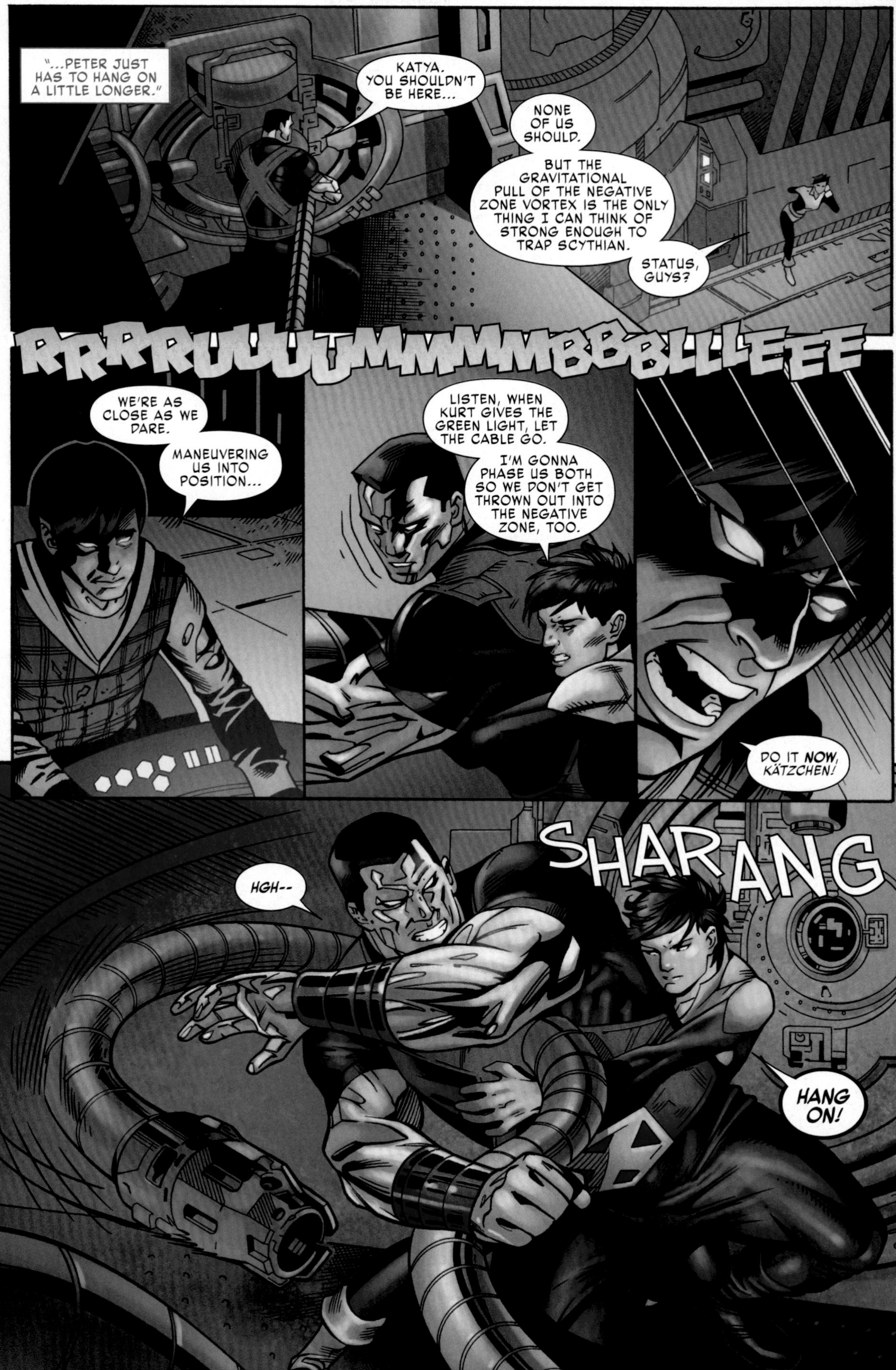
"...PETER JUST HAS TO HANG ON A LITTLE LONGER."
KATYA. YOU SHOULDN'T BE HERE...
NONE OF US SHOULD.
BUT THE GRAVITATIONAL PULL OF THE NEGATIVE ZONE VORTEX IS THE ONLY THING I CAN THINK OF STRONG ENOUGH TO TRAP SCYTHIAN.
STATUS, GUYS?
RRRRUUUUMMMMMBBBLLLEEE
WE'RE AS CLOSE AS WE DARE.
MANEUVERING US INTO POSITION...
LISTEN, WHEN KURT GIVES THE GREEN LIGHT, LET THE CABLE GO.
I'M GONNA PHASE US BOTH SO WE DON'T GET THROWN OUT INTO THE NEGATIVE ZONE, TOO.
DO IT NOW, KÄTZCHEN!
SHARANG
HGH--
HANG ON!

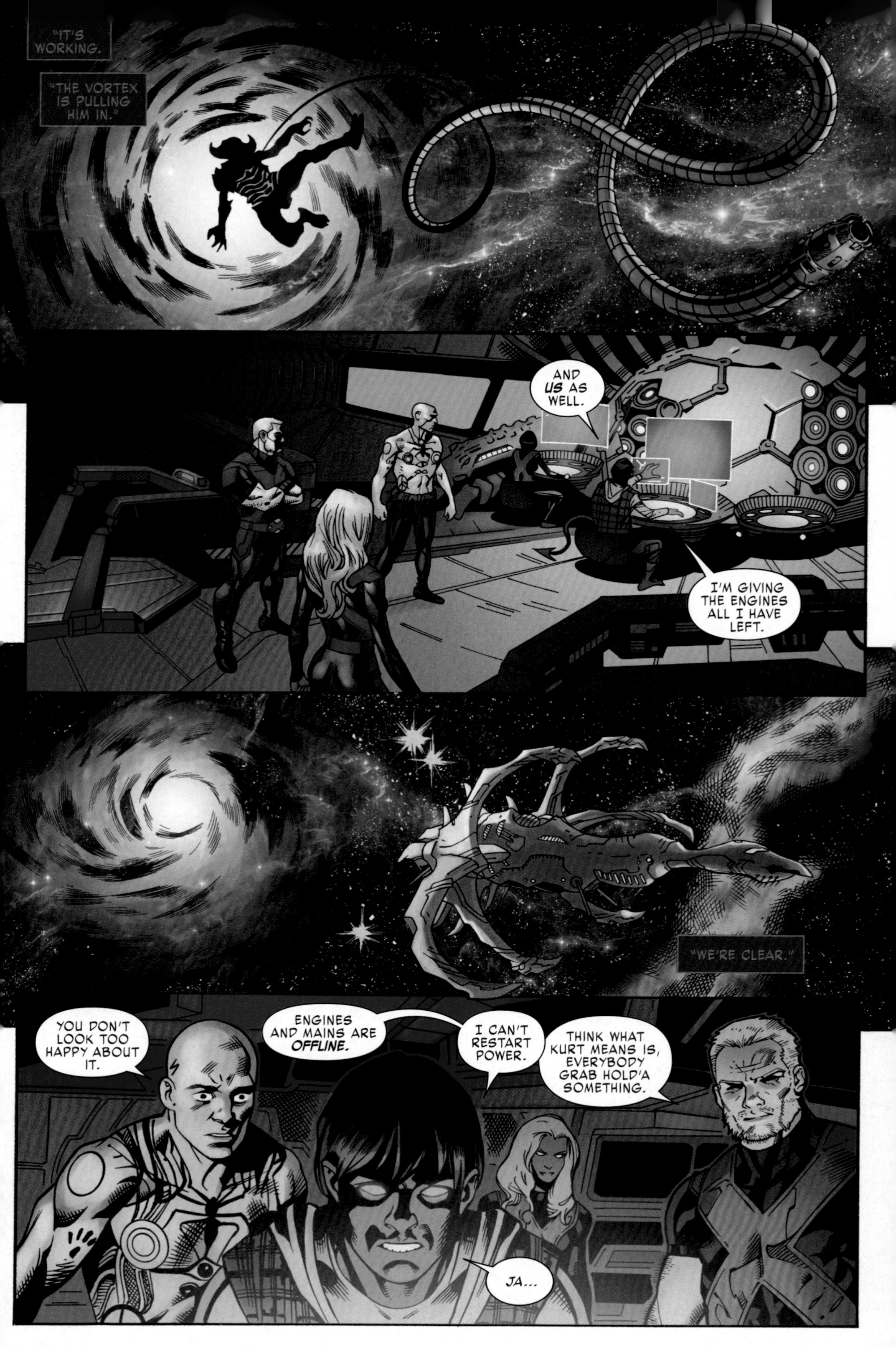
"IT'S WORKING.
"THE VORTEX IS PULLING HIM IN."
AND US AS WELL.
I'M GIVING THE ENGINES ALL I HAVE LEFT.
"WE'RE CLEAR."
YOU DON'T LOOK TOO HAPPY ABOUT IT.
ENGINES AND MAINS ARE OFFLINE.
I CAN'T RESTART POWER.
THINK WHAT KURT MEANS IS, EVERYBODY GRAB HOLD'A SOMETHING.
JA...

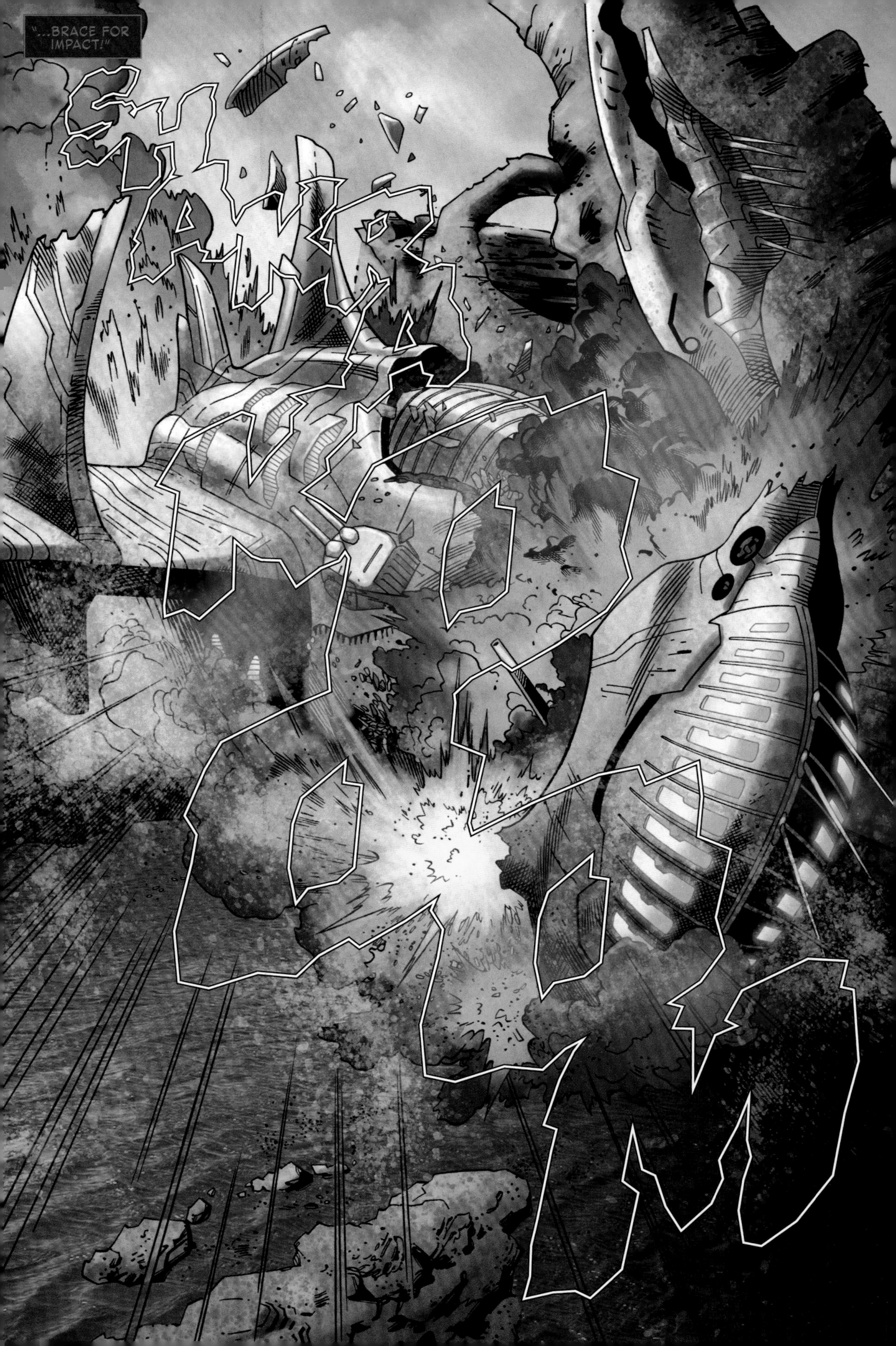
"...BRACE FOR IMPACT!"

20

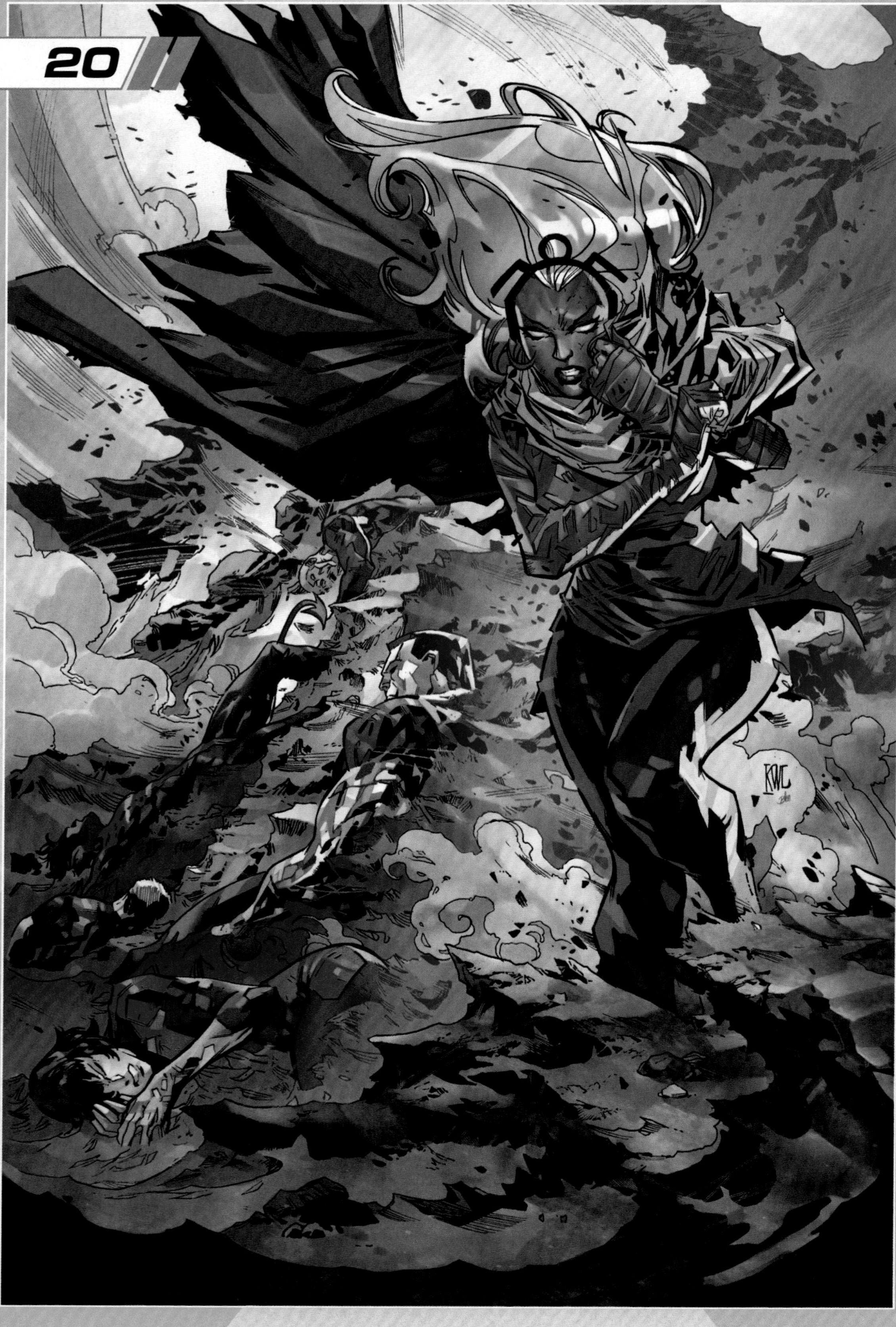

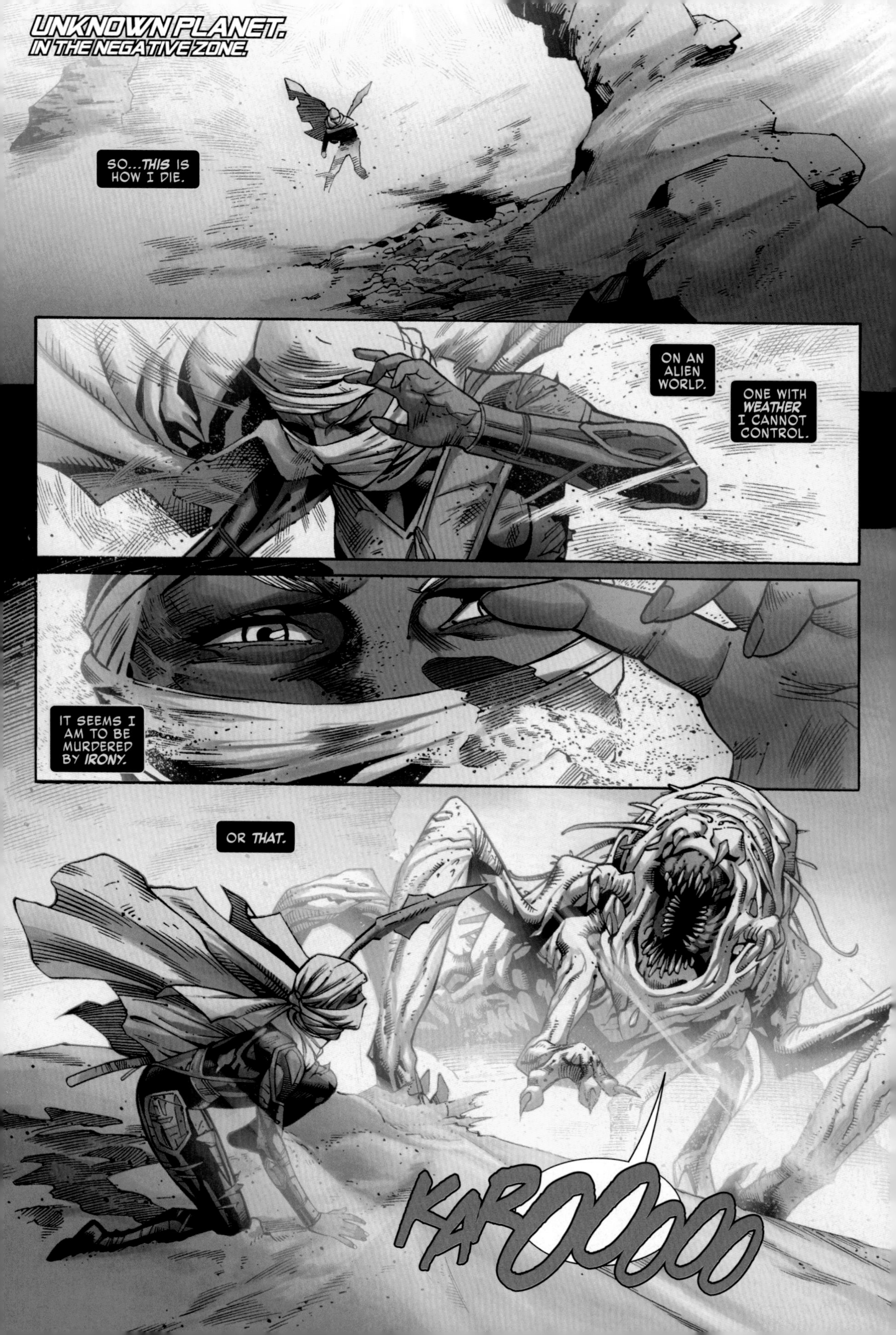
UNKNOWN PLANET.
IN THE NEGATIVE ZONE.
SO...THIS IS HOW I DIE.
ON AN ALIEN WORLD.
ONE WITH WEATHER I CANNOT CONTROL.
IT SEEMS I AM TO BE MURDERED BY IRONY.
OR THAT.
KAROOOOO

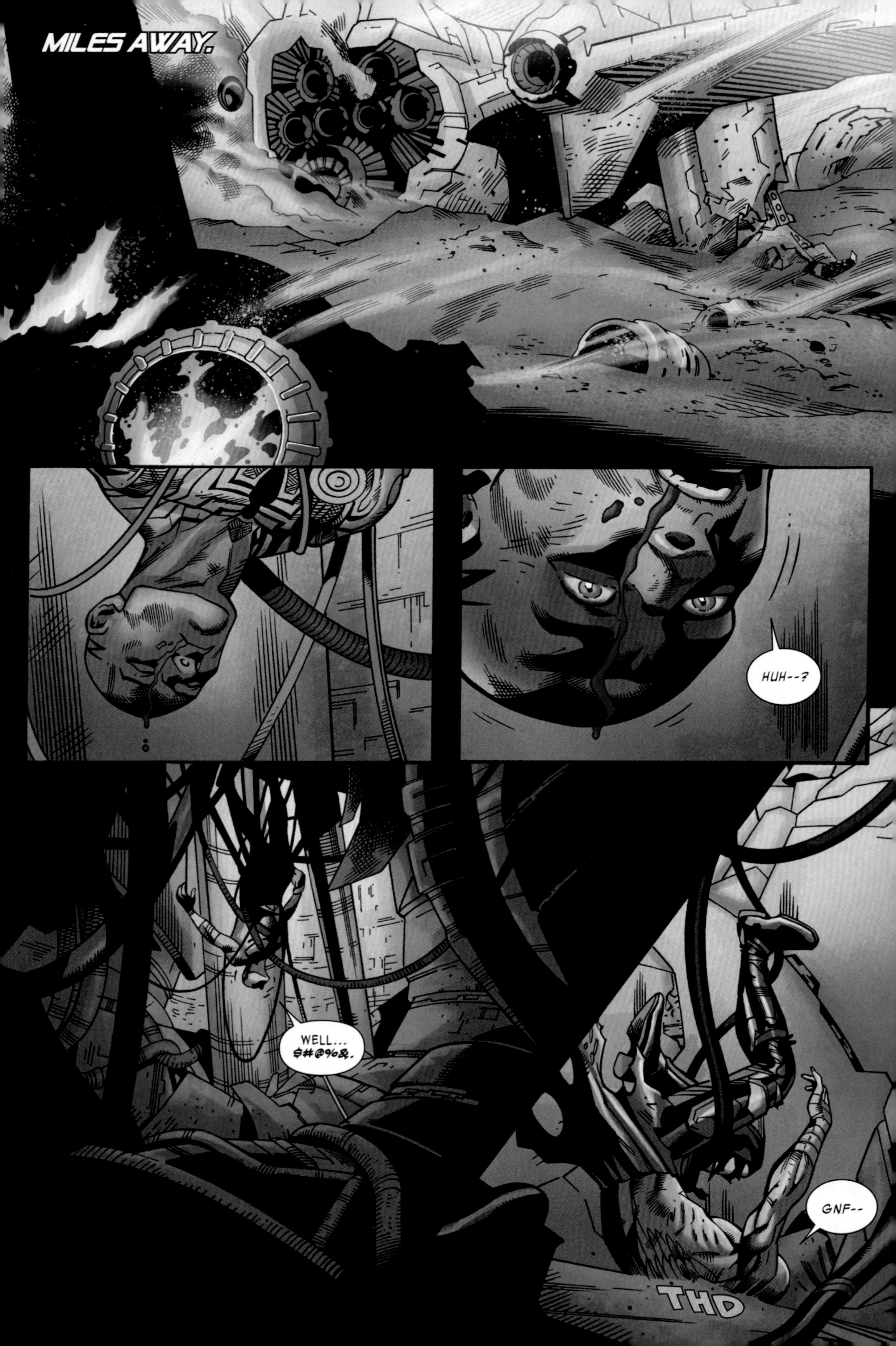
MILES AWAY.
HUH--?
WELL... $#@%&.
GNF--
THD

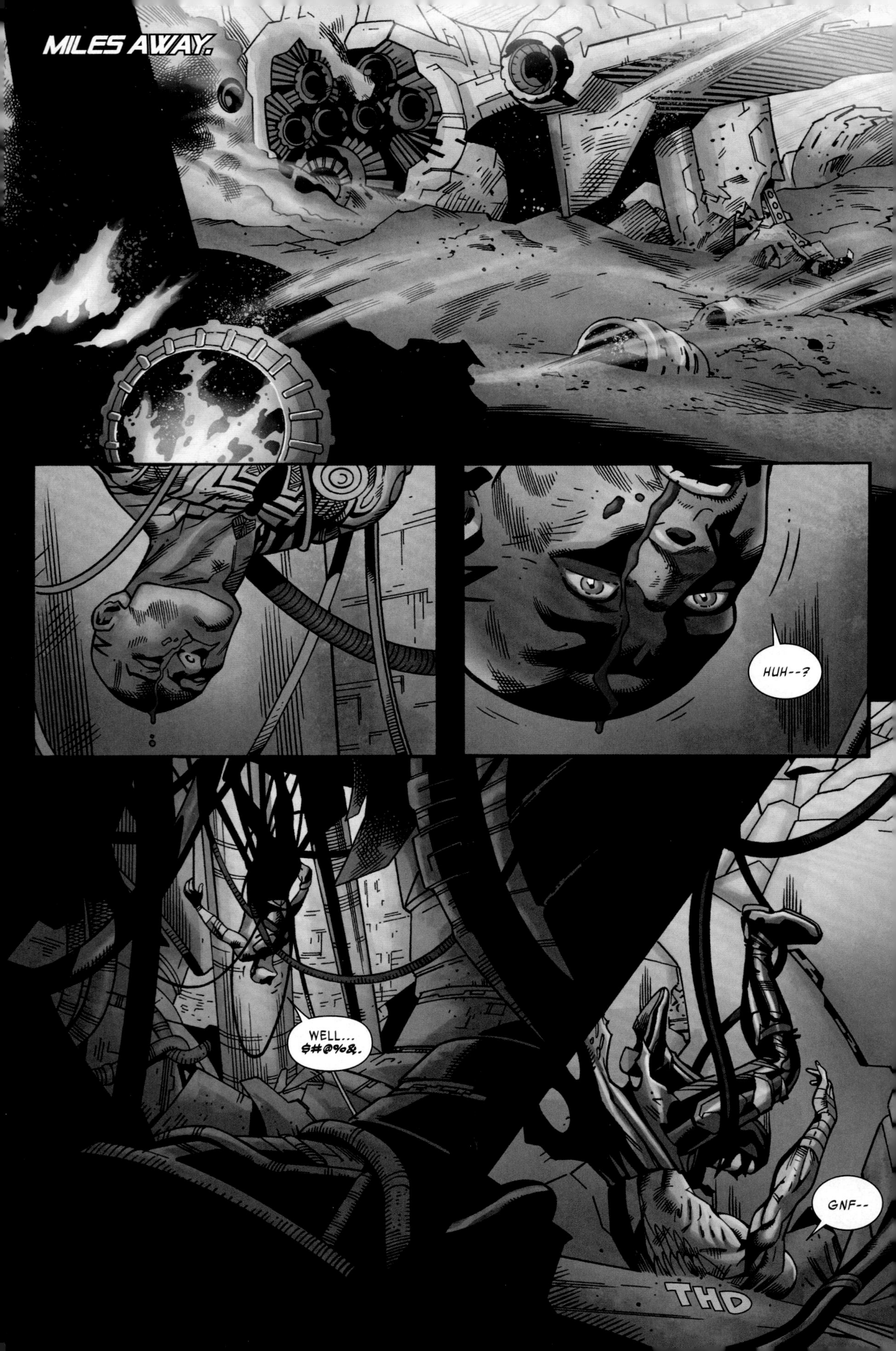
MILES AWAY.
HUH--?
WELL...
$#@%&.
GNF--
THD

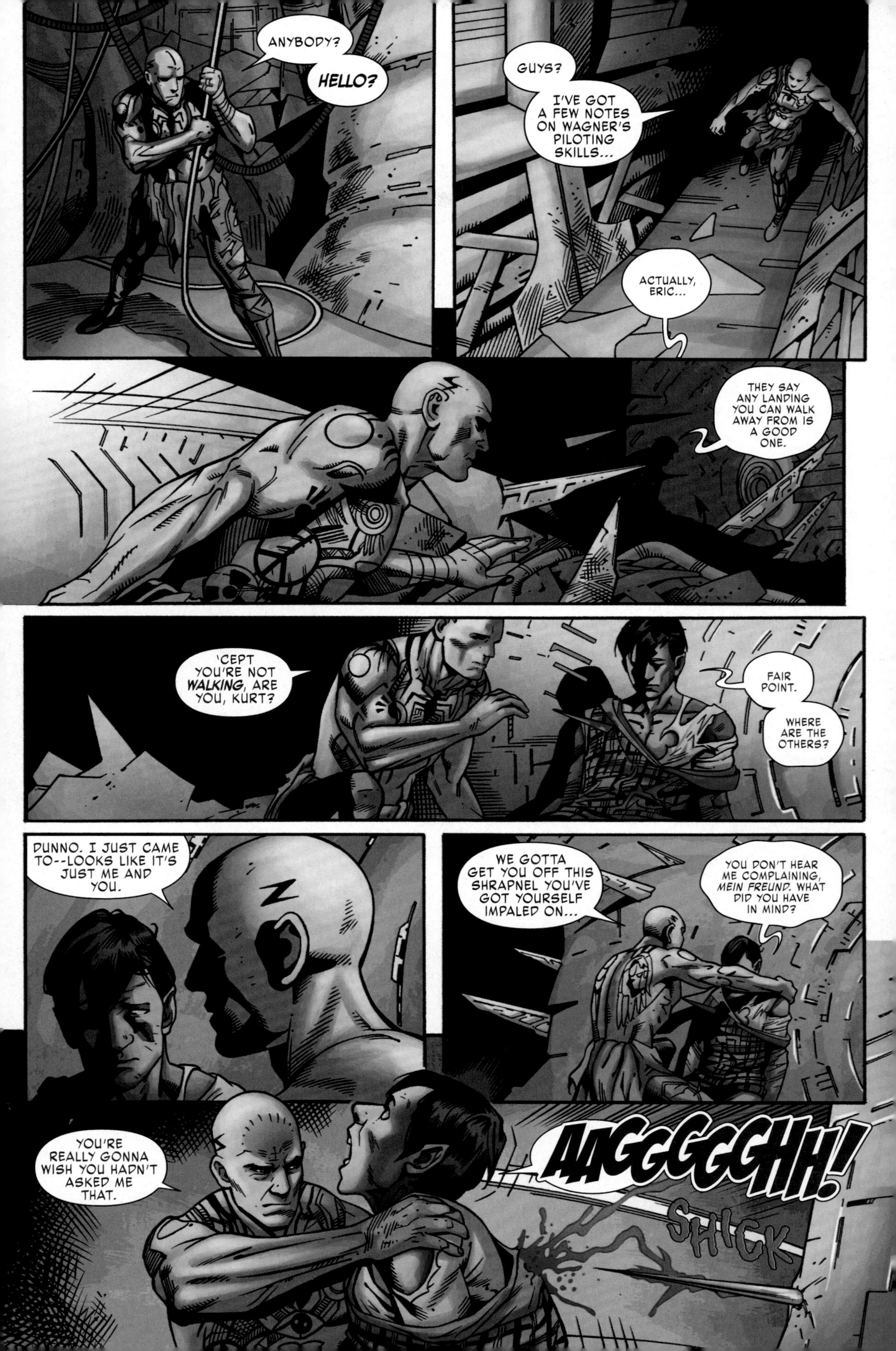
ANYBODY?
HELLO?
GUYS?
I'VE GOT A FEW NOTES ON WAGNER'S PILOTING SKILLS...
ACTUALLY, ERIC...
THEY SAY ANY LANDING YOU CAN WALK AWAY FROM IS A GOOD ONE.
'CEPT YOU'RE NOT WALKING, ARE YOU, KURT?
FAIR POINT.
WHERE ARE THE OTHERS?
DUNNO. I JUST CAME TO--LOOKS LIKE IT'S JUST ME AND YOU.
WE GOTTA GET YOU OFF THIS SHRAPNEL YOU'VE GOT YOURSELF IMPALED ON...
YOU DON'T HEAR ME COMPLAINING, MEIN FREUND. WHAT DID YOU HAVE IN MIND?
YOU'RE REALLY GONNA WISH YOU HADN'T ASKED ME THAT.
AAGGGGGHH!
SHICK

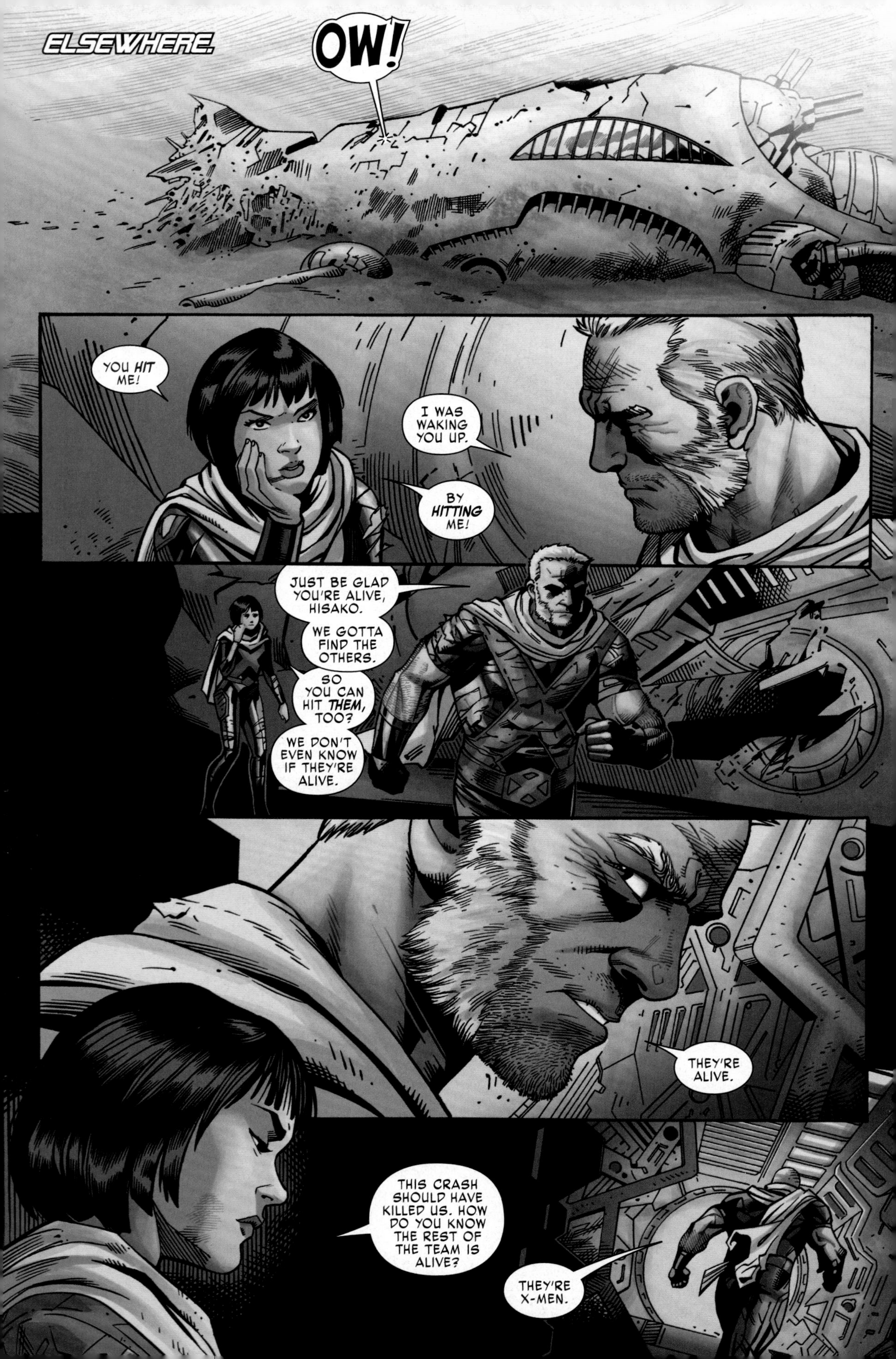
ELSEWHERE.
OW!
YOU HIT ME!
I WAS WAKING YOU UP.
BY HITTING ME!
JUST BE GLAD YOU'RE ALIVE, HISAKO.
WE GOTTA FIND THE OTHERS.
SO YOU CAN HIT THEM, TOO?
WE DON'T EVEN KNOW IF THEY'RE ALIVE.
THEY'RE ALIVE.
THIS CRASH SHOULD HAVE KILLED US. HOW DO YOU KNOW THE REST OF THE TEAM IS ALIVE?
THEY'RE X-MEN.

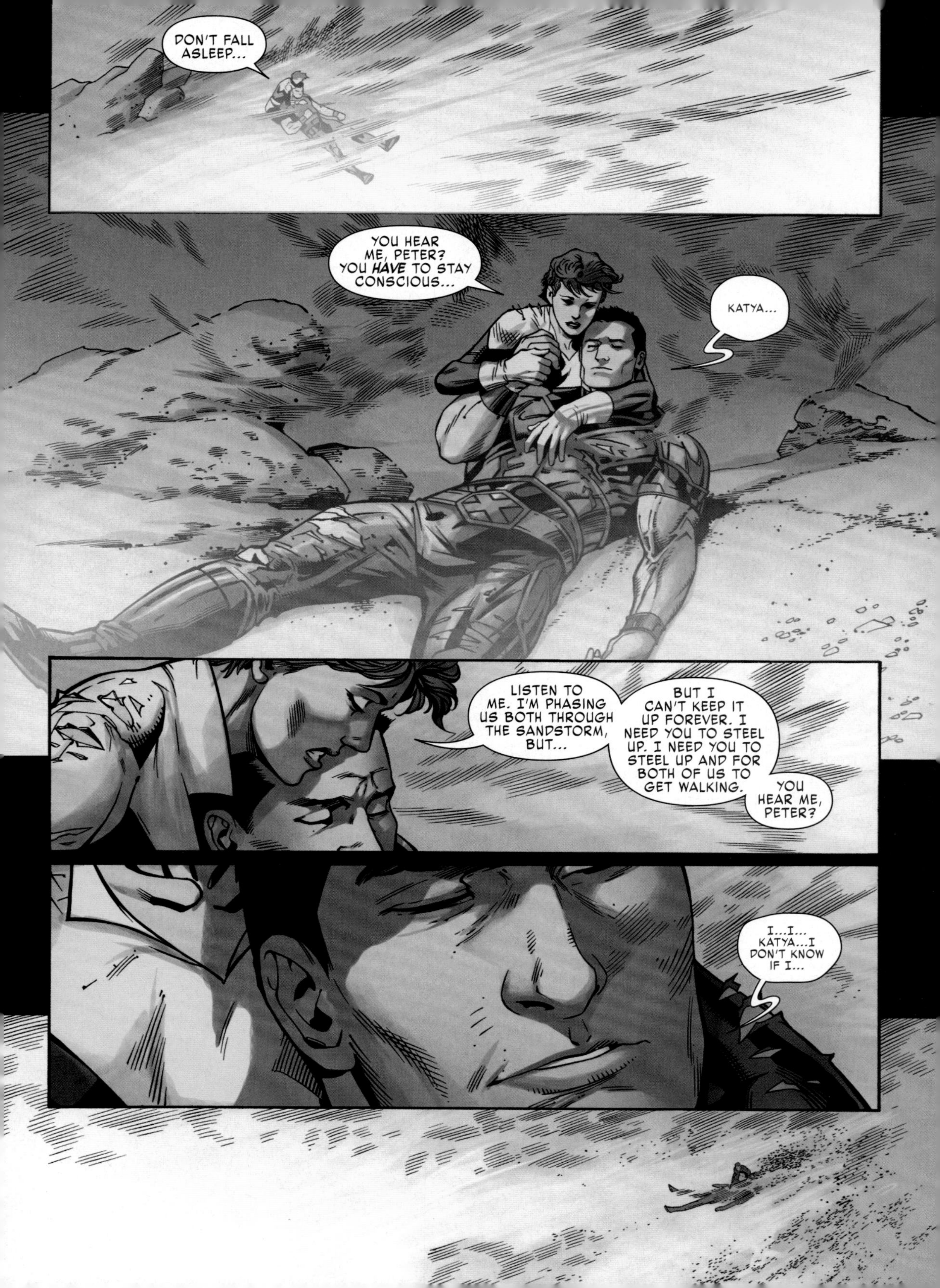
DON'T FALL ASLEEP...
YOU HEAR ME, PETER? YOU HAVE TO STAY CONSCIOUS...
KATYA...
LISTEN TO ME. I'M PHASING US BOTH THROUGH THE SANDSTORM, BUT...
BUT I CAN'T KEEP IT UP FOREVER. I NEED YOU TO STEEL UP. I NEED YOU TO STEEL UP AND FOR BOTH OF US TO GET WALKING.
YOU HEAR ME, PETER?
I...I... KATYA...I DON'T KNOW IF I...

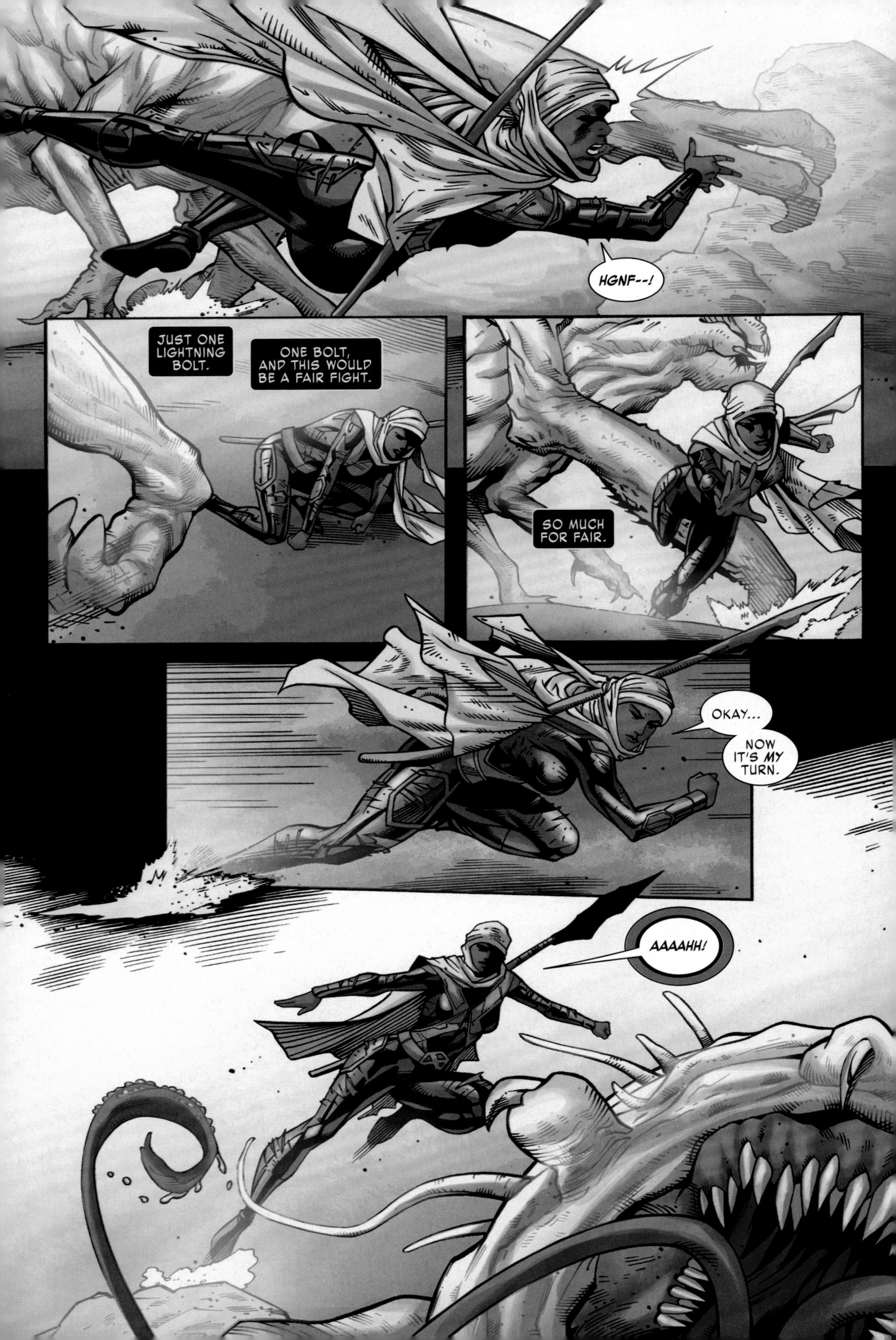
HGNF--!
JUST ONE LIGHTNING BOLT.
ONE BOLT, AND THIS WOULD BE A FAIR FIGHT.
SO MUCH FOR FAIR.
OKAY...
NOW IT'S MY TURN.
AAAAHH!

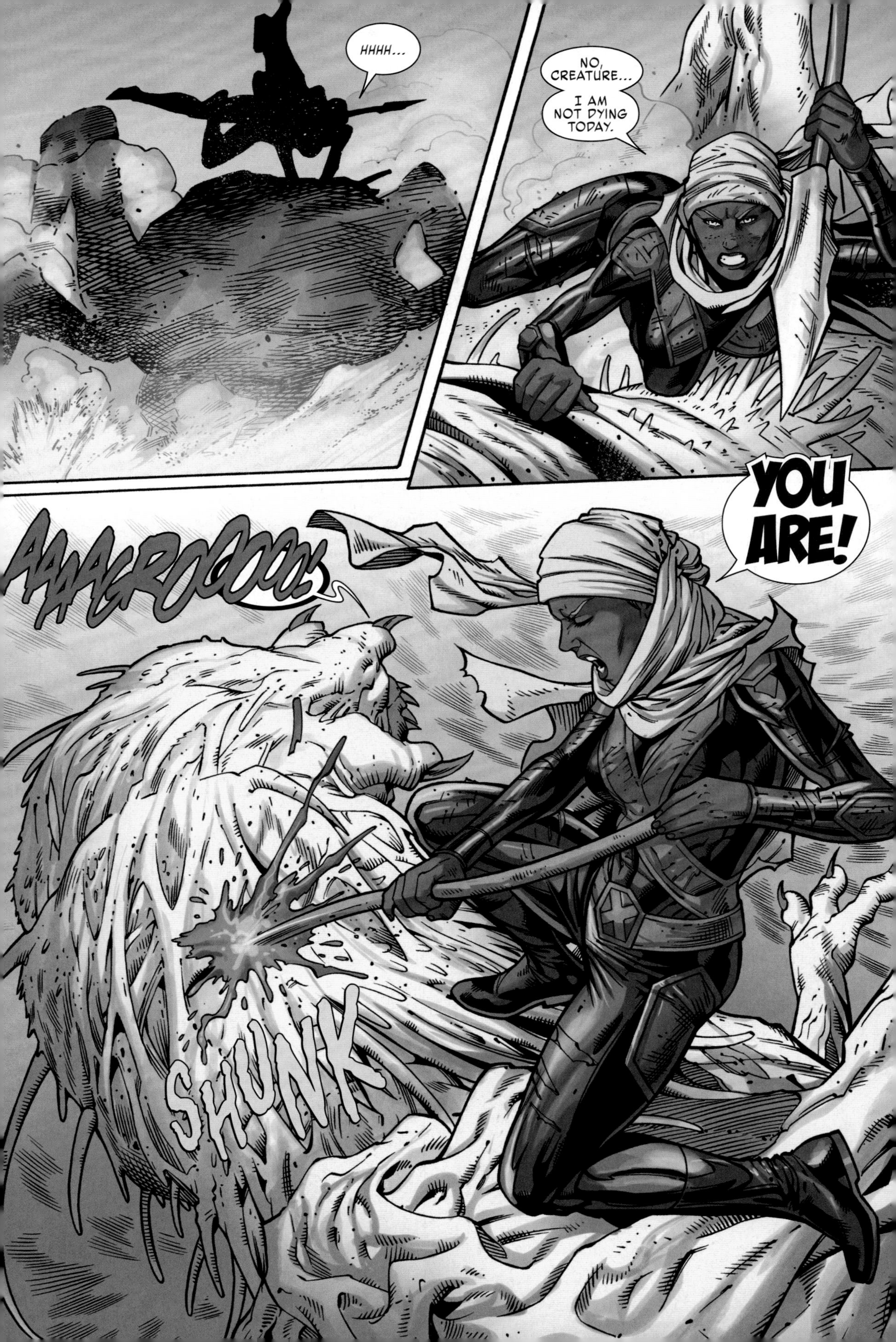
HHHH...
NO, CREATURE...
I AM NOT DYING TODAY.
YOU ARE!
AAAAGROOOOO!
SHUNK

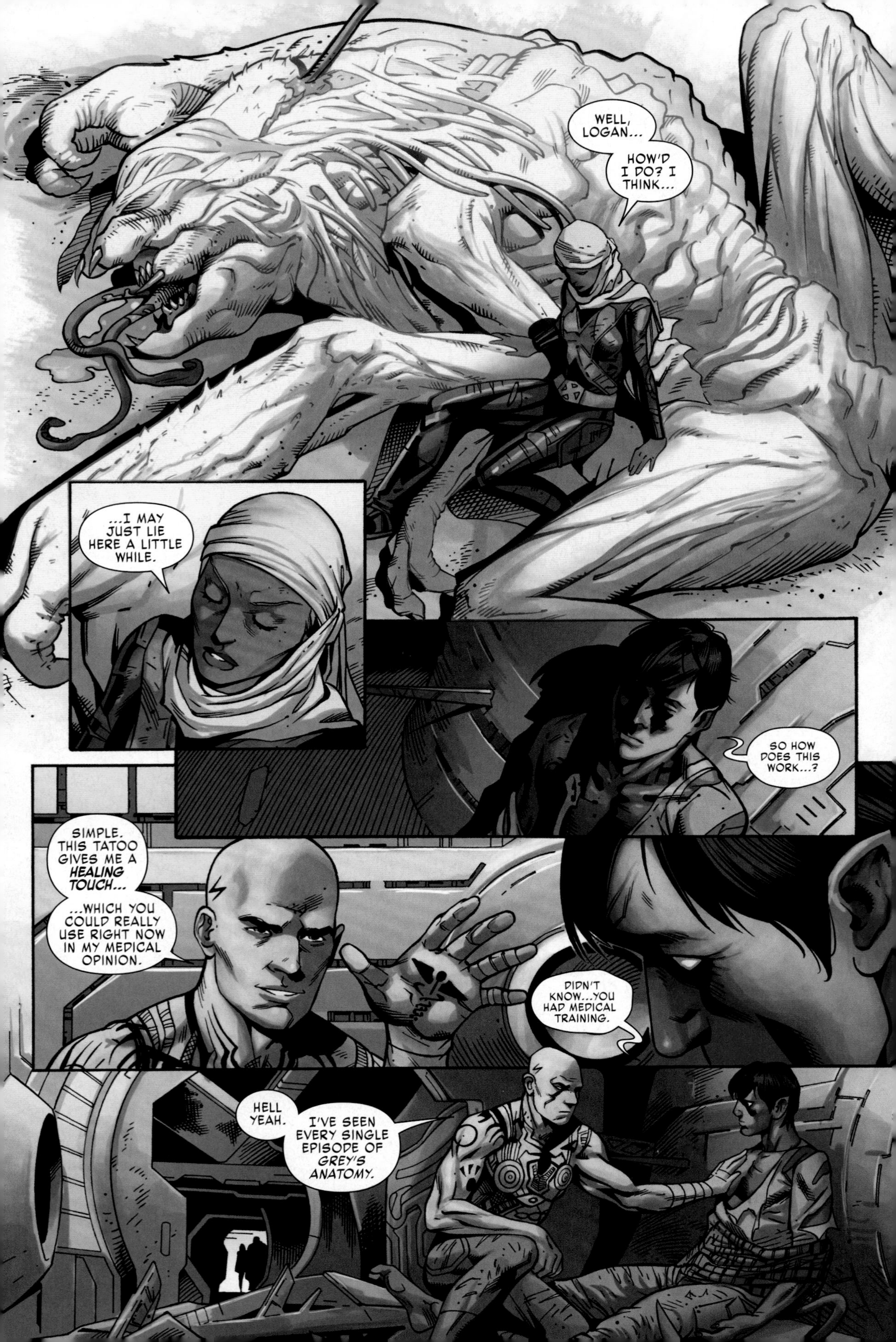
WELL, LOGAN...
HOW'D I DO? I THINK...
...I MAY JUST LIE HERE A LITTLE WHILE.
SO HOW DOES THIS WORK...?
SIMPLE. THIS TATOO GIVES ME A *HEALING TOUCH...*
...WHICH YOU COULD REALLY USE RIGHT NOW IN MY MEDICAL OPINION.
DIDN'T KNOW...YOU HAD MEDICAL TRAINING.
HELL YEAH.
I'VE SEEN EVERY SINGLE EPISODE OF *GREY'S ANATOMY.*

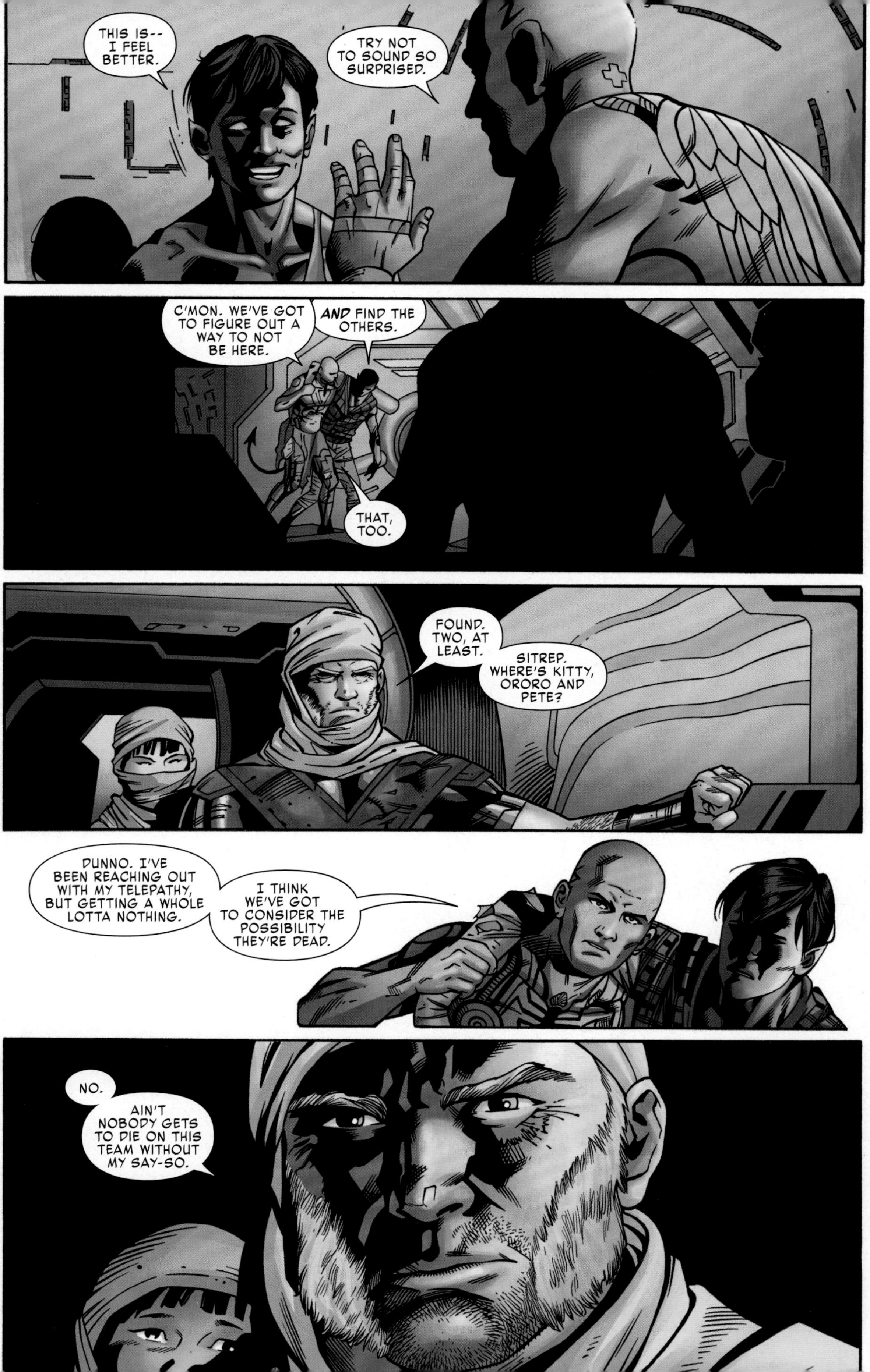
THIS IS-- I FEEL BETTER.
TRY NOT TO SOUND SO SURPRISED.
C'MON. WE'VE GOT TO FIGURE OUT A WAY TO NOT BE HERE.
AND FIND THE OTHERS.
THAT, TOO.
FOUND. TWO, AT LEAST.
SITREP. WHERE'S KITTY, ORORO AND PETE?
DUNNO. I'VE BEEN REACHING OUT WITH MY TELEPATHY, BUT GETTING A WHOLE LOTTA NOTHING.
I THINK WE'VE GOT TO CONSIDER THE POSSIBILITY THEY'RE DEAD.
NO.
AIN'T NOBODY GETS TO DIE ON THIS TEAM WITHOUT MY SAY-SO.

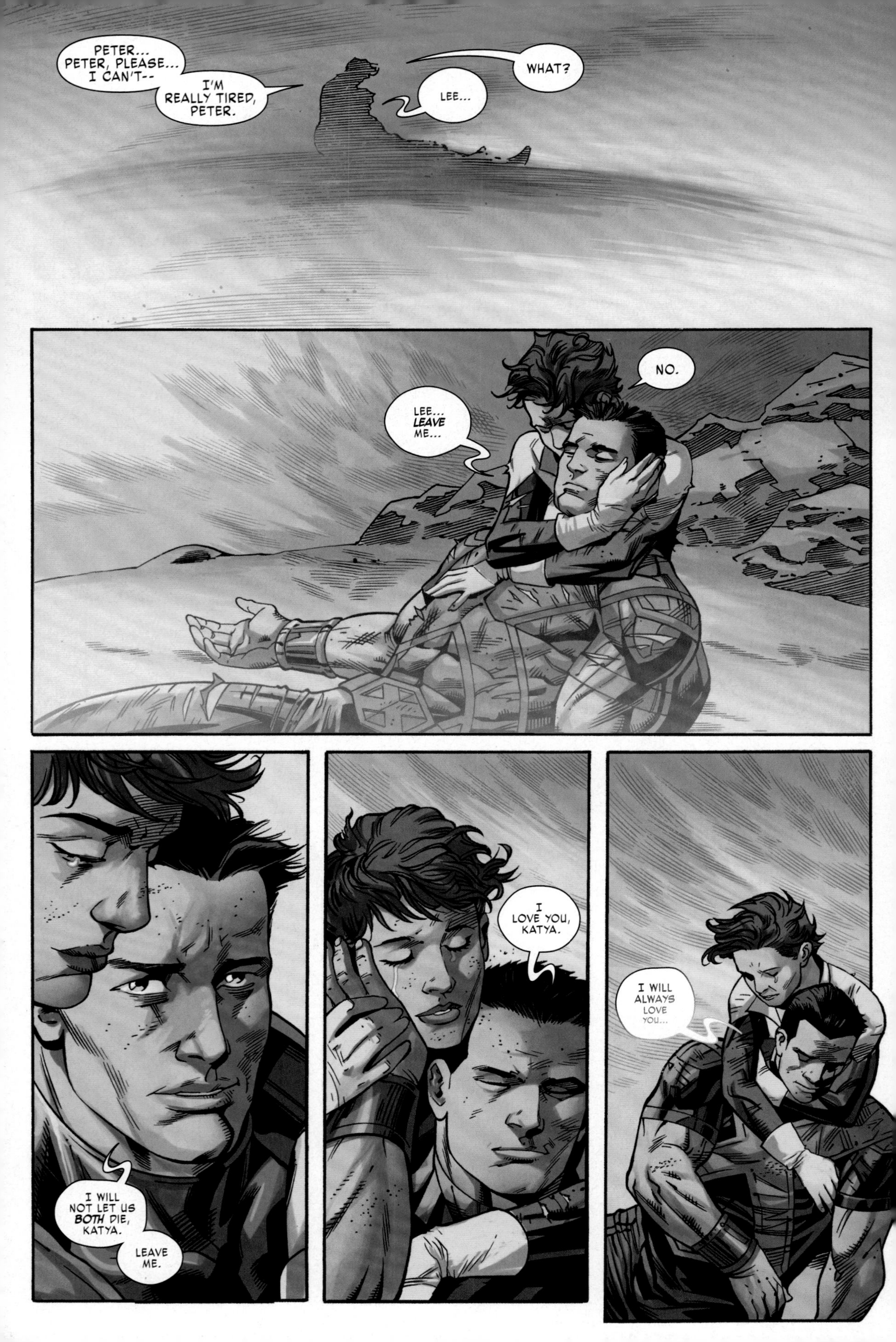

PETER... PETER, PLEASE... I CAN'T--
I'M REALLY TIRED, PETER.
WHAT?
LEE...
LEE... LEAVE ME...
NO.
I WILL NOT LET US BOTH DIE, KATYA.
LEAVE ME.
I LOVE YOU, KATYA.
I WILL ALWAYS LOVE YOU...

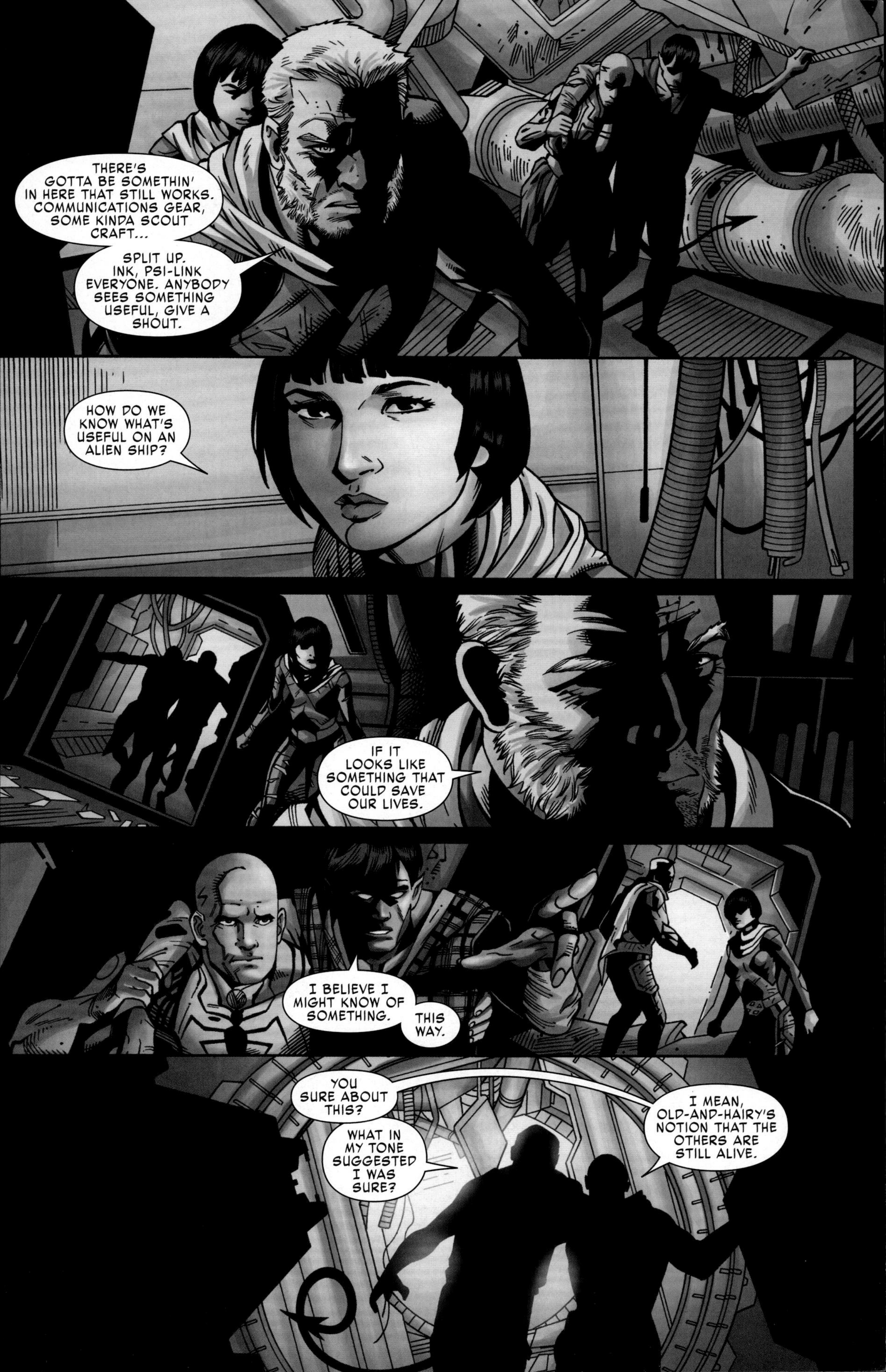
THERE'S GOTTA BE SOMETHIN' IN HERE THAT STILL WORKS. COMMUNICATIONS GEAR, SOME KINDA SCOUT CRAFT...
SPLIT UP. INK, PSI-LINK EVERYONE. ANYBODY SEES SOMETHING USEFUL, GIVE A SHOUT.
HOW DO WE KNOW WHAT'S USEFUL ON AN ALIEN SHIP?
IF IT LOOKS LIKE SOMETHING THAT COULD SAVE OUR LIVES.
I BELIEVE I MIGHT KNOW OF SOMETHING.
THIS WAY.
YOU SURE ABOUT THIS?
I MEAN, OLD-AND-HAIRY'S NOTION THAT THE OTHERS ARE STILL ALIVE.
WHAT IN MY TONE SUGGESTED I WAS SURE?

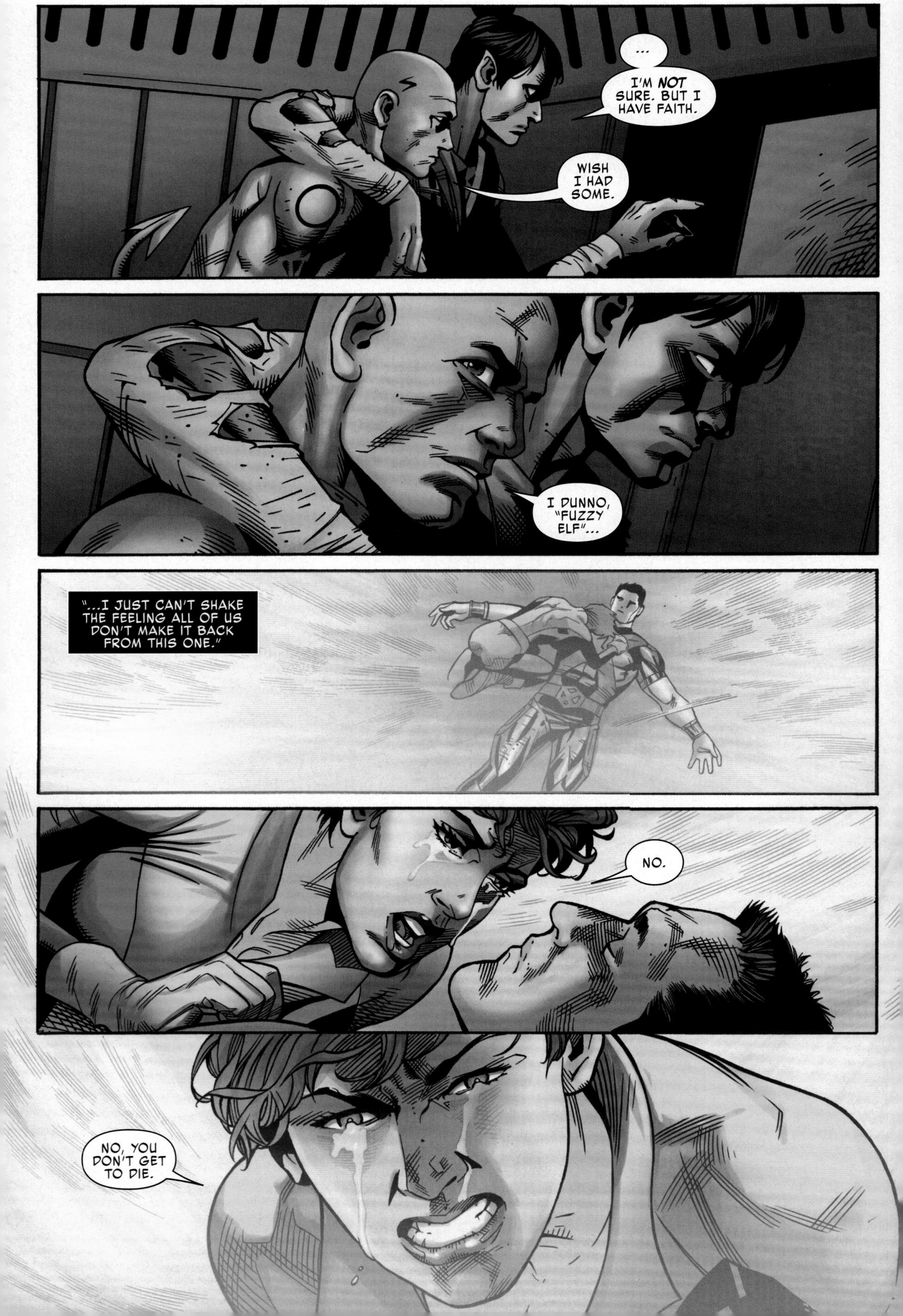
...
I'M NOT SURE. BUT I HAVE FAITH.
WISH I HAD SOME.
I DUNNO, "FUZZY ELF"...
"...I JUST CAN'T SHAKE THE FEELING ALL OF US DON'T MAKE IT BACK FROM THIS ONE."
NO.
NO, YOU DON'T GET TO DIE.

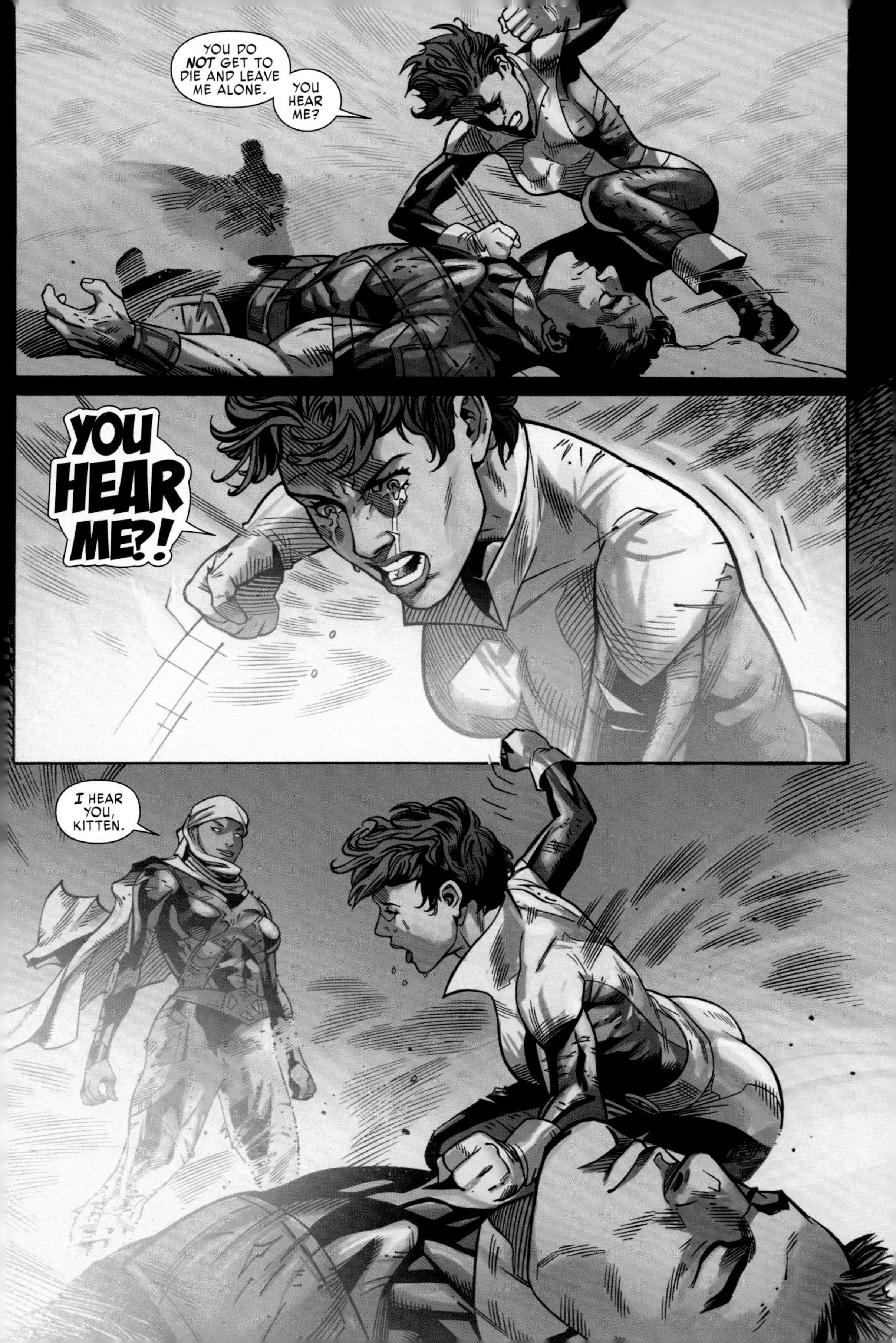
YOU DO NOT GET TO DIE AND LEAVE ME ALONE.
YOU HEAR ME?
YOU HEAR ME?!
I HEAR YOU, KITTEN.

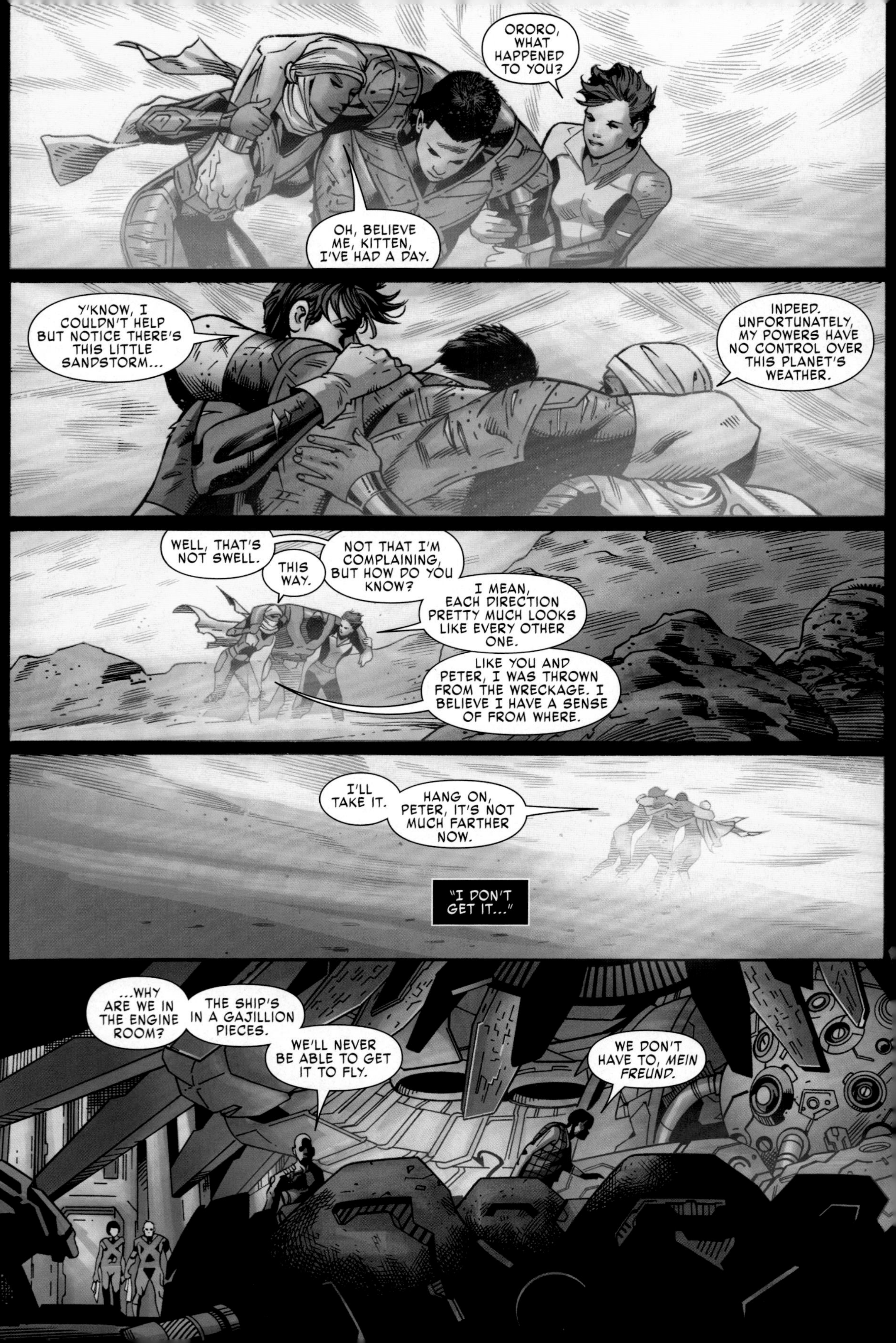
ORORO, WHAT HAPPENED TO YOU?
OH, BELIEVE ME, KITTEN, I'VE HAD A DAY.
Y'KNOW, I COULDN'T HELP BUT NOTICE THERE'S THIS LITTLE SANDSTORM...
INDEED. UNFORTUNATELY, MY POWERS HAVE NO CONTROL OVER THIS PLANET'S WEATHER.
WELL, THAT'S NOT SWELL.
THIS WAY.
NOT THAT I'M COMPLAINING, BUT HOW DO YOU KNOW?
I MEAN, EACH DIRECTION PRETTY MUCH LOOKS LIKE EVERY OTHER ONE.
LIKE YOU AND PETER, I WAS THROWN FROM THE WRECKAGE. I BELIEVE I HAVE A SENSE OF FROM WHERE.
I'LL TAKE IT.
HANG ON, PETER, IT'S NOT MUCH FARTHER NOW.
"I DON'T GET IT..."
...WHY ARE WE IN THE ENGINE ROOM?
THE SHIP'S IN A GAJILLION PIECES.
WE'LL NEVER BE ABLE TO GET IT TO FLY.
WE DON'T HAVE TO, *MEIN FREUND*.

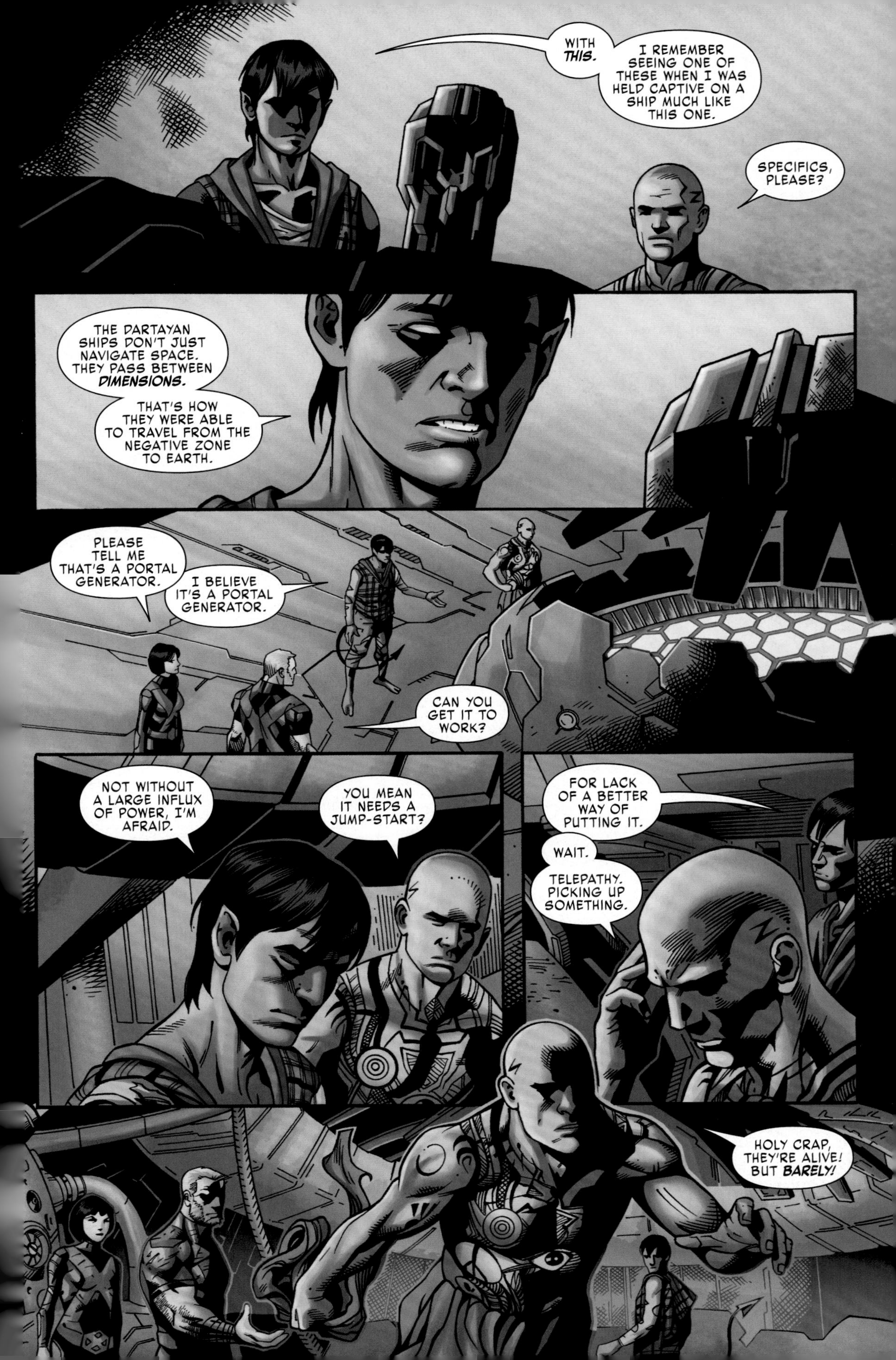

WITH *THIS.*
I REMEMBER SEEING ONE OF THESE WHEN I WAS HELD CAPTIVE ON A SHIP MUCH LIKE THIS ONE.
SPECIFICS, PLEASE?
THE DARTAYAN SHIPS DON'T JUST NAVIGATE SPACE. THEY PASS BETWEEN *DIMENSIONS.*
THAT'S HOW THEY WERE ABLE TO TRAVEL FROM THE NEGATIVE ZONE TO EARTH.
PLEASE TELL ME THAT'S A PORTAL GENERATOR.
I BELIEVE IT'S A PORTAL GENERATOR.
CAN YOU GET IT TO WORK?
NOT WITHOUT A LARGE INFLUX OF POWER, I'M AFRAID.
YOU MEAN IT NEEDS A JUMP-START?
FOR LACK OF A BETTER WAY OF PUTTING IT.
WAIT.
TELEPATHY. PICKING UP SOMETHING.
HOLY CRAP, THEY'RE ALIVE! BUT *BARELY!*

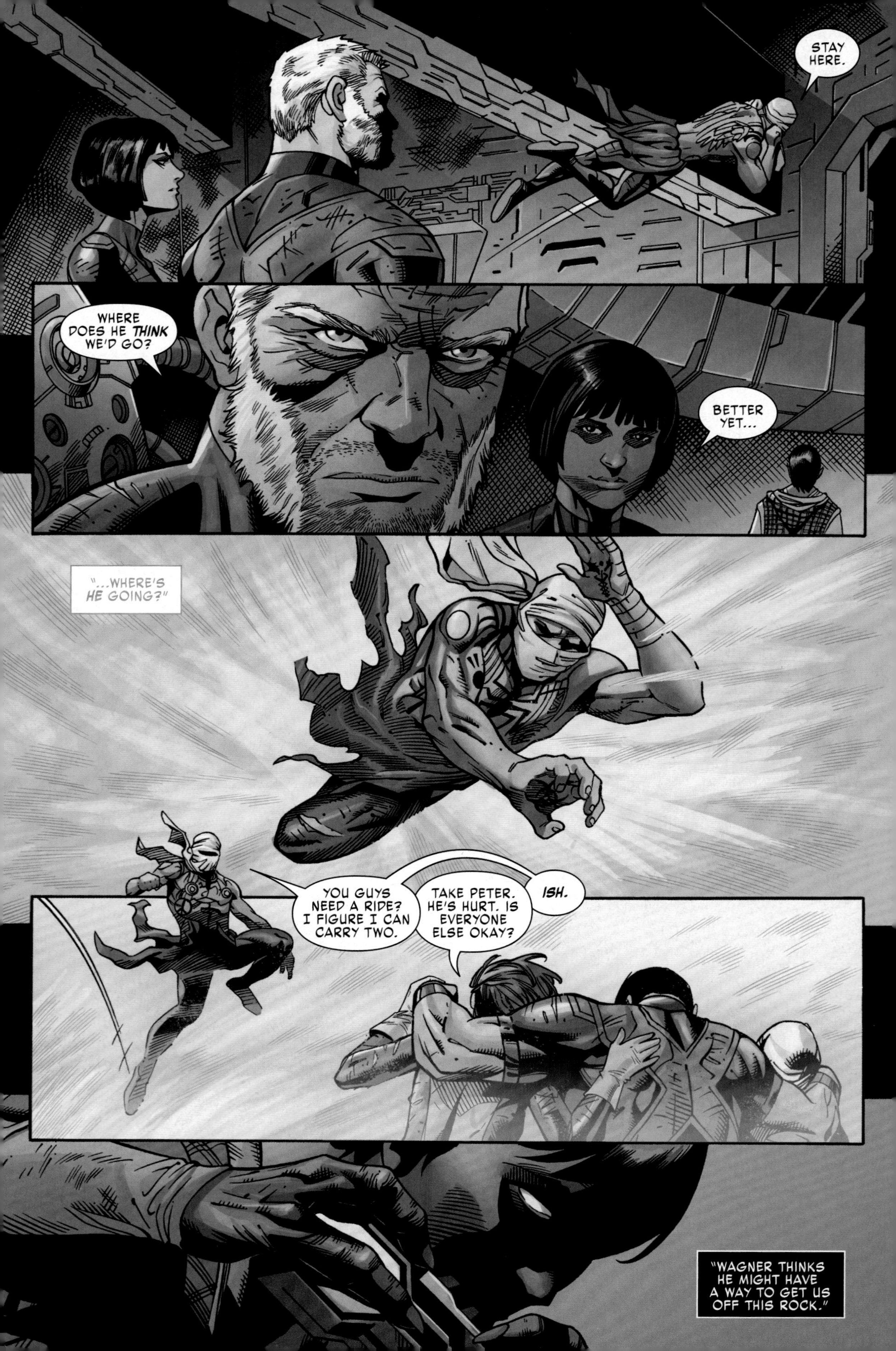
STAY HERE.
WHERE DOES HE THINK WE'D GO?
BETTER YET...
"...WHERE'S HE GOING?"
YOU GUYS NEED A RIDE? I FIGURE I CAN CARRY TWO.
ISH.
TAKE PETER. HE'S HURT. IS EVERYONE ELSE OKAY?
"WAGNER THINKS HE MIGHT HAVE A WAY TO GET US OFF THIS ROCK."

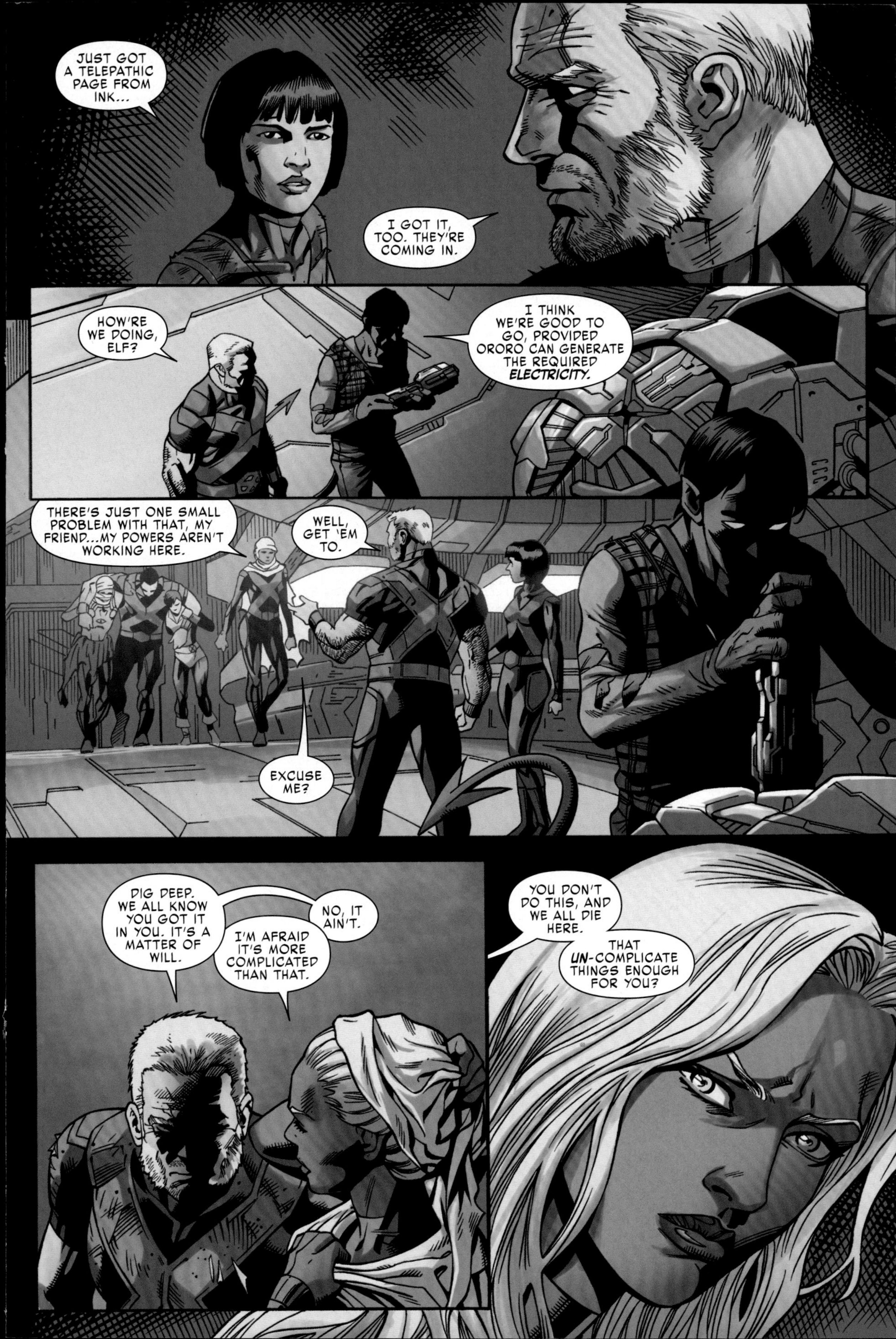
JUST GOT A TELEPATHIC PAGE FROM INK...
I GOT IT, TOO. THEY'RE COMING IN.
HOW'RE WE DOING, ELF?
I THINK WE'RE GOOD TO GO, PROVIDED ORORO CAN GENERATE THE REQUIRED ELECTRICITY.
THERE'S JUST ONE SMALL PROBLEM WITH THAT, MY FRIEND...MY POWERS AREN'T WORKING HERE.
WELL, GET 'EM TO.
EXCUSE ME?
DIG DEEP. WE ALL KNOW YOU GOT IT IN YOU. IT'S A MATTER OF WILL.
NO, IT AIN'T.
I'M AFRAID IT'S MORE COMPLICATED THAN THAT.
YOU DON'T DO THIS, AND WE ALL DIE HERE.
THAT UN-COMPLICATE THINGS ENOUGH FOR YOU?

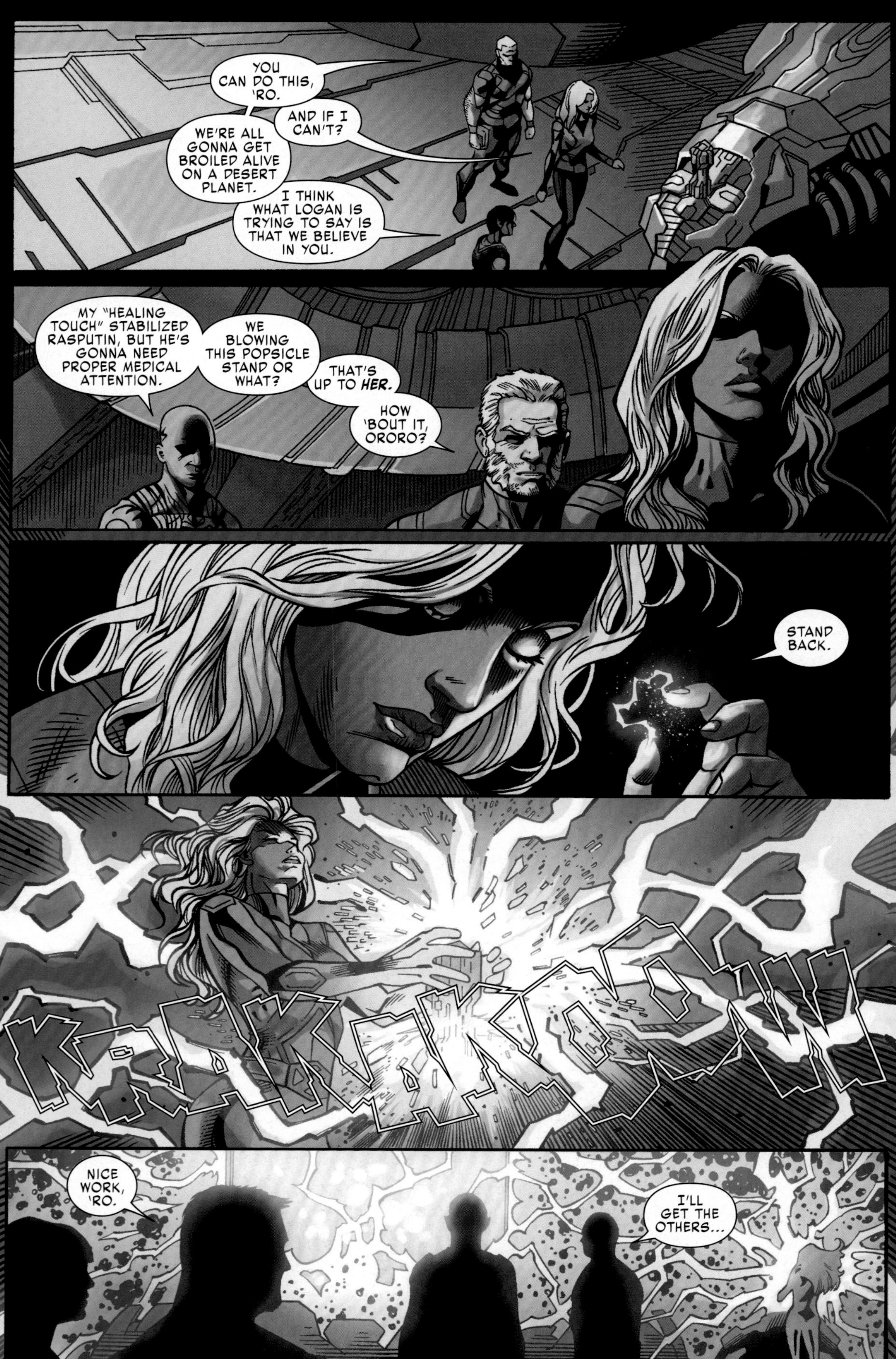
YOU CAN DO THIS, 'RO.
AND IF I CAN'T?
WE'RE ALL GONNA GET BROILED ALIVE ON A DESERT PLANET.
I THINK WHAT LOGAN IS TRYING TO SAY IS THAT WE BELIEVE IN YOU.
MY "HEALING TOUCH" STABILIZED RASPUTIN, BUT HE'S GONNA NEED PROPER MEDICAL ATTENTION.
WE BLOWING THIS POPSICLE STAND OR WHAT?
THAT'S UP TO **HER**.
HOW 'BOUT IT, ORORO?
STAND BACK.
K-RAKKOOOM
NICE WORK, 'RO.
I'LL GET THE OTHERS...

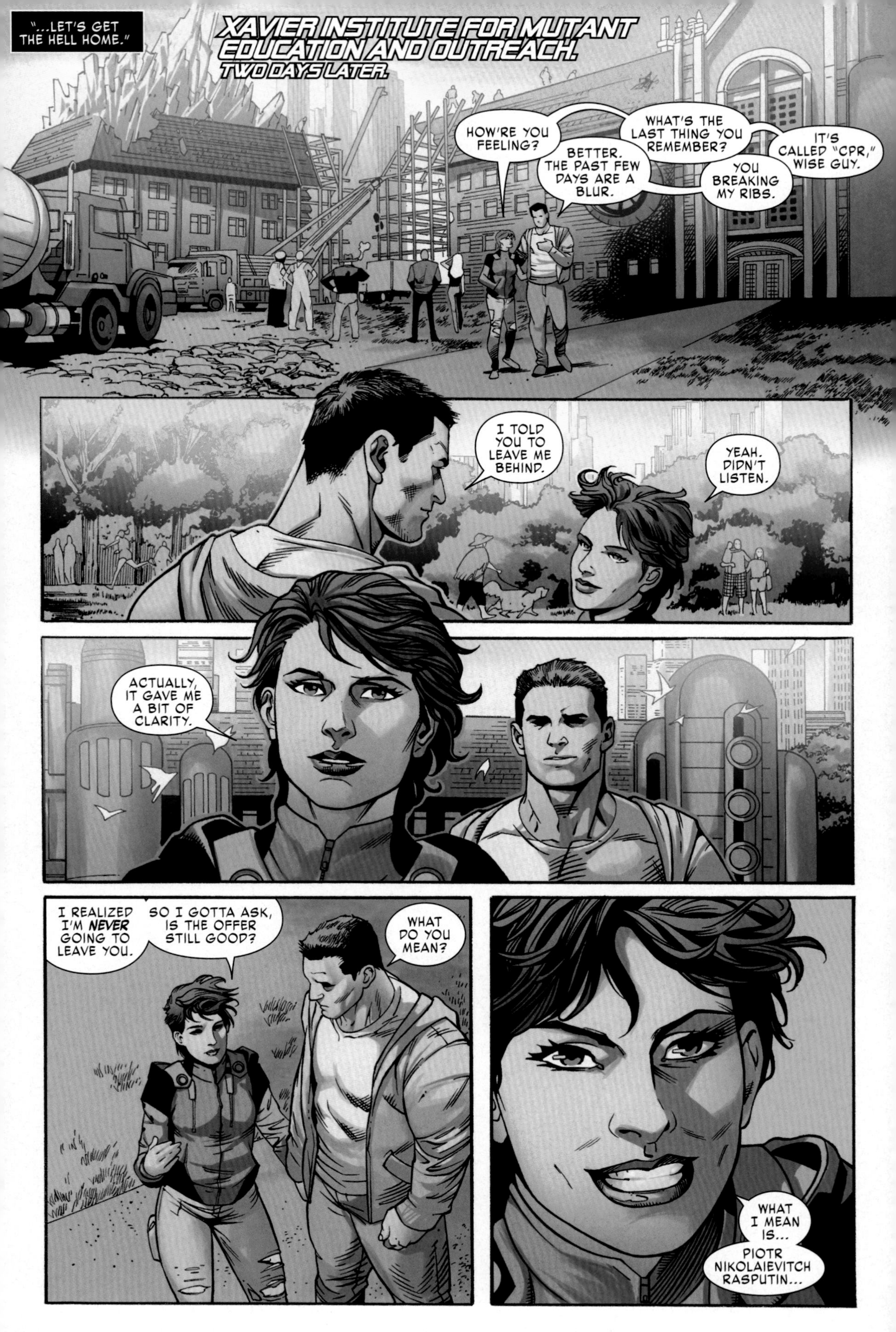
"...LET'S GET THE HELL HOME."
XAVIER INSTITUTE FOR MUTANT EDUCATION AND OUTREACH. TWO DAYS LATER.
HOW'RE YOU FEELING?
BETTER. THE PAST FEW DAYS ARE A BLUR.
WHAT'S THE LAST THING YOU REMEMBER?
YOU BREAKING MY RIBS.
IT'S CALLED "CPR," WISE GUY.
I TOLD YOU TO LEAVE ME BEHIND.
YEAH. DIDN'T LISTEN.
ACTUALLY, IT GAVE ME A BIT OF CLARITY.
I REALIZED I'M NEVER GOING TO LEAVE YOU.
SO I GOTTA ASK, IS THE OFFER STILL GOOD?
WHAT DO YOU MEAN?
WHAT I MEAN IS... PIOTR NIKOLAIEVITCH RASPUTIN...

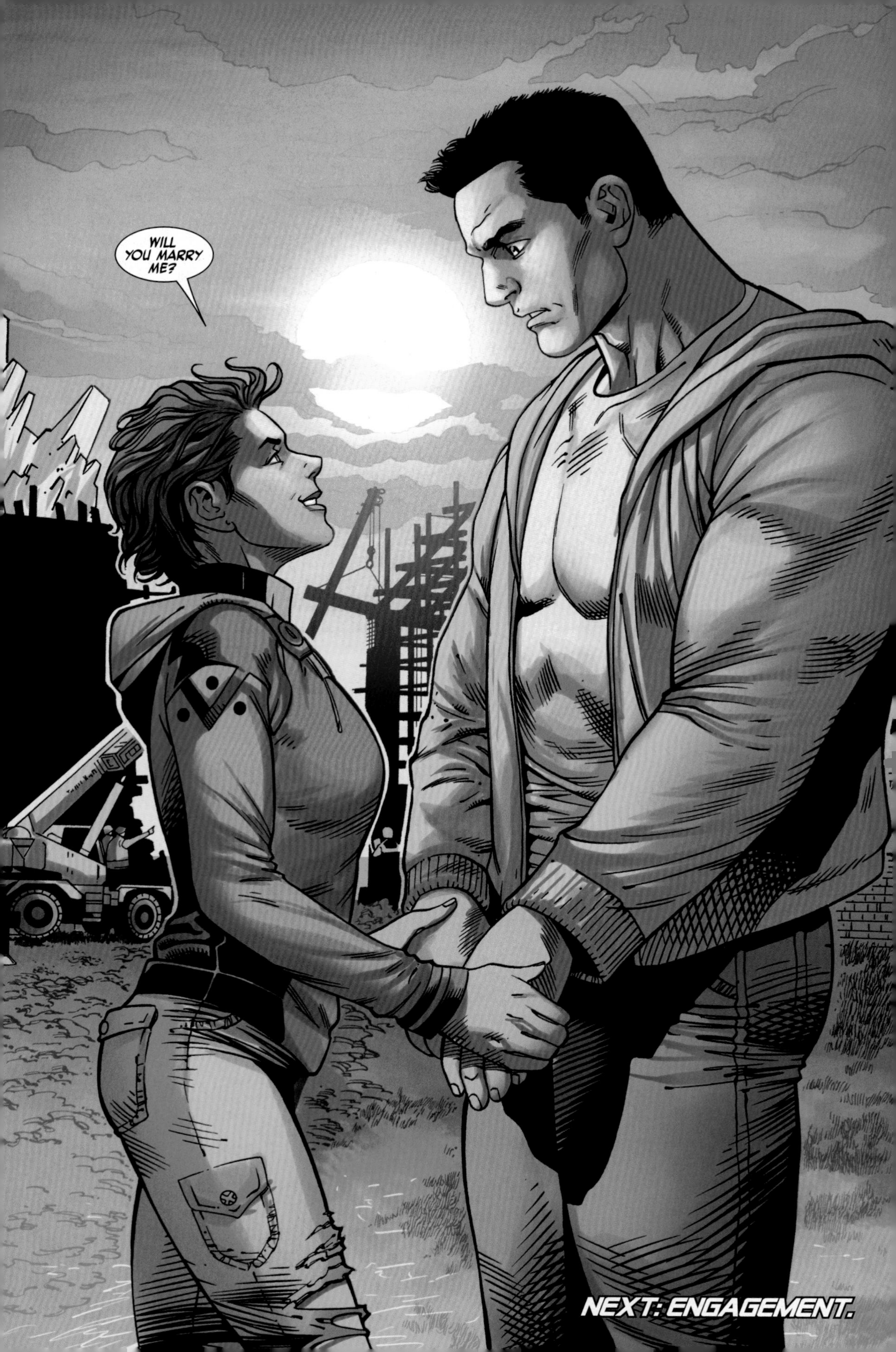
WILL YOU MARRY ME?
NEXT: ENGAGEMENT.

#17 COVER ART BY **KEN LASHLEY**

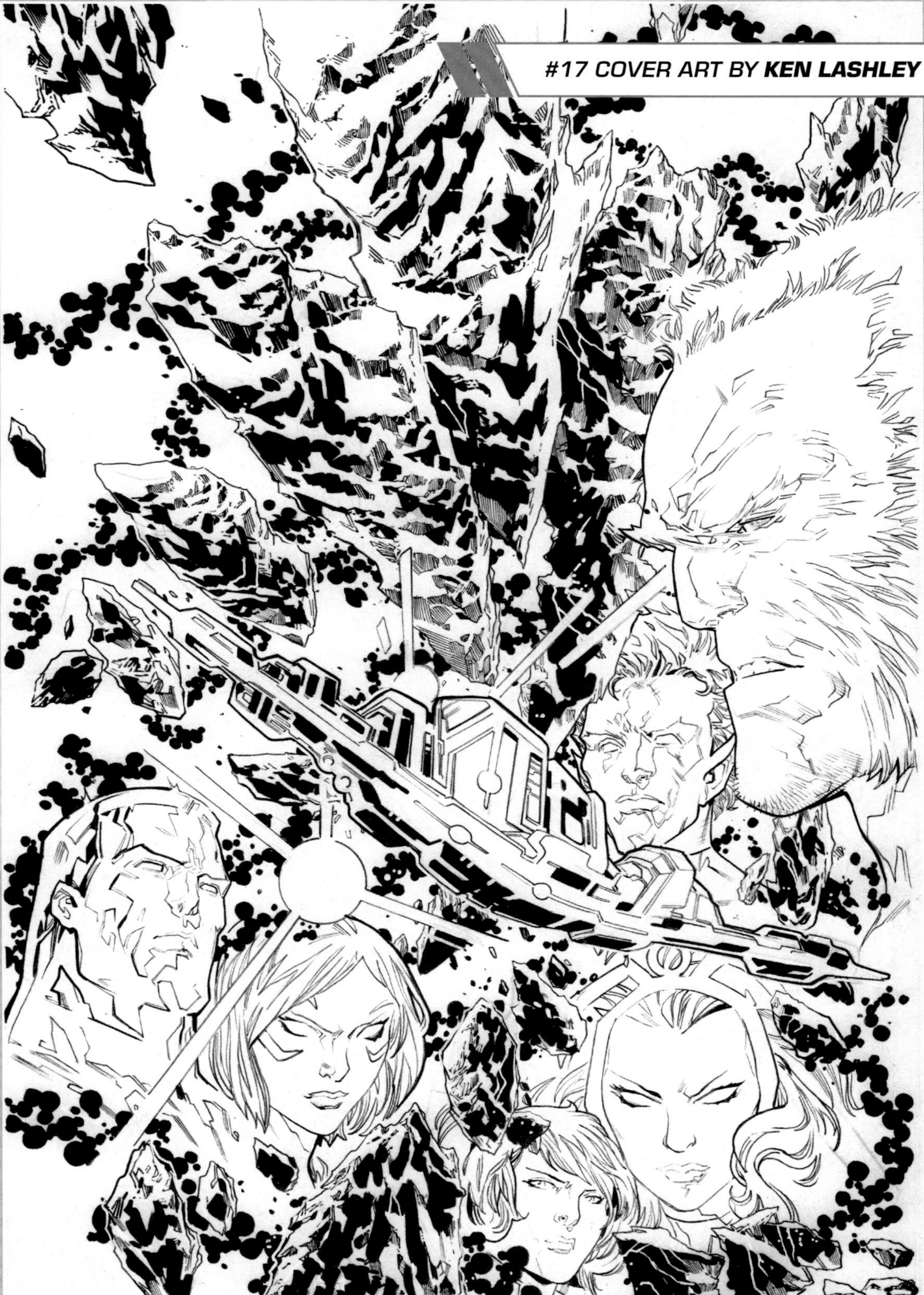
KWL

#19 COVER ART BY **KEN LASHLEY**

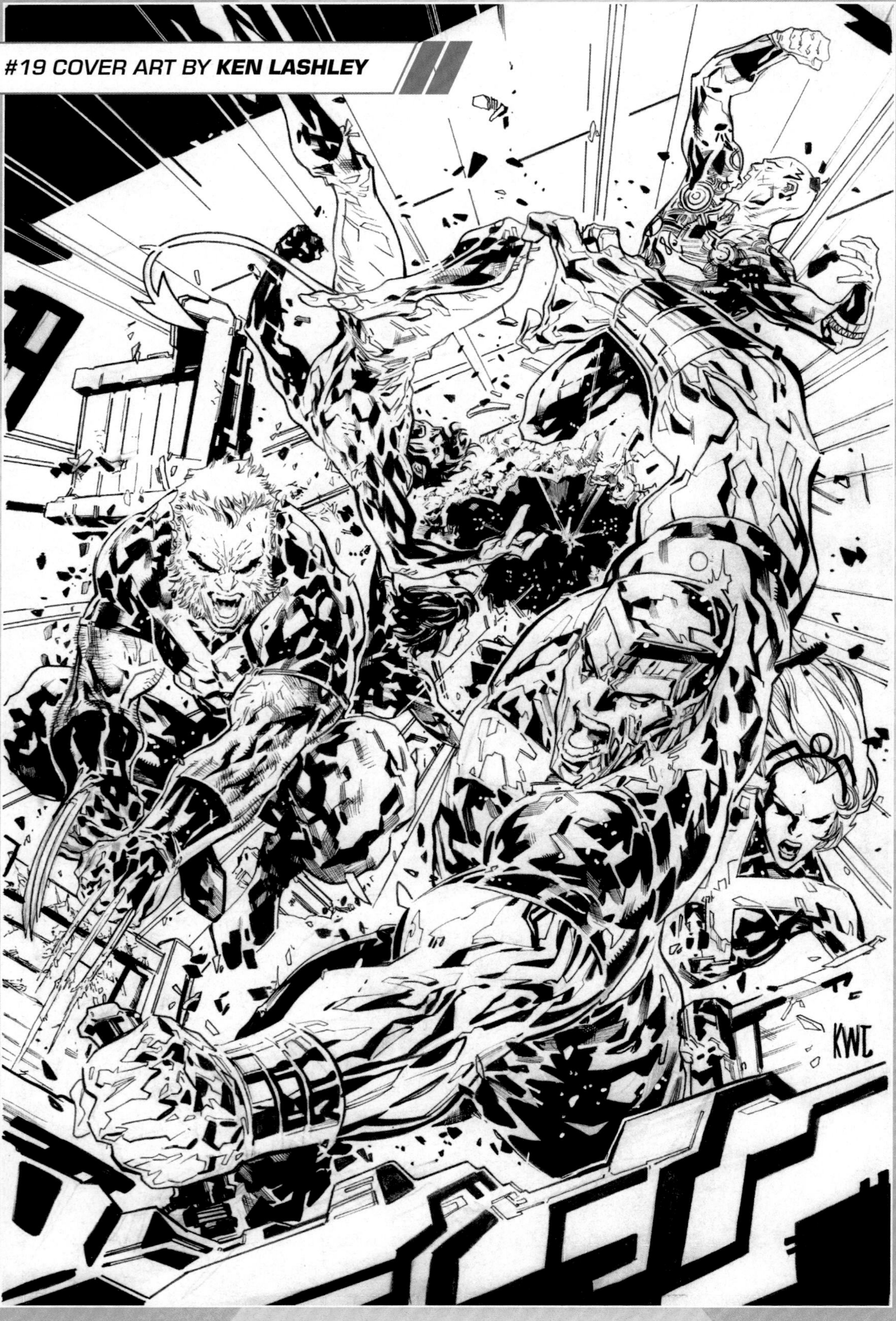
KWL

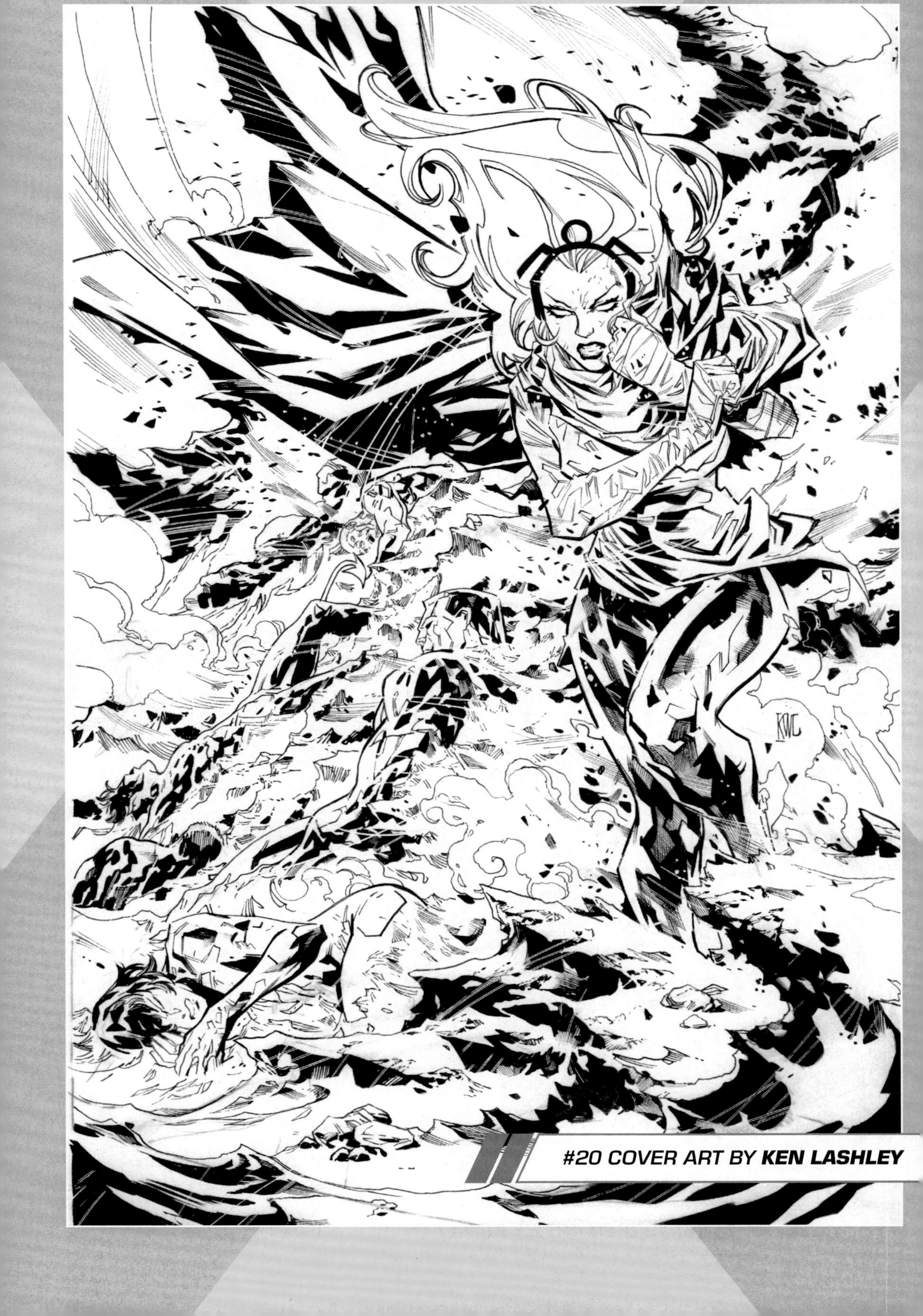

#20 COVER ART BY **KEN LASHLEY**

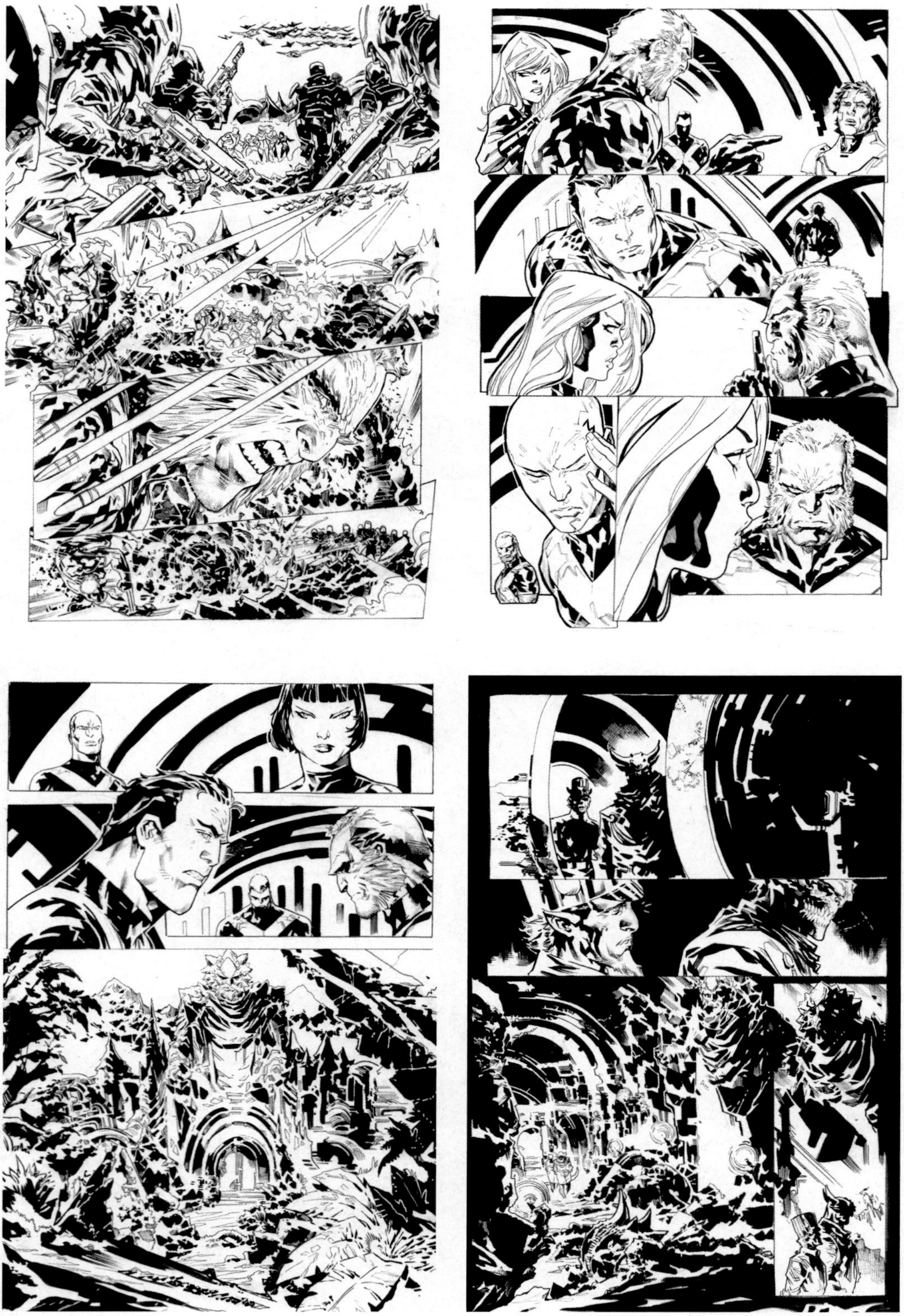

#17, PAGES 10, 15-16, 18 & 20 ART BY **KEN LASHLEY**

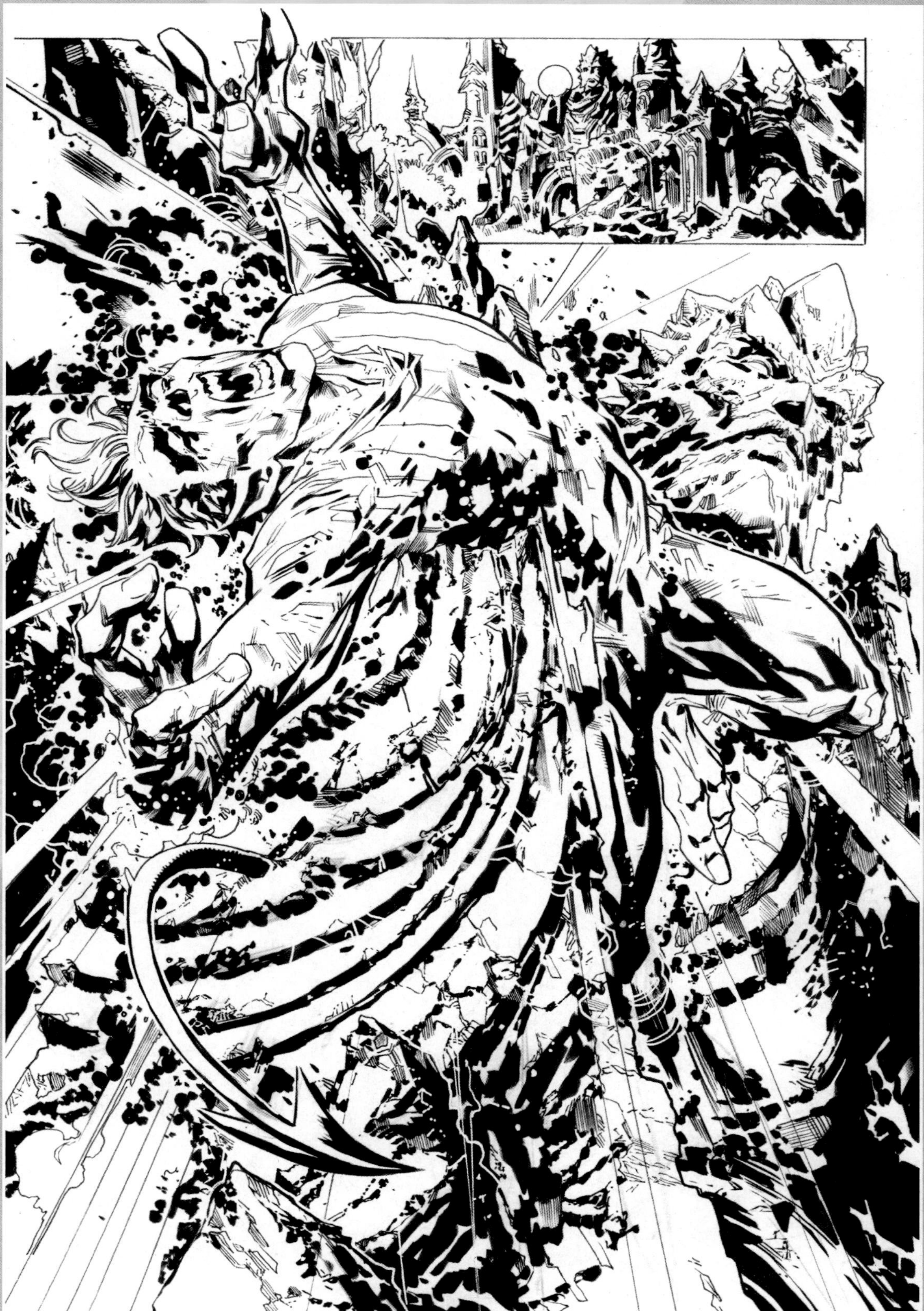

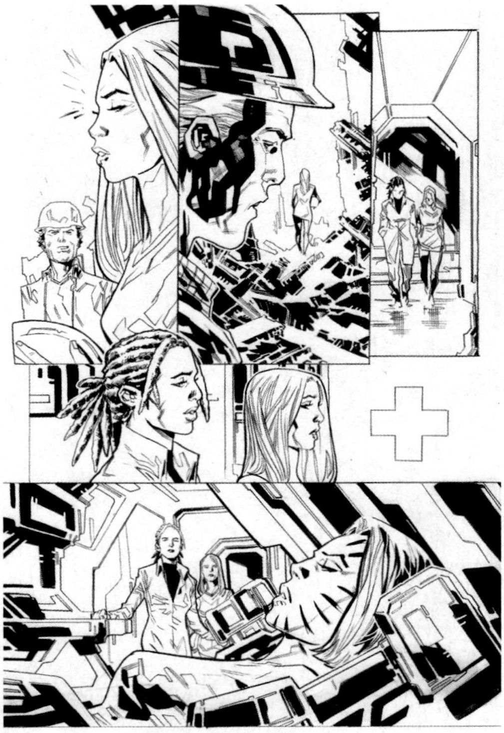

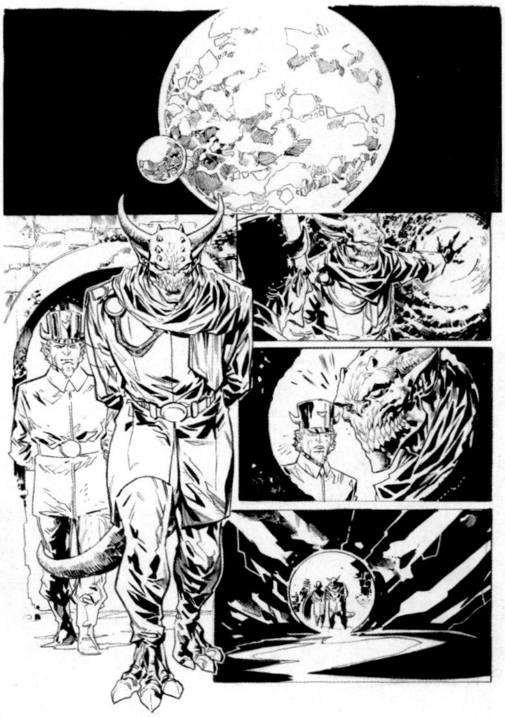

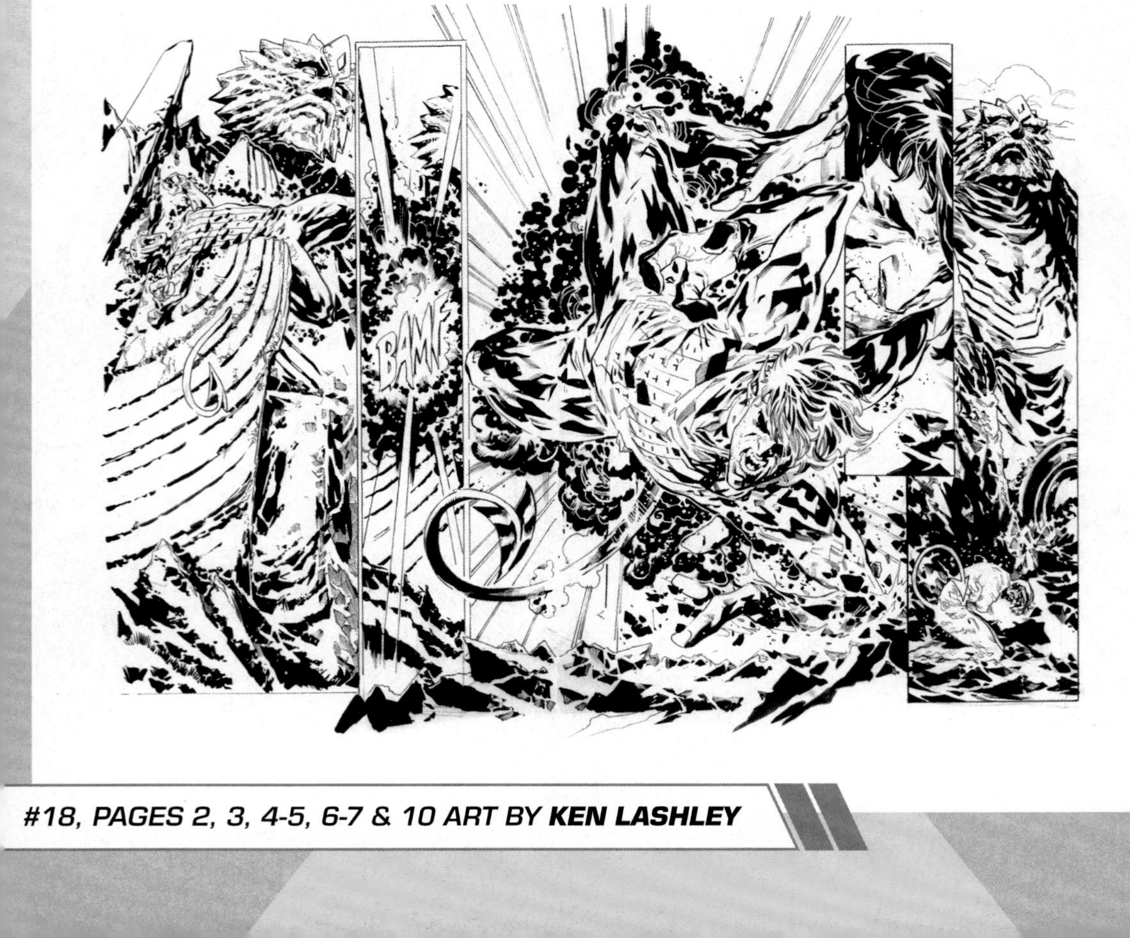
BAM!

#18, PAGES 2, 3, 4-5, 6-7 & 10 ART BY ***KEN LASHLEY***